COUNT AXEL VON FERSEN.

SWEDEN

AND THE

AMERICAN REVOLUTION

By

ADOLPH B. BENSON

Associate Professor in Yale University

NEW HAVEN

THE TUTTLE, MOREHOUSE & TAYLOR COMPANY

1926

Copyright, 1926
By
ADOLPH B. BENSON

NILS SAHLIN, Distributor
Box 1068, Yale Station, New Haven, Conn.

To
the memory of
those Swedish officers
who with the French fought
and died in the American
War of Independence

THE EVACUATION, 1783.
IN MEMORIAM, November 25, 1783.

" . . . Here in New York, on the 25th of November, 1783, was performed the last act of the war of liberation . . . . .

In the evening there was a memorable dinner at Fraunce's Tavern, on the corner of Broad and Pearl streets. The room is still shown, almost unchanged, where WASHINGTON, CLINTON, and the heroes of New York met at this triumphal banquet . . . . Toasts were pledged to all who had aided the cause of freedom—the French king, the United Netherlands, *the Northern powers* . . . . ."

Eugene Lawrence in *Harper's Weekly* for November 24, 1883.

TABLE OF CONTENTS

PAGE

PREFACE xi

INTRODUCTION

The problem and method of investigation. The importance of the naval operations. 1-6

CHAPTER I

The Swedish motives for participation. Attitude toward
the American colonists 11

CHAPTER II

Sweden and the Armed Neutrality 25

CHAPTER III

Swedish Commercial relations with America during the
Revolution. Treaty of amity and commerce 40

CHAPTER IV

Gustav Philip Creutz 56

CHAPTER V

Descendants of the Delaware Swedes in the struggle for
independence. John Hanson and John Morton 66

CHAPTER VI

A list of Swedish officers in the French and Colonial
service for American independence 87

CHAPTER VII

Colonel Axel von Fersen 129

CHAPTER VIII   PAGE

Baron Curt von Stedingk 147

Concluding remarks 167

BIBLIOGRAPHY 169

APPENDIX

1. Full English text of treaty of amity and commerce, 1783 182

2. Address on John Hanson 198

3. An outline of the French participation, etc. 203

INDEX OF NAMES 209

LIST OF ILLUSTRATIONS

Portrait of Count Axel von Fersen ....*Frontispiece*

Our First Treaty with Sweden ....*Between pages* 50 and 51

Portrait of Count de Creutz ....*Opposite page* 56

Statue-Portrait of John Hanson .... " " 78

Alexander Contee Hanson .... " " 80

The Hanson Coat-of-Arms .... " " 80

The Nicholas Brown House .... " " 132

PREFACE

This study is the work of a layman who was attracted to the subject a few years ago by his general interest in all relations between Sweden and the United States. A specific interest in the literary relations between the two countries led gradually and naturally to investigations of some historical connections. This monograph is one result of such research. It does not claim to be exhaustive; but the author hopes that it contains enough information, suggestions, compilations, quotations, and criticism to serve as a helpful introduction to the subject as a whole. A *thorough* study of Swedish public opinion regarding the American Revolution—aside from the more practical attitude in Swedish commercial and diplomatic circles—still remains to be done, as does also an exhaustive survey of the accomplishments of the Swedish Delaware descendants. This work is intended to show, however, that the American colonies profited during the Revolution by the Swedish maritime policies and by the volunteer enlistments of Swedish officers in the French service.

This study purposes—to be more exact—to describe some of the outstanding features of the Swedish interest and participation in the American War of Independence. It purports to outline the official and, in some degree, the non-official Swedish attitude toward the American colonists; to indicate in a general way, by the estimation of numbers, the part played by the descendants of the Delaware Swedes; to point out what share the Swedish government had in directing European policies that influenced the final results; to show that commercial relations existed between the American colonies and Sweden during the period of the Revolution; and—most important of all—to give as complete list as possible of the names of Swedish officers who directly or indirectly fought for American Independence.

To Professor Charles M. Andrews, professor of American history in Yale University, who read the first chapters in their original, crude form; to Hanna Astrup Larsen, editor of the *American-Scandinavian Review;* to Mr. James Creese, Secretary of the American-Scandinavian Foundation; and to Dr. Amandus Johnson of Philadelphia; all of whom have read the manuscript, in part, I acknowledge gratitude for helpful suggestions. Miss May Atherton Leach has kindly consented to let me reproduce in this work an article by her on John Morton; Herr Matts Juhlin-Dannfelt of Kloten, Sweden, has been of service to me in some important preliminary work; Herr Thorsten Laurin of Stockholm has shown a friendly and helpful attitude toward the undertaking; and Professor Axel Johan Uppvall of the University of Pennsylvania has contributed some necessary negative data, thereby saving me not a little labor. Under the able and willing direction of Dr. Erik Naumann, chief archivist of Riksarkivet, Stockholm, Fröken Jutta Jahn has with painstaking care copied the first-hand sources that were inaccessible to me. To this investigation in its final scope, the coöperation of Dr. Naumann and Fröken Jahn, as noted more specifically later, has been indispensable.

To the librarians and assistants of the Rhode Island Historical Society, the John Carter Brown Library, the John Hay Memorial Library of Brown University, the Providence Public Library—all of Providence, Rhode Island—and to the staff of Yale University Library, I express my thankfulness for ever-ready assistance.

Lastly, I am grateful to my wife for all interest and encouragement, for substantial aid in research, for help in proofreading and indexing, and for advice in matters of form.   A. B. B.

New Haven, Conn.
September, 1926

INTRODUCTION

The Problem and Method of Investigation

Volumes have been written on the timely aid of the French auxiliary army; many histories have eulogized the gallantry of the Polish volunteers in America; the German participation in the American Revolution, whether for or against, has been investigated and duly apotheosized or condemned; and the Irish have reaped their share of glory for active encouragement in our struggle for freedom. But, so far as we know, no attempt has been made in America to identify the Swedish volunteers who helped to fight our battles on sea and land; and they have therefore never been mentioned, as such, in our general histories, or been given credit for their assistance. Occasionally, a large work or specific treatise on the American Revolution contains a brief reference to Count von Fersen, the friend of Marie Antoinette and Rochambeau's first aid-de-camp, whose letters on his American campaign have been translated into English at least three times; and a few works in English mention Count von Stedingk. The other Swedish officers are passed over in silence, for the simple reason that their participation has never been investigated, and they are not known. Besides, history has but little space for soldiers below the various grades of general, and there seems to have been no Swedish volunteer who held a rank above that of colonel.

There are, also, more definite reasons why we have such meagre knowledge of the Swedish officers in America. First of all, the great majority of them—probably *all* of those who came direct from Europe during the Revolutionary period—served (as did some of the Irish and Germans) under the French flag, and merged with the French, temporarily losing their identity as Swedish subjects. Secondly, the records of the French Army and Navy in America are notoriously incomplete with little hope of ever filling up the gaps. The lists of men and officers of some companies are lost entirely; no official documents have been found concerning Duc de Lauzun's famous legion, in which there were many foreign officers; and there are few, if any, records of non-official voluntary enlistments or engagements. And even such

sources as we have, whether in print or manuscript, are so full
of orthographic distortions and chaotic discrepancies, not to mention actual errors, that only the most vigilant linguistic study can
detect the nationality of the names. Many of these would seem
to baffle all knowledge, guess-work and imagination. It is not
unusual to see an officer's patronymic spelled in half a dozen
different ways, with variances wide enough to indicate separate
individuals under ordinary circumstances. Thus *Carl Raab* (see
page 108) becomes in the French records *Riaub, Rhaale, Ahaab,*
Haab, Raoul, and *Charles Rabb;* yet there is not the slightest
doubt that these are all one and the same person. In most cases
the Christian names of the Swedish officers are wanting entirely,
and all one has to work on, in French sources, is a distorted surname. *Nangof* is an unintentional French simplification of
Nauckhoff (Henric Johan); and *Logenhausen, de Houguenou-*
sem, and *M. Houguen-Houzen* are three interesting variants,
obviously heretofore considered as three separate individuals, of
one and the same Swedish nobleman, Carl Johan von Hohenhausen. Even the well-known Fersen is referred to by Claude
Blanchard as *de Ferry.* In like manner, *Aron Sjöstjerna,* an
ensign, becomes simply *Scalierna* in the French version; and
Johan Herman *Schützercrantz,* appears as *Schuzsleirans,* with
three other similar variants.

But are not some of these German names? the reader will
ask. This brings us to the heart of one important phase of the
problem, and to the third reason for difficulties and some previous false deductions in the matter.

After the Swedish successes in the Thirty Years' War, where
men and officers of all nationalities had served under the banner
of Gustavus Adolphus, or his surviving generals, hundreds of
foreign families followed his victorious armies to Sweden and
settled there. Among these were English, Scotch, German,
Polish, and French Huguenot emigrants, many of whom had
distinguished themselves in the war in Germany, and several of
whom were eventually—if they had not been so already—honored
with titles and property by the Swedish government. Not a few
were raised to the peerage for military accomplishments, and
almost all of them retained their ancestral family names. Also,
Sweden during her period of military greatness possessed extensive territories in the Baltic provinces and northern Germany,

whose inhabitants had long been Swedish subjects. Finland had belonged to Sweden for several hundred years. And so it came about, especially in army and navy circles, that a large proportion of the Swedish gentry had foreign names. One needs only to be reminded that two hundred upper-class British families alone settled in Sweden during the seventeenth century. Consequently such names as *Bruce, Douglas, Hamilton, Key,* and *Montgomery* are fairly common to this day in Sweden, most of them belonging to the old nobility. Likewise, *Charlier, de la Gardie, de Laval, Lewenhaupt, Löwenadler, von Platen, Richter, Ruhe, Rosen, Schwartz, Wachtmeister, von Wrangel,* and *Wravrinsky* are cognomens of bona fide Swedish subjects whose ancestors have been Swedes for several generations. About the time of the American Revolution, *Hall* was the name of a notable Swedish miniaturist in Paris; *Sinclair* was the name of a colonel in the Swedish army; *Chapman, Fleetwood,* and *Gilbert Sheldon* were prominent Swedish naval officers; *Ramsay* was a governor; *Corvin* was another English-sounding name of a Swedish citizen; and Adolph *Wertmüller* was a Swedish artist in America, who in the course of time had the opportunity to paint Washington, and who deemed it necessary to sign his canvases "Wertmüller, Suédois," to indicate his original allegiance. *La Vreince* was a successful Gallicism for the Swedish *Lafrensen,* another artist; in 1810 the clergyman officiating at Count von Fersen's funeral was Gustaf *Murray;* and a few decades later Carl *Snoilsky,* of Polish ancestry, became one of the most characteristic Swedish poets that the North has ever produced. Such names as Karl *Warburg* and Henrik *Schück,* famous Swedish citizens and historians of Swedish literature, show of course Jewish origin; but the name *Cesare* (the name of the well-known cartoonist of the New York *Times*) would hardly lead anyone to suspect that the bearer was born in Sweden. The examples could be multiplied many times.

In 1775 the number of such extraneous names in Swedish society was still exceedingly large—out of all proportion, in fact, to the indigenous patronymics. In other words, in examining the names of Swedish officers of that period we find that there are scores whom a foreigner would never suspect as being of Scandinavian nationality. It has quite naturally been taken for granted, that men bearing such names as *Zachaud, Brummer,* and *Colquhoun* were anything but Swedish. Very often, as the records show, the French themselves either did not know or did not care to designate the nationality of the officers. It must be admitted, however, that in the printed French *naval* records, which are much more complete than those of the army, an unrecognizable combination of vowels and consonants is often followed by the dubious explanation in parenthesis that it represents an "officier suédois."—It has been the writer's task and pleasure to solve the majority of these strange combinations and, wherever possible, verify them by Swedish sources.

There is also another phase of the problem, which helps to explain the situation. Contemporary Frenchmen, either consciously or unconsciously, were singularly cautious in their references to foreigners in their ranks. This partiality, though natural enough under ordinary conditions, and in this case unintentional perhaps, is in any case astonishing when we recall the traditional popularity of Swedish officers in France throughout the eighteenth century. It would not be courteous to imply that they were, conceivably, *too* popular. At all events, not even Fersen's name is mentioned in the published campaign memoirs of his friend, Duc de Lauzun (Biron); the memoirs of Count de Moré give no information about Swedish officers; nor do the travel accounts of the Chevalier de Chastellux or Abbé Robin furnish enlightenment. One is equally disappointed in examining the four volumes on "des troubles de l'Amérique anglaise" by François Soules; and L. F. B. Robertnier in his manuscript journal on the war in America from 1780 to 1783 (which is found in the Shepley Historical Collection in Providence, Rhode Island) either ignores or knows nothing about the Swedes. Many of the available contemporaneous French narratives—probably influenced by the idle functions at Newport—show more interest in social entertainments than in military operations. Many Frenchmen in Newport were more concerned with the charms of Miss Hunter than with the problems of General Washington. Lafayette, though deeply interested in the possibility of securing Swedish ships for belligerent purposes, has nothing to say about the Swedish officers, and he must have known some of them. Rochambeau's memoirs record two minor missions of his aid, Colonel von Fersen; but that is all.

Nevertheless, subsequently printed compilations from the surviving official French documents provided a sufficiently large num-

ber of names to inspire a more profound study of the subject.[1]
The method of compilation and identification has been as follows:
First; all French names in properly suspicious medium that had
the remotest resemblance to a Scandinavian surname, or were
definitely cited as Swedish, have been examined, reconstructed, if
possible and necessary, and traced in available Swedish records.
Since a surprisingly large proportion of the Swedish survivors of
the war subsequently attained prominence in their own land, it
often became a simple matter to look up biographical material
about them either in the general *Biografiskt Lexicon* or in the
Nordisk Familjebok; and inasmuch as the majority of the participants either were already or eventually became noblemen,[2] one
could almost always find some illuminating and definite facts in
the four volumes of Anrep's *Svenska Adelns Ättar-Taflor,* a biographical catalogue of the Swedish nobility, a Swedish *Almanach
de Gotha,* which has been a most valuable source of identification.
Secondly; through the courtesy and able direction of Dr. Erik
Naumann of Riksarkivet in Stockholm, a number of names have
been obtained directly from original papers, letters and dispatches
in the Swedish archives. Those by Count de Creutz, the Swedish
ambassador in Paris during the American Revolution have, of
course, been my most reliable source. It has proved impossible
thus far to obtain the full name of all Swedish officers discovered
to date; but there is no doubt about the existence, or nationality,
of the individuals mentioned in each case, or about the minimum
number. Only two or three names have not been positively
identified. Of course, the total number of foreign officers who
served us during the Revolution will never be known. In the
interim let a commensurate honor and justice be paid to the
Swedish officers whom we already know. They performed a
part worthy of our consideration and gratitude!

---

[1] In the Bibliography and in the list of officers, Chapter VI, the more
important sources are indicated.

[2] For instance: after September, 1781, all successful candidates for a
second lieutenancy in the French cavalry or infantry were obliged, per
order of "His Majesty," to submit a genealogical certificate showing
noble birth of at least four ancestors. See letter by Creutz, preserved
in *Riksarkivet,* Stockholm, of September 2, 1781.

THE IMPORTANCE OF THE NAVAL OPERATIONS

The large majority of the Swedish officers served in the French navy, and in order to understand their service it is necessary, first of all, to recall the relative value to us of the French auxiliary army and the French navy. The American War of Independence was fought in all parts of the world, and we know now that the burden of our foreign aid rested with the French fleet. It was a comparatively easy matter to recruit forces for land duty on American soil; authorities in Paris were swamped with requests for early service in the American Continental forces, and, later, for duty in the expeditionary French army. The number of more or less able volunteers anxious to go to America became a dire nuisance, and most of them had to be turned away. Creutz complained to his king, on February 3, 1780, that so many Swedes arrived in Paris that it was difficult to get them well placed; and Count de Maurepas urged moderation in the "solicitations" of positions for the Swedish officers. "If it were a land war," he said—thereby implying that at least so far as the French were concerned it was a naval war—"it would be different, but it was only right, considering how few troops could be employed, that the French should be given preference." But this was for service on land. It was a different matter to serve in the French navy, and much more difficult to get able men and officers for duty on water. The British squadrons watched closely, and the French ships had the double duty, with constant danger, of engaging or frightening the enemy and transporting land troops. The second division of the French expeditionary force never reached America at all, because it was blockaded in home harbors by the English fleet. The problem was not so much how to get adequate infantry or artillery, as, after the financial difficulties had been straightened out, how to get them to the United States. The control of the seas was an enormous advantage for the British, and it became imperative to harass the English in all parts of the globe. Those who could be kept busy in European, African, or Asiatic waters, would not bother the Americans, and it was infinitely more practical from our viewpoint to damage the English nearer home than to wait until they had had the opportunity to do injury in the American states or waters. A tremendous responsibility, then, fell on the shoulders of the officers of the French navy; and the writer has never read of any contemporaneous stampede to enlist in this service. The glory and promises for the future seemed less certain and brilliant. On land, a foreigner might possibly obtain some high rank, such as that of general, in the American army—Lafayette did; but America could offer nothing very attractive in her own inadequate navy, and in the French service no foreigner might legally command a warship, no matter how capable he was.[1] The highest rank that he could obtain was that of *lieutenant de vaisseau*. The only advantages possible for a stranger serving on a French man-of-war were naval experience, the satisfaction of having a position, and the remote possibility of some honor or pension at the end, if still alive, with a chance for promotion in the navy of his native country. There could be no meteoric rise into positions of recognized command either in the French or the American employ.

Les Combattants Français de la Guerre Americaine 1778-1783

---

[1] After the summer of 1780, however, exceptions might be made under certain conditions in the case of the Swedish officers. While the Swedish king and Count de Creutz were at Spa, in July, 1780, the acting Swedish minister to the French court, Staël von Holstein, wrote the following (apparently undated) message to his king about the position of the Swedes in the French naval service:

"The ambassador (de Creutz) had demanded that the Swedish officers serving in the French navy should be granted the privilege of commanding (a vessel), in case their superior officers, or those of equal rank, were killed or otherwise disabled. (The French minister of Naval Affairs) de Surtine wrote me a letter a short time afterward in which he told me that in his opinion the ambassador's demand was liable to cause embarrassment, and that he believed it would be much better to follow the old established plan. Since this was very disadvantageous for the Swedish officers, I sent a new communication in which I again called attention to what the ambassador had pointed out, and showed the Minister that it was not only unjust but also detrimental to the good of the service to deprive capable officers of the honor of commanding in their turn, and that this exclusion could only injure the honor of the individual who in an extreme emergency saw himself compelled to obey his inferior in rank whom he had commanded the moment before.

I was more fortunate in this negotiation than I had dared to hope. Monsieur de Surtine has just advised me that the king of France has granted my request, and that orders to that effect will be given and sent out to all ports in France."

recognizes the proper importance of the operations on water, and lists first of all the naval men and officers, who of course out-numbered the land forces that fought for us by at least five to one. Only a small part of the army could be used, but practically the whole of the navy.   And all naval actions by the French and their Spanish allies contributed something to the success of the cause. Only lack of space compels the compiler of the above-cited work to limit the enumeration of French participants to those who served on the western continent.   Says Merou, the author of the Introduction: "The exploits of de Suffren, for example, in the Indian Ocean have perhaps contributed just as much to the final result as those in the Chesapeake."[1]   When peace negotiations were going on, the English won a signal victory over the French fleet in the West, but this was to a great extent offset by the simultaneous reports from the far East which told of British reverses in India, where de Suffren was threatening "that other colonial empire, which it would ruin them to lose."[2]   The West Indies became a favorite field of operations.   Spain joining France extended the theatre of war "far beyond the colonies, with the consequent inability of England to employ the greater part of her forces upon this (American) continent," C. H. Russell points out in *The French Alliance*.[3]   Through naval coalition against her, England found herself necessitated to defend Florida, the Mediterranean, the British Channel, the coast of Africa, and even England itself   To quote from Mr. Russell:

Necessarily England's attention was in a great degree diverted from America, and her capacity actively to prosecute the war there was corre-spondingly reduced.   The battle for American independence was in-directly fought on many seas and in many lands, where the English met their European enemies.   To the Americans of that day, impatient and discouraged, and from time to time disappointed at not receiving from France the military and naval aid upon their own continent and upon their own coasts which they desired, these important facts were not so clear as they now are to us.   But their importance to the cause of American inde-pendence cannot be over-estimated.[4]

In short, despite serious blunders and reverses, the navy played a "rôle considérable," as the French said.

---

[1] Introduction, xi.
[2] Paul Gaulot, *A Friend of the Queen,* I, 100-101.
[3] P. 17.
[4] *The French Alliance,* p. 30.

We can now understand why the Scandinavian sailors,[1] the direct descendants of Viking seafarers, were so welcome to the French authorities. Their proffered services were more needed and were accepted with less hesitancy. In the above-quoted letter to Gustavus III, by Count de Creutz, of February 3, 1780, after declaring that there were too many Swedish officers who were candidates for land duty, he continues: "But in the navy it is a different situation, if Your Majesty should send me *fifty officers more,* I could place them all. Besides, all Your Majesty's naval officers have distinguished themselves in such a marked way and shown such evident talent that they are eagerly sought, by preference, in all fields of (naval) activities." Most of these Scandinavians had had previous training of an especially intensive character and were immediately assigned to active duty against the English. Obviously, from the geographical nature of marine warfare, they could not all insist upon being sent forthwith to American coasts; they readily accepted assignment to vessels and waters where they could do most good. Some of them undoubtedly never saw America; yet others whose names appear toward the end of the war as serving on vessels in the East Indies under Bailli de Suffren were probably here at the beginning of the French operations in 1778 and 1779, when de Suffren and his squadron carried off the chief honors in American waters outside of Rhode Island, although we have not as yet any definite proof of the fact.

At all events, dozens of Swedish naval officers secured leaves of absence from their own country, or resigned from other for-

---

[1] Among the Scandinavians in French service during the American Revolution were several Danish officers also, such as Bille, Fisher, Hauch, Koefoed, and Krieger. Of these Hauch and Koefoed are sometimes designated in French records as Swedish.

On August 30, 1778, de Creutz writes to his king: "Eight Danish naval officers have arrived here (in Paris) and request employment in the French navy. We do not know yet whether they will be admitted as volunteers or as supernumeraries."

The remainder of the same letter is also of interest: "All the Swedes who have arrived have been suitably employed and have embarked on the fleet. All those who come in the future will also be employed in like manner. If peace is not made this winter, the next campaign will be as terrible as it is instructive, because the preparations going on are enormous. . . ."

eign service, to participate in the war under the French flag. And these did not belong to the class of idlers and adventurers who, allured by promises, first flocked to Paris to overwhelm the American agents with offers of aid. They were for the most part serious men, a few of them unemployed perhaps, whose subsequent record in life proved their sterling qualities. Several of them later became admirals in the Swedish navy, a navy which during the American Revolution and for a considerable time afterwards was, relatively, as we shall see, of considerable consequence, and enjoyed the respect of all naval powers, England included. Her officers were, therefore, a valuable acquisition to the American and French cause. Many who distinguished themselves in our war later became heroes in the Swedish struggle against Russia, and among the officers who fought on American soil, one became Grand Marshal, or chancellor, of Sweden, and another led the Swedish forces against Napoleon in the battle of Leipzig, 1813.

But, first—before we treat of the Swedish officers in detail— let us examine the Swedish attitude in general toward the American colonies, and see what relations existed between Sweden and the United States during the Revolutionary period.

CHAPTER I

THE SWEDISH MOTIVE FOR PARTICIPATION

ATTITUDE TOWARD THE AMERICAN COLONISTS

Since this brief monograph aims to treat historical facts from an objective, though sympathetic, standpoint, avoiding so far as is humanly possible the frequent pitfalls of the exaggeration of minorities and the deification resulting therefrom, we shall not hesitate to dwell for a moment on the *motives* for Swedish participation in our Revolution, remembering, however, that we are more concerned with accomplishments than with motives, and that, whatever the latter may be, the facts and ultimate results remain essentially the same.

We may assume that the Swedish friendship for France furnished a strong impulse for aid; lack of enthusiasm for England and revolt against her maritime policies on the high seas gave another; the personal desire of officers to gain naval and military experience and honor provided a third motive for enlistment in our cause; and then also, the unusual opportunity for adventure undoubtedly attracted the Vikings of 1780, as it had those of the year 1000, and as it did so many others. But the motives were probably not all selfish. Lack of employment, though it played a part, probably did not figure very largely in the case of the Northern volunteers, certainly not among the naval officers; there was much to do in the Baltic and in the Gulfs of Finland and Bothnia during those troublous times, and at least one Swedish officer in the Franco-American service was called back home to help enforce the decree of the Armed Neutrality.

It may be argued that the Swedish officers, most of them born aristocrats, with no love of democracy such as the insurgent American colonists dreamed of, would never have fought for a republic in Europe. This is unquestionably true! It was quite safe to do for America what they would never have done for their own country. But this was true of other foreign participants as well. To be an aristocrat in Europe and a republican in America—so long as one could do some tangible damage to England—was the fashion of the day, and Sweden was more in the mode than the rest. Such was the inconsistent if not illogical spirit of an age which prattled vaguely in high circles about freedom and the rights of man, little realizing that monarchial despotism was soon to receive a mortal wound. And, in France, noblemen did not escape the guillotine because they had fought for American liberty. They had remained, or were thought to have remained, intrinsically monarchists. The same tendency obtained in a considerable degree among the Swedish gentry. It was the natural result of heredity and circumstances.

Yet there were more deeply rooted reasons for Swedish sympathy with the American colonists. Like other Scandinavians, the Swede was *par excellence* a liberty-loving individual who would never suffer oppression for any length of time or be subject to outside domination. Servility in any political form was against his nature, and tyranny prompted immediate revolt. Montesquieu in his *L'Esprit des Lois* had located the cradle of European liberty in the North. It was contended that liberty dwelt on the mountains and near the seas; the Scandinavian peninsula had both. And, in the past all Swedish classes had sponsored freedom both in the abstract and the concrete, even if sometimes one estate had done so at the expense of another. *Independence* was a word that appealed instinctively to rich and poor, nobleman and democrat.[1]

Thus the people would, *a priori,* naturally look with favor upon the new nation across the sea, and we shall learn that Swedish representatives at foreign courts were decidedly friendly to the American agents. In reality—though not officially perhaps, for Sweden was ostensibly a neutral nation—she was ever ready to offer refuge in her harbors to American vessels; and despite the initial reluctance of her king she became the first *neutral* country to recognize, unsolicited, the United States by negotiating a treaty of amity and commerce.[2] Then when we recall that Sweden as a neutral had, officially, but little direct political or Pan-Swedish interest in the contest, we may conclude that some of its citizens participated in the American war with more altruism than other foreigners, with the possible exception of Baron von Steuben and the Polish patriots. And the Swedes probably loved America as much as the French, if not more. That Sweden

[1] Cf. second paragraph, Chap. V.
[2] See Chapter III, pp. 48 ff. and note 2 on p. 48.

could not officially become America's ally will be understood by anyone who has studied European history and Scandinavian geography.

Nevertheless, aside from personal motives of individuals, Sweden, as a nation, had, like other nations, her affiliations and antipathies which were destined to influence her attitude toward France and America during their war with England.

In the Thirty Years' War, France, disregarding any religious aspects, had helped finance the armies of Gustavus Adolphus to aid in the humiliation of Austria; and since that time the political and cultural relations between the two countries had been very intimate. Reciprocal eulogies were the order of the day. Yet Sweden was never the vassal of France. During the eighteenth century scores of Swedish officers had served in the French armies, and one regiment, called significantly the Royal Suédois, was commanded almost entirely by Swedish officers, up to the time of the French Revolution. Swedish ministers were popular at the French court, and the outbreak of the American war found the Swedish ambassador to France, Count Gustav de Creutz, the favorite and, though young in years, the most experienced foreign diplomat in Paris. It was in some degree his seniority as a foreign representative, the respect for his opinion, and his own enthusiasm for Franklin and the American colonies, which created such a friendly feeling for America in diplomatic circles. Besides being his country's envoy, de Creutz, at a time when literary prestige often took precedence over titles of nobility, was also a poet and a gentleman of the French style, whose friendship and judgment were sought in the literary salons of the capital. His own weekly salon "became one of the circles most sought by philosophers and literary men," says the Duc de Broglie of the Swedish ambassador, although, according to the testimony of Prince Talleyrand, Marmontel read so many tragedies at these meetings that he drove away all the guests.[1]

Politically, Sweden needed and solicited the friendship of the French government. Her possessions south of the Baltic had more than once brought her into complications with Germany; in the east Russia had for centuries been a menace, and it was only a question of time when Finland would become Russian

---

[1] *Memoirs*, p. 35.

territory; and because of ancient family quarrels, several of them serious, Sweden and Denmark regarded each other with more or less suspicion. Thus it happened that Gustavus III, upon his accession to the Swedish throne, looked more and more to France for political coöperation. His culture was perhaps more French than Swedish; he felt drawn toward the splendor of the French court, whose magnificence he had copied, if not excelled, in his own capital. Also, he had entertained plans of curbing the power of the stubborn Swedish nobility, and for their execution had obtained the backing of France. Therefore, when America solicited French aid for her struggle with England, France counted in turn on both moral and, in some form, active encouragement and assistance from Sweden. In fact, judging from previous relations, one might have expected to see Sweden drawn into the war. "In Gustavus III of Sweden, the nephew of Frederic of Prussia," writes Bancroft, "France might expect a friend. The (bloodless) revolution of 1771 (-1772 in Sweden), in favor of the royal prerogative, had been aided by French subsidies[1] and the counsels of Vergennes, who was selected for the occasion to be French minister at Stockholm."[2] It is not without some significance for us that in 1776 the former French envoy to the Swedish court was the French minister of foreign affairs, in whose hands lay largely the final decision to recognize our independence and enter the war on the American side.

There may have been another contributory reason why France sought the good will of Sweden and Spain. In 1776 Swedish credits in Holland, the European banking-house of the time, were higher than her own, a condition which the American agent in Amsterdam, William Carmichael, considered of sufficient import to make a report of it to the Committee of Secret Correspondence. He writes on November 2, 1776, that the French credit "has been

---

[1] France on her part, was anxious to maintain the friendship of Sweden, and Louis XVI fulfilled the subsidy agreements made by Louis XV. In 1776 the subsidy agreement of 1773 was declared in force for three years more and Sweden received 700,000 livres more in 1778. On December 2, 1778, in return for a renewal of the treaty of 1738, France secretly guaranteed Gustavus III 1,500,000 livres a year for six years. After 1783, following a journey to Italy and France, Gustavus III got increased subsidies from France, and on July 1, 1784 the island of St. Barthélemy in the West Indies.

[2] *History of United States* VI. Revised edition of 1876, p. 92.

very low of late." The financial standing of Spain is extremely good. "Sweden and Denmark have both good credit; the former the best; they have money at four per cent; and it is not long since the King of Sweden borrowed three millions of guilders at this interest to pay off old debts at five per cent. His interest is paid punctually." . . .[1] The American agent probably did not know that the financial condition of the Swedish government was in some measure dependent upon the payment of French subsidies. However, if French credit was low at Amsterdam, Swedish credit must have been based on some independent sources, and not entirely on the uncertain French subsidies.

The continuation of Carmichael's letter from Amsterdam may serve to introduce specific evidences of the Swedish attitude toward the American war of independence. He writes:

If it should be determined to send any cargoes of Tobacco here on the public account, it will perhaps be thought proper to convoy them. The frigates destined to that service might retaliate the injuries we have received. *Should there be a necessity of seeking shelter or refreshments, I have it from the Swedish ambassador (Baron de Geer) here that we shall find both in their ports.*[2]

This was in 1776. The secret offer requires no comment, except to point out that it could hardly have been made by an accredited representative without some knowledge of the feelings and inclinations of his people and government.

On March 31, 1779, Franklin writes from Passy to the American agent, Stephen Sayre:

Sir; I have received your favor of the 10th inst. from Copenhagen. The account you give of the disposition of the Swedish Court is very agreeable. I saw in the newspapers that a deputy of the Congress was at Stockholm. Did you obtain the audiences you mention by assuming that character? The information you did not choose to venture by the post from Copenhagen may be safely sent from Amsterdam.[3]

The Swedish court at first could do nothing publicly that might be interpreted as official. But as we have noted, her representatives abroad seldom hesitated to defend and champion the Americans, and Carmichael's letter shows that this was done two years before the official French entrance into the conflict. To indicate

---

[1] Wharton, *Diplomatic Correspondence*, II 186.
[2] *Ibid.*, 188. The italics are not in the original.
[3] Wharton, III, 107.

to what extent the Swedes were willing to go, secretly, to harass
the English, and help the colonists, we need only read the following testimony by Carmichael to Livingston, dated at Madrid,
December 20, 1781. After reporting that the capture of Cornwallis was not at all pleasing to the foreign ministers of Germany,
Russia, and Denmark, who considered the surrender a blow deciding the independence of the States, Carmichael continues:

> The new minister of Sweden is open in declaring his partiality for our
> cause. . . . and signified that he would have waited on the American
> representative Mr. Jay on his arrival here, as it is the custom of these
> last come to do, if no other minister had arrived since Mr. Jay's residence
> who had not done it. His conduct to myself shows that this was not a
> mere compliment, for he has invited me several times to dine with him,
> and visited me. . . . The Imperial (Russian) and Swedish ministers
> declare that their respective sovereigns will reclaim all vessels under their
> colors, going to or returning from America, which comply with the articles
> of the armed neutrality,[1] and it has been hinted to me that it was not
> difficult to obtain letters of naturalization for the crews of American
> vessels, provided the nominal officers are subjects of either country.[2]

No European took a keener interest in the American war than
the Swedish minister in Paris. And he was interested not only
in the engagements in which Swedish officers participated but in
the war as a whole. His correspondence with Gustavus III and
others shows how closely he followed all the events of the conflict. A study of his letters will illustrate this. The following
quotation indicates an intimacy with the French minister of foreign affairs which was probably not shared by any other foreign
diplomat. Creutz became virtually an unofficial adviser to Count
de Vergennes:

> With great intensity France has redoubled her war preparations at Brest
> and Toulon, and it is the belief that some important expedition is pending.
> I have pointed out to Count de Vergennes the necessity of exerting efforts
> proportional to the power and position of France, efforts which sustain the
> opinion that is current about her resources. I have added that all true
> friends of France should like to see energetic action, and that no success
> can be expected except through an offensive war and by transporting to the
> (West Indian) Islands a corps of troops for destroying the English power
> in that region. The Minister replied that he agreed with me entirely, and
> that when the plan of the campaign had been put into effect, it would
> show that it had been conceived on a grand scale with hope of a successful
> issue.

---

[1] See Chapter on the Armed Neutrality.
[2] Wharton, V. 62.

This was written on February 24, 1780. On the second of March, Creutz reports that Admiral Rodney had broken through the enemy's naval line at Gibraltar and started for American waters; that Rochambeau had been chosen commander of the expeditionary force, which was now to be sent to America; and that de Ternay, with ten warships, was to convoy the French troops across the Atlantic. Creutz hopes that Spain will turn its attention to Florida and India instead of wasting its time at Gibraltar, and that after Halifax and New York have been captured, the French army will be able to crush the English power in the Antilles. He is glad that the war has finally assumed a more active character, speaks of the French and German regiments that are to set out for the West, and expresses faith in the ability of Rochambeau.

On the eleventh of June, 1780, Creutz reports that no details have been received from Count Guichen, French naval commander in the West Indian waters, but that he has continued his campaign, and that France expects to hear soon about successes near Martinique. A naval battle there has been "murderous," since the number of wounded transported to Guadeloupe amounts to eight hundred. . . .

"Two frigates from the Orient (i. e. from the French squadron in Eastern waters) are being fitted out for service in America under the command of the famous Paul Jones. They are the *Union* and the *Ariel*. They will carry with them ten thousand rifles and clothing for as many men."

Washington is only waiting for the arrival of Rochambeau, writes Creutz eleven days later, in order to attack New York. "We are impatiently waiting for news from the various scenes of war. Never before have so many attacks been made in so many different places. They can not all be failures; some must be decisive and force a treaty of peace. This campaign, it seems to me, has the potentialities of the most momentous results. And if these do not produce peace, we can never tell when the war will end."

In a dispatch to the Swedish king of March 28, 1781, Creutz announces that Admiral de Grasse had left six days before with twenty-six vessels of war. At the same time a convoy with eight thousand men had been sent along as reinforcements for the army. "Never before has such a formidable fleet, equipped in such a

short time, left the ports either of France or of England." Says
Creutz: "This is where the activity of Monsieur de Castries
(French Secretary of the Navy) can be recognized. The departure of this fleet has silenced the rumor of peace, and I believe
that in reality the difficulties have multiplied to such an extent
that, despite the English and French desire to cease hostilities, this
autumn will see the war again in all its furor. The deplorable
part is that nothing decisive happens, and I still fear that the
next campaign will witness many battles but few defeats. . . ."

Let these samples suffice to show what may be called the
Swedish diplomatic interest in the war.[1]

We have indicated that the Swedish people should be favorably
disposed toward the United States, both by inheritance and circumstances. Bancroft has referred to another ground for support. "The oldest colonizers of the Delaware were Swedes, and
a natural affection bound their descendants to the mother country."[2] The Swedish settlements on the Delaware from 1638 on
had not been very large, but their number has constituted a sturdy
and thrifty group, the descendants of whom in 1776 were spread
over several states, and, as we hope to show later, were unquestionably more numerous than some writers and census-calculators
might imagine. Sweden had kept up a sporadic communication
with these descendants—it is not true that they had been forgotten—and during the eighteenth century had sent several
clergymen, with books, to New Sweden. Now and then, a few
Swedish emigrants had arrived in America. For instance, in
1711 Gustaf Hesselius, an artist, had followed his clerical brother
to these shores, and had become a father of American art,
especially of portrait-painting.[3] In 1748-1750 Pehr Kalm, the
Swedish botanist who had been sent out by the Swedish Academy
of Sciences to gather seeds for his government and study American plants and animals, could be seen discussing problems and
conditions with the Delaware descendants, and upon his return he
had published a three-volumed report of his voyage and findings
which was eventually translated into English, German, and French.
It was a translation of this report which first brought Benjamin

---

[1] For a more personal account of Count de Creutz see special chapter.
[2] *Op. cit.*, VI, p. 92.
[3] Cf. Willetta Goddard Ball, *Scandinavian Contribution to Early American Art, The American-Scandinavian Review*, III, 7-15.

Franklin's name before the German public. Besides, for two decades thereafter, Kalm had published scientific articles on American subjects, thus keeping the name of America constantly before the learned classes. He had also brought back to Sweden information about his friend Franklin, who thus continued to enjoy the respect and sympathy of the Swedish cultured bodies. It was only natural, then, if Swedish volunteers in the French army and navy felt they knew something about us, and that in some degree they were fighting the battles of their own sons and daughters.

It must be admitted that the innermost convictions of the Swedish king were not favorable to the Americans, any more than those of George III, or Louis XVI, because of his inherited regal prejudices about the rights of kings. He regarded the colonists, technically, as rebels, who could become free and independent only through the release of their oath of allegiance to the King of England. It was an opinion easy to understand, and based on tradition and environment. On October 19, 1778, Gustavus III writes from Drottningholm, to his minister at Paris:

> The action of the French ministry (in recognizing American independence) it seems to me, has deviated both from the principles of justice and practical interests, and from state principles of nations that have been in force for centuries. I cannot admit that it is right to support rebels against their king. The example will find only too many imitators in an age when it is the fashion to overthrow every bulwark of authority. But I presume I shall have to give in in this matter.

Gustavus III, however, was not the only one to hold this political opinion. "All Europe," writes C. H. Russell, "whether friendly or otherwise, had regarded the colonists simply as insurgents. It must be remembered that there were grave doubts among many of the Americans themselves as to whether the declaration (of independence) was wise or justified."[1] Some regarded it as a premature step, if not open rebellion.

Yet Gustavus III could separate practical foresightedness—and maybe certain personal sympathies—from his political principles as a regent. He was an astute, farsighted monarch. Despite traditional prejudices, common to others as well, he was wide awake to the progress of the world, being held as "one of the foremost in the advancing ranks." So it was not long before he began to

---

[1] *The French Alliance,* p. 13.

consider the acknowledgment of American independence by in-
structing his ambassador in Paris to enter into negotiations for
a treaty with the new power beyond the sea. Still in 1778 he had
offered to mediate between England and France and did not care
to be accused of double dealing. So, in December, 1782, he
reiterates his former ideas to Creutz and cautions him to carry on
his negotiations carefully. But his sympathies were with France;
the heroic struggle of the colonists procured his respect; he liked
Franklin; and English methods irritated him. Thus it happened
that the American cause profited by the practical attitude of
Gustavus III. Some Englishmen accused him of duplicity.

Russell, who certainly knew nothing specific about Swedish
interest in the war, admits that "even in monarchial countries outside of France"—where there was no such sympathy with the
American cause as existed in that country—the progress of events
caused sympathy to be alienated from England and turned toward
the Colonies.[1]

Perhaps the best proof of sympathy for us is the English
exasperation at the Swedish attitude and actions. Englishmen
called Sweden "a constant appendage to French policy and interest." It is true, as we shall see, that Sweden did practically
the same things for which, in the case of Holland, England
declared war. It was Sweden rather than Russia which took the
leading, effective part in the Armed Neutrality, aimed primarily
against England; she opened her harbors to American privateers;[2]

---

[1] *Ibid.*, p. 30.

[2] Officially, however, it was only in Marstrand, a free port open on equal
terms to all belligerents, that Americans—after their independence had
been recognized by Sweden—might dispose of prizes captured on the high
seas. From some American reports it would seem as though more than
one Swedish port were open to privateers, but it is possible that reports
of Swedish hospitality were sometimes intentionally exaggerated for
moral effect. We know that once, in 1780, Gustavus III yielded to a
vigorous protest by the English minister relative to the Americans finding
refuge in Marstrand, and ordered their privateers out of the harbor.

Also, before Sweden recognized American independence, American warships were considered and treated as private vessels, and therefore not
entitled, for instance, to the regular official salutes.

Cf. C. T. Odhner, *Sveriges politiska historia under konung Gustaf III:s
regering*, II, pp. 92 and 123. Also, Arnold Munthe, *Svenska Sjöhjältar*,
VI. p. 100.

her sentiments friendly to the colonists were openly revealed; she entered into negotiations for a treaty with the States while the belligerent nations were yet at war; and she helped America, commercially, as did Holland, both directly and indirectly. A communication from London of March 30, 1780, reproduced in the American press, announced that "Sardinia, Sweden, and Naples, are ready to commence hostilities upon us whenever France and Spain call for their assistance." The following report from London of October 18, 1781, bearing an unmistakable stamp of truthfulness, was reproduced in the Providence *Gazette* for January 26, 1782, as evidence of Swedish moral support and coöperation on the French and American side:

The Swedes are now waging hostilities against us (English) in such a matter, as can scarcely any longer be called clandestine, and though their neutral masque is attended with double injury, our Ministers are afraid to open their eyes on those transactions.

What an intolerable insult to be tamely born by the British flag, blocking up a large Dutch fleet in the Texel, to see a single Swedish ship of 74 guns, purchased for the audacious purpose, quietly convoy the Dutch fleet under protection of its flag, and proudly bid defiance to ten English sail of the line, to touch the prey they had been so long waiting in vain.— This tale is so unusually ignominious, that it may seem the extravagance of fiction, but we again pledge our utmost credit to the public for the strict truth in it. . . . What madness is it thus to resign our ancient honor and interest, while through an inhuman revenge we are fighting for a shadow in a distant world!

The American press valued the coöperation of Sweden and scrupulously reported favorable news from that country. The same *Gazette* announced on October 26, 1782: "The King of Sweden has manifested, by some generous overtures to Congress, a most friendly disposition toward us, and has requested that an ambassador from these States may be sent to his Court."

Previously, on March 25, 1780, the same paper had printed the following information, which may be inserted here as showing the attitude and pride of the Swedish king in conferring honors upon those of his subjects who had already won laurels in America. "Stockholm (Sweden) Oct. 8. The King has been conferring honors on several Swedish officers who served under Count d'Estaing, and distinguished themselves by their bravery, particularly in the naval action off Grenada, and some others who were at the taking of the ship *Ardent,* by the French frigate *Juno.*"

This item was obviously published to show Americans the Swedish participation in the struggle for whatever encouragement it might give.

Early in the war the colonists were in sore need of increasing their naval and maritime forces, but were too poor to purchase ships outright. Lafayette suggested procuring some by loan, from Sweden, under certain guarantees, as a temporary relief, and on April 26, 1779, wrote to Count de Vergennes about the advisability of obtaining from Sweden "four ships of the line, with the half of their crews." He continues:

United States would engage to return them within a year upon certain conditions.—The vessels might come to us under the Swedish flag. France need not be implicated at all. We could supply them in part, provide them with officers in blue, and send them out under the American flag. It would only be necessary to know, whether France would engage to be responsible for the hire, and would help to complete the equipment. . . . I have not yet spoken to Dr. Franklin about the scheme, but I have sounded the Swedish ambassador on the subject, much to my satisfaction; he asked me for a letter, directed to him, which might be sent to his king; and since I saw that this important project might result in something advantageous, I was constrained to confide it to you, and ask your opinion. The Swedish ambassador states that the vessels may be here in two months and a half . . . .[1]

Though this proposition was finally rejected as adventurous and impracticable, involving too many elements of danger, the letter itself shows the coöperative attitude of the Swedish ambassador and his willingness to further a scheme fraught with perilous possibilities for his own government.

Although the French negotiations with Sweden concerning the loan of her ships for the United States had not brought the desired results, they had rekindled in the mind of the Swedish king an ambition which became another, more potent reason for

---

[1] Cf. following item from Henry Doniol, *Histoire de la Participation de la France à L 'Établissement des États-Unis d'Amérique,* Tome 4, pp. 230, 231: "On aurait chargé le corsaire Paul Jones de transporter des troupes audacieuses que La Fayette aurait commandés. Bristol, Liverpool, les cités riches de ces côtes se seraient vu surprendre et auraient fourni de l'argent aux Américains. Cette idée fut bientôt abandonné. La Fayette lui en substitua une autre, grâce a des encouragements de l'ambassadeur de Suéde, qui lui offrit de faire prêter aux États-Unis quatre vaisseaux par son souverain. Il se serait alors agi d'engager des hommes et des officiers par les Français.

supporting the anti-English side of the conflict—the ambition to obtain for Sweden a colony in the West Indies.[1] And it seems to have been Lafayette who, in anticipation of Swedish favors to the Allies, such as the possible loan of ships, first suggested a plan for the realization of such an ambition. Says C. T. Odhner:

Believing that England would finally succumb to her many enemies and at the treaty of peace be obliged to surrender several of her colonies, the king (Gustavus III) took up again his plan of 1775,[2] that of attempting to procure for Sweden a colony in America.[3] The first suggestion of this idea was given by the Marquis de la Fayette, who in the beginning of 1779 had returned from America and was entertaining all kinds of schemes for the benefit of the united colonies. One of these plans was that Sweden should transfer some of their warships to the Americans and in return receive one of the West Indian islands to be taken from the English.[4] Obviously, Sweden could not accept a proposition which could have but one result—war with England; yet, on the other hand, the king zealously cherished the thought of obtaining an island in the West Indies. Such a possession would furnish a market for our manufactured products, provide an opportunity for our naval officers to get training, and offer a place of diversion for all the restless minds of the land. He preferred Porto Rico. Others mentioned were Tobago, St. Vincent, Grenada, and St. Christopher. An effort was made to interest Vergennes in the matter and through him to exert an influence on the court at Madrid. Also, a way was sought to enter into negotiations with the united colonies, and one hoped that the young Count Fersen, when he left for America as

---

[1] Cf. p. 14, note. See also pp. 62, 108 and 110.

[2] C. T. Odhner, *op. cit.,* I, p. 393.

[3] Bancroft, *op. cit.,* VI, p. 92, says: "The adventurous king (of Sweden) had the ambition to possess a colony, and France inclined to gratify his wish. His people, as builders and owners of ships, favored the largest interpretation of the maritime rights of neutrals; and we shall see their king, who had dashing courage, though not perseverance, now and then shows himself as the boldest champion of the liberty of the seas."
This championing of the rights of neutrals, as we shall see, was very valuable to France—and America—and France was willing to do something in return.

[4] In a letter by Creutz of May 20, 1779, it appears (1) that Lafayette had made his proposition in the name of Americans, and (2) that there were perhaps other means of winning over the American Congress—and induce it to grant Sweden a colony—than by selling warships to the United States.
Again referring to the same matter, Creutz wrote as follows to Gustavus III on March 2, 1780: When he arrives in America, "Count de Fersen, in concert with the Chevalier de la Luzerne, will be able to act with all the prudence and precaution that such a delicate matter demands, and be certain of success if the plan is at all feasible."

General Rochambeau's adjutant, would be instrumental in effecting a cession of some island or continental stretch of land to Sweden. Perhaps he had in mind the old Swedish colony on the Delaware, which still kept up an ecclesiastical relation with the old motherland.[1]

The following communication throws some more light on why the Swedes should favor America in the war:

John Adams to the President of Congress, Braintree, August 4, 1779:

Russia, Sweden, and Denmark comprehended under the denomination of the northern powers, have been thought by some to be interested in our return to the domination of Great Britain. Whether they consider themselves in this light or not, their late declarations against the right of England to interrupt their navigation, and their arming for the protection of their commerce on the ocean, and even in the English Channel, are unequivocal proofs of their opinion concerning the right in our contest and all their intention not to interfere against us. It is not probable that the courts of Petersburg, Stockholm, and Copenhagen have viewed with indifference the present revolution, if they have been apprehensive of being hurt by it in some respects, which, however, I think must have been a mistaken apprehension; yet the motive of humbling the pride of the English, who have endeavored to exercise their domination over the northern seas and to render the Danish and Swedish flag dependent on theirs, has prevailed over all others, and they are considered in Europe as having given their testimony against the English in this war.[2]

This brings us to the subject of the Armed Neutrality.

---

[1] Odhner, *op. cit.,* pp. 79-80.
[2] Wharton, *Diplomatic Correspondence,* III, 285.

CHAPTER II

SWEDEN AND THE ARMED NEUTRALITY[1]

By an extraordinary combination of circumstances the most despotic Courts of Europe united against Great Britain to give liberty to the armed and revolted Colonists. The Danes and Swedes seemed to have laid aside mutual animosities; they joined in alliance with Russia.

This testimony by the Britisher, John Brown, in *Memoirs of the Court of Sweden*[2] refers to what is generally known as the Armed Neutrality, a confederation of the Northern Powers to protect their commerce against the high-handed methods of the English.

"During the summer (of 1778)," writes Bancroft, "the flag of Denmark, of Sweden, of Prussia, had been disregarded by British privateers, and they severally demanded of England explanations. Vergennes seized the opportunity to fix the attention of Count Panin (the Russian ambassador), urged him to persuade the Empress Catherine to make common cause with Sweden, Denmark, Prussia and Holland. Denmark announced it would send out a squadron for convoy in the spring, and said Sweden would have to do the same."

Bancroft goes on to point out that in an interview with Panin the Swedish envoy invited the Russian court to join that of Stockholm in "forming a combined fleet to protect the trade of the North. Denmark," he said, "would no doubt subscribe to the plan and the commerce of the three countries, now so interrupted, would no longer be molested." Panin listened willingly and brought the matter before the English minister late in December. In 1779—to continue Bancroft's account—

the oppressed maritime powers continued to lay their complaints before the Empress of Russia; so that the study of neutral rights occupied her mind till she came to consider herself singled out to take the lead in their

---

[1] In regard to the general subject of Swedish negotiations with America during the Revolution, including the Armed Neutrality, cf. chap. I of *Relations of the United States with Sweden,* by Knute Emil Carlson, University of Pennsylvania dissertation, 1921. This brief monograph substantiates my own conclusions with respect to Sweden's part in the Armed Neutrality, conclusions which had been reached and written down before I had become acquainted with Dr. Carlson's work.

[2] I, p. 230.

defense, and could with difficulty be withheld from sending to England very disagreeable remonstrances on the subject.[1]

In order to understand Sweden's part in this enterprise, however, we must first glance at the personnel, the policies, and the political and commercial conditions in the countries most concerned. The nations of the North had different interests, and were not what we should call close friends. Prussia seems to have kept aloof and out of the militant struggle entirely until the League of the Armed Neutrality had been in operation for almost a year, at least so far as any effective measures were concerned. Her trade with America was slight, and most of it of an indirect character. She had little to lose in the first place, and took no chances. Denmark was defiant toward her Swedish neighbor, and had "the worst possible opinion" of her king. Denmark needed coöperation, but at first believed an entente impossible. So she hesitated when it came to bid defiance to Great Britain, though she desired Swedish help in case of eventual action. Then, too, she had no fixedness of administration, and the Danish ministry was ultra-monarchial, whatever the sentiments of the people might be:

Count Bernstorff, (Danish) minister of foreign affairs, a Hanoverian by birth, professed to believe (like Gustavus III, George III, and Louis XVI) that the repose, the strength, and the happiness of civil society depend upon the principle that a people (like the American colonists) can never be justified in renouncing fidelity, obedience, and subjection to its lawful government, and declaring itself independent. He watched, therefore, that the Danish government should not favor, or even seem to favor, any step which promised help to the Americans. Complying with the suggestion of the English Court, Danish subjects were forbidden to send, even to Danish West Indies Islands, munitions of war, lest they should find their way to the United States. The Danish and Norwegian ports were closed against prizes taken by American privateers, yet, from its commercial interests, Denmark was forced to observe and claim the rights of a neutral.[2]

In other words, Denmark, like Holland, being geographically nearer to England, found itself, in 1778, more or less between the devil and the deep sea, and did not like to take radical steps unless necessitated to do so. As in the case of Holland, her

---

[1] *History of the United States of America from the Discovery of the Continent.* Vol. VI (1876), 238.
[2] *Ibid.,* pp. 92-93.

policy was to a large extent a matter of proximity and fear. So, for a considerable time Denmark never fully committed herself; she kept her former alliances, adopted a policy of watchful waiting, while spasmodically talking vigorously of concerted efforts; and, although the astute Bernstorff had no objections to curbing British naval and commercial power—in fact he strongly favored it—nevertheless, there were the political bonds with England, and he preferred English supremacy on the seas to French; at all events he doubted whether one would be any better than the other. He had valid reasons to be worried. As for the colonists, he believed they hated the Frenchmen at the bottom of their hearts, and would only use them for a purpose. Besides, he regarded their revolution as "the least excusable and most pernicious that could exist." Yet, England's pride deserved to be humbled, and Bernstorff had foreseen in December, 1777, that England and France would come to war.

Russia had nothing to fear from her immediate neighbors, and, as it proved, worked for her own interests to an extent which can scarcely be imagined from that final formal result which was heralded to the world as the work of the Empress of Russia. It is evident from the diplomatic correspondence that she was concerned, naturally enough perhaps, with the protection of her own coasts only; and it took much long and persistent outside pressure to produce a satisfactorily workable plan that would benefit all members of the proposed League. Russia was by no means so favorably disposed toward a joint armed proposal, for such a league was aimed against England. In the interim, Sir James Harris had been sent as English ambassador to St. Petersburg to court the favor of Russia, to enter into an alliance, if need be, and thus to offset and neutralize the alliance between France and the United States. That Russia, too, may have had real fear of being dragged into the war with England is a plausible view held by some historians. The same condition obtained in the Netherlands. For a long time, while feebly and nominally asserting their commercial rights and freedom of the seas, the Dutch withheld convoys when it involved danger of a conflict with Great Britain.

Thus it came to pass, that for the first two years Sweden took relatively the boldest part in this hazardous revolt. She adopted an independent foreign policy and "raised her voice in defense of

not only her own but also of general European interests"; and
in order to make herself heard, she "let her words be followed
by action."[1] It was in this Swedish attitude toward the scheme
that France found something worth while. It was Sweden, says
Doniol in his voluminous *Histoire de la participation de la France,
etc.,* which was "particularly inclined to adopt the views of France
with respect to neutrals."[2] As has been mentioned before, it was
in Gustavus III that Vergennes found a staunch supporter of his
conception of a union of neutrals "au profit de la France," and,
incidentally, *au profit de l'Amérique.* It was Sweden which
championed, and virtually from the very beginning put into practice, an efficacious program against what was regarded as English
insults. She held, as we do to-day, that disrespect for neutral
flags was a sign of barbarism and piracy. At all events, on the
15th of September, 1778, the French ambassador to Sweden
could report to his government that the exasperated Swedish
monarch had told England to better her ways under penalty of
harsh measures. The English were pirates who did not respect
a treaty, he had told them in substance. Stockholm informed
London that it would protect its commerce at all costs, as it was
impossible to accept the laws imposed by England.[3] The French
envoy reported also that Sweden had diplomatically sounded
Russia on the matter of joint action in case Great Britain did not
heed her protests.

These were courageous plans—it would take a strong convoy

---

[1] C. T. Odhner, *Sveriges politiska historia under Konung Gustaf III:s
regering,* II, 63. On this page begins an excellent Swedish account of the
Armed Neutrality.

[2] III, 713.

[3] The relations between Sweden and England at this time were strained
almost to a rupture. "Every one knows that, during the American war,
England claimed the right to search neutral vessels for contraband of war,
and that she exercised this right in a high-handed manner which con-
trasted most unfavorably with the liberality of the French in this respect.
Finding it impossible to obtain redress from England, the Northern Powers
exchanged notes as to the advisability of meeting force by force, and
Gustavus (December, 1778) instructed his Minister at London to deliver
a remonstrance to the English Government couched in such sharp terms
that Lord Suffolk expressed himself unable to distinguish it from a
formal declaration of war." R. Nisbet Bain, *Gustavus III and His Contemporaries,* I, 210.

to make them effective. But, through the genius of the king, Sweden during his reign had relatively the biggest navy in her history; she had many merchant ships to protect; hoped eventually to get some assistance somehow; and, besides, had been brought to a point of desperation. Consequently, Sweden and her regent became jointly the soul of the Armed Neutrality, when it most needed a soul, and when it did France and America most good. But let us examine further the first-hand evidence.

In the Diary of Gustavus III for September, 1778, we find this entry:

The French ambassador has told me about an interview with the Danish minister, Baron Gyldenkrone, on a topic concerning which Bernstorff has commissioned the latter to sound my ministry, namely to find out whether I would be inclined to unite with Denmark for effective measures and regulations for the projection of our trade against English privateers, and if I would be willing to have jointly a few ships cruise in the Channel for this purpose. I answered that protests which I had lodged with the English ministry gave me hopes of a favorable reply and adequate compensation; that the proposition of the Danish court might be advantageous, provided one could actually rely on this court; and that in the interim I would think it over and discuss the matter with Count Ulrik Scheffer (the Swedish minister of foreign affairs).[1]

Here it would seem to appear that Denmark gave the first verbal impulse in the North for a formal armed neutrality (1778). But mutual distrust and Danish vacillation frustrated all prospects for immediate naval action; and we noted above that previous to Denmark's suggestion Gustavus III had lodged an individual protest with Great Britain. The Danish proposal proved, temporarily, but a diplomatic whim, for nothing further was done on Denmark's part.[2] But in Sweden the idea bore fruit. In a letter by Bernstorff to Ditlev Reventlou, of March 27, 1779, we learn that the Swedish minister to Denmark, von Sprengtporten, had orders from his government to let Denmark name her own conditions in order to join in a convention that would prove to England and Russia that their measures were united. Certainly, here was a spirit of coöperation the sincerity of which

---

[1] E. G. Geijer, *Des Königs Gustav III Nachgelassene . . . Papiere,* II, 118.

[2] Later also, at the same time that she joined the Armed Neutrality, she made a secret treaty with Great Britain, "through which the most important exports from Sweden were made contraband," an action which naturally irritated her neighbor. See Odhner, *op. cit.,* II, p. 96.

might have been accepted. Maybe the very fact that Sweden showed her willingness to consider a Danish proposition at all was in itself a cause for suspicion. At all events, Sweden then proceeded *alone,* and in the beginning of the following year *published* an intrepid resolution to convoy its merchant vessels.[1] Count de Creutz informs Vergennes on April 11, 1779:

It is with an infinite satisfaction that I have the honor to inform Your Excellency of the firm resolution which the King of Sweden has taken to put into immediate execution the measures already announced for protecting his commerce and navigation, without, however, rejecting the project of Russia. For this purpose he will order a few vessels to cruise along his coasts near Gothenburg, which will serve also as a depot for fitting out convoys. Your Excellency will surely find that this act is a masterpiece of moderation, prudence and firmness, and that one could scarcely make a decision with more promptness and mature deliberation. The declaration which we shall make in concert with Russia will be modified according to the particular situation of Sweden and its commerce. The regulations governing merchandise which enjoy the protection of the convoys will be printed directly, and will follow the principles established in the Treaty of Utrecht. Your Excellency will recognize in the conduct of my master, the King, the good faith, the abandon, and the confidence in his ally, of which all his demands will bear abundant testimony.

This boldness by the French "ally" was hailed in some parts of Europe as practically synonymous with suicidal stupidity. Bernstorff wrote to Reventlou from Copenhagen, May 4, 1779:

The king of Sweden has just published his resolution of furnishing a convoy to the vessels of his nation navigating through the Channel. This is one of the things which could happen that excites most my attention and curiosity. It may have very serious consequences. The English will surely not respect the Swedes more than the Dutch. A couple of frigates will not frighten them; they will then arrogate to themselves the right to search vessels under convoy, and if Sweden does not sustain its measure, she will only reap cares and the gravest affronts, instead of the coveted glory and plaudits which she is ambitious to have. *Her efforts to drag us into making common cause with her have been numberless.* We should well like to have done so under certain conditions, but it is impossible to acknowledge the principles, and I doubt that Sweden will emerge successfully from a plan so dangerous and delicate.[2]

---

[1] C. T. Odhner, *op. cit.,* II, p. 76: "Although scorned by Denmark and but little supported by Russia, Sweden had thus, on her own responsibility, taken a very important step forward in the plan of armed neutrality, a step far in advance of the neighboring governments."

[2] *Bernstorffsche Papiere,* edited by Aage Friis, III, 597. (The italics are

In a subsequent letter in the same month Bernstorff was still anxious to see how the Swedish enterprise was coming out.[1]

It is obvious that Sweden was the first nation to make the proposed plan effective by actual deed (1779); that she made "numberless" attempts to have Denmark join her; that she had urged Russia to adopt the proposal; that she remained, as we shall see, consistent in her purpose; and that instead of reaping affronts, she saw, to Bernstorff's great astonishment, her navy respected, trade relations improved, and, the following year, the nominal union consummated. To "accept" Russia's "invitation" to join the League became only a matter of modifications and diplomatic form. Both her word and deed had preceded those of Russia; and the American press, which reported the progress on the plans for an armed neutrality with great faithfulness, felt that Sweden, or the Scandinavian countries—it was of course impossible for America at the time to make any sharp distinction between Sweden and Denmark—took the initiative in the matter. The Providence *Gazette* prints on Christmas Day, 1779, a letter from London, of August 30, in which it is heralded that Russia intended "to follow the example of Sweden and Denmark, and to protect their trade with France." Her Imperial Russian Majesty, "determined to put an end to this violence (of taking neutral ships into English ports on 'frivolous pretexts'), is necessitated to follow the example of the Kings of Sweden and Denmark, by equipping a squadron to protect the trade of her subjects."

The following letter by an American agent will serve to illustrate the importance of Sweden's part in inaugurating the Armed Neutrality: The message is by John Adams, and is addressed to the President of the second Continental Congress, from Amster-

---

not in the original. Unless otherwise stated, all translations, including this extract, are by the present writer.)

Apropos of Bernstorff's depreciatory reference to the Swedish navy, it should be noted here that, in 1780, Sweden had in all 23 vessels of the line and 24 frigates to protect her commerce. Of these ten ships of the line and six frigates were especially equipped for the purpose. See p. 36.

[1] Gustavus III himself was a little uncertain whether the British would respect the Swedish convoys. If they did not, the Swedes, he believed, would be obliged to help themselves, and could not depend on aid from France. Odhner, II, 76.

Apropos of the Swedish convoys, Lord North is supposed to have said: "Who is going to escort the Swedish war vessels?" *Ibid,* II, 76.

dam, August 14, 1780. After transmitting the text of the new
declaration by Sweden in regard to the defense of neutral trade,
Adams continues:

The King of Sweden is at Spa, from where, in the letter of the 30th of
July, the public are informed that his majesty, *the first who during the
present maritime war has given validity to the rights of neuters, by means
of the declaration which he caused to be made last year (1779) to the belligerent powers* and by means of the protection which he granted from that
time to the commerce and the navigation of his subjects in sending out
from his ports a *numerous squadron,* has manifested the consistency of
his sentiments and disposition in this respect by a new declaration lately
made to the courts of Madrid, Versailles, and London, an authentic copy
of which follows.[1]

The declaration is reprinted in full, and shows that "a certain
number" of Swedish vessels had been armed the year before, and
that of these some had been employed along the coasts of the
kingdom, and others had been sent to convoy Swedish boats "in
different seas where the commerce of his subjects called them to
navigate." Then follows the declaration by Denmark.

The Swedish historian Erik Gustaf Geijer, who published the
posthumous papers of Gustavus III already quoted, declares
frankly that the proportion of honor due the various Northern
Powers and individuals for inaugurating the Armed Neutrality
may be disputed, but that Sweden, following an indirect verbal
suggestion from Denmark, was, beyond the least shadow of a
doubt, the first country to make the plan a reality,

while Denmark withdrew and Russia intended to limit herself to a protection of her own coasts against the violence of privateers, until Catherine
II, upon advice of Count Panin, made the proposal her own. This time
the proposal came from Russia, which communicated its decision to Sweden
in March, 1780, namely the decision to protect the commerce of its subjects,
by a squadron of fifteen ships-of-the-line and four frigates, and desired
that Sweden make common cause with her. This offer was regarded in
Stockholm with suspicion, since it contradicted their view of the year
previous. However, after the prospect had been more closely investigated,
the king gave his consent and communicated to Russia a new plan of an
armed neutrality convention based on the two principles that free ships
made free goods, and that nothing could be considered contraband except
what had been designated as such in treaties.[2]

This was signed at St. Petersburg, August 1, 1780, by both parties,

---

[1] Francis Wharton, *Diplomatic Correspondence,* IV, 30-31. The italics
are my own.
[2] *Des Königs Gustavus III Nachgelassene Papiere,* II, 195.

and new declarations were sent to England and the Powers fighting against it. Holland's final disposition toward it made England declare war. According to its provisions, the purpose of the Armed Neutrality was to protect trade and further restoration of peace.

The full significance of the Armed Neutrality for France and America may be gathered from a study of the official diplomatic correspondence on the matter, and the scrupulousness with which the records of the facts and proceedings in the case were reported to Congress by the American representatives. That neutral aid was much needed may be seen in a letter dated at Au Pardo, February 26, 1779, and reproduced in the third volume of Doniol's compilation. That Sweden was in earnest and scorned idle talk is convincingly substantiated in the following extraordinary communication. Sweden delivers nothing less than an ultimatum to Great Britain:

John Adams to the President of Congress, Paris, March 18, 1780. . . . . "They (the French) talk of a quintuple alliance which has been concluded between Sweden, Denmark, Russia, Prussia, and the United Provinces for the maintenance of the honor of the flags of these powers. (In regard to the English seizure of a Swedish convoy) the Baron de Nolcken, envoy extraordinary from Sweden, had declared that if the convoy of his nation was not released forthwith, with an indemnification for expenses and losses, he had orders to quit the court of London in twenty-four hours . . . .

By a letter I just now received from Holland I am told that the grand business is done between the northern powers on a footing very convenient for Holland, as it must compel the English to cease interrupting the trade of the neutral powers. This would be more beneficial to France and Spain (allies of America) than Holland, by facilitating the acquisition of ship timber, hemp and all other things for the supply of the arsenals of the marine. A principal brand of the British policy has ever been to prevent the growth of the navies of their enemies by intercepting their supplies."[1]

This explains the necessity for trading with the North, and it applied to America, as we shall see, as well as to her allies. Each and every power was struggling for trade advantages, and these trade advantages had to be maintained if the war was to be waged successfully. But, to proceed chronologically with a record of the negotiations:

On April 9, 1780, J. Adams writes from The Hague to the President of Congress a letter sent from Paris, April 14:

In the meantime . . . . it is given out that the convention between the

---

[1] Wharton, *Dip. Corr.,* III, 558.

courts of Petersburgh, Stockholm, and Copenhagen, will in a little time
be confirmed, and that Denmark will procure, on certain conditions, five or
six thousand seamen for this (Dutch) republic.[1]

Adams to the President of Congress, Paris, April 24, 1780.

Sir: There is intelligence from Stockholm of the 4th of this month that
the envoy extraordinary of the Empress of Russia has given notice to that
court of the declaration made by his Sovereign, as well as to the States-
General of the United Provinces, as to the powers actually at war, demanding at the same time that Sweden would accede to it, and to this end join
herself to Russia, by augmenting the Swedish marine, to the end to concur
by this means in the maintenance of a neutrality.[2]

Adams to Congress, Paris, May 2, 1780:

The royal college of the admiralty of Stockholm has sent to all the
agents and consuls who reside in foreign countries an ordinance, by which
it is announced to all masters of Swedish ships that necessary convoys
would be given for the protection of the commerce of the subjects of his
kingdom.[3]

That is, Sweden keeps up her independent action, while verbal
negotiations are going on. The pending formality could at the
most but add strength to the *enforcement* of the agreements, and
increase the moral effect upon the world, since in Sweden the
fact had preceded the paper signatures for joint action.

John Adams to Digges, May 13, 1780:

Sweden and Denmark are in the same system with Russia and Holland.
Indeed, if the English ministry had only common information, they would
have known that this combination of maritime powers has been forming
these eighteen months, and was nearly as well agreed to a year ago as it
is now.[4]

Adams to Congress, Paris, May 20, 1780:

P. S. . . . The Charge d'affaires of Denmark has notified the ministry
at Stockholm, the 28th of April, that this court had acceded to the armed
neutrality to which the Empress of Russia had invited it, and he has
requested, in consequence, in the name of his sovereign, his Swedish
majesty to enter into the same confederation.[5] Although no positive

---

[1] Wharton, III, 614.

[2] *Ibid.*, III, 626.

[3] *Ibid.*, III, 647.

[4] *Ibid.*, III, 676.

[5] After rejecting "numberless" invitations from Sweden to do the same
thing, Denmark finally changed tactics when Russia agreed to the plan,
and now in turn invites Sweden to join in the common action. Denmark
had, however, considered such a plan in 1778 as we have seen.

answer has as yet been given him, it is nevertheless not at all doubted that Sweden will concur with the other neutral powers to restrain the excesses of the armed ships and cruisers of the belligerent powers; an excess of which the rencounter of the (Swedish) frigate *Illerim* with a cruiser from Mahon furnished new example, as was remarked at the head of the relation which the court has published of it.[1]

Adams to Congress, Paris, May 23, 1780:

Sir: The public papers (in France) announce that all the maritime powers have acceded to the proposition of Russia respecting an armed neutrality.[2] The article from Stockholm is of the 2d of May:

"Our court has accepted the plan of an armed neutrality which the Empress of all the Russias has proposed to it; and in consequence has given orders to equip six more ships of the line—so that our naval force will

---

[1] *Ibid.*, III, 695-6. This unfortunate attack by the English on a Swedish vessel—it was said the *Illerim* was taken for a French boat—was reported to Congress by Adams in a communiqué from Paris of April 4, 1780. The attack took place on the 28th of February, and the Swedish captain, Anckarloo (see Anckarloo in biography of his brother, chap. VI) was mortally wounded. The American press reported whatever facts could be gathered for the psychological effect of the incident. Says the Providence *Gazette* for Saturday, July 29, 1780, quoting an extract from a letter dated at Paris, April 4, and communicated from Philadelphia on July 18th: "There is an anecdote from Malaga which ought to be mentioned, because it cannot fail to have serious consequences. 'The Swedish frigate the Illerim, of 34 guns, commanded by Capt. Ankarloo, on the 28th of February, at half after eight at night, met an English privateer belonging to Minorca, of 28 guns. The Swedish captain, after hailing the privateer, let her continue her course, and went on quietly his own. About half an hour after, the privateer returning, ranged herself astern of the frigate, and unexpectedly discharged both her broadsides, loaded with langrage, which killed three sailors, broke the thigh and right leg of the Captain, wounded his lieutenant, and some people of the crew. Ankarloo, who in the evening had been obliged by a violent gale of wind to draw in his guns, and shut up his ports, not finding himself prepared for battle, his officers took immediate measures, with the utmost alertness, for repulsing the privateer, which in fact did receive at least one broadside from the frigate; but upon the whole she escaped in the night by the force of sails and of oars. After this perfidy on the part of the English, Ankarloo would have entered Marseilles, for the sake of dressing his wounds; but having met with contrary winds and bad weather for three days, he put into Malaga, where he went ashore to the house of the Swedish Counsul, and he is since dead of his wounds.'"

[2] At first, however, only two powers, Denmark and Sweden, formally accepted the proposition; the other nations joined later.

consist, like that of Denmark, of ten[1] ships of the line and six frigates, whereof six vessels of war will remain in the port Karlskrona, equipped and ready to be employed on the first order."[2]

Apropos of the *Illerim* affair, Adams notifies Congress three days later that advices from Hamburg, of May 19, indicate a firm attitude of the Swedish king to "defend and maintain, with his arms and his hands, the system of neutrality" already adopted by his majesty.[3]   A notice from Hamburg to Paris, of May 26, tells of Sweden's positive acceptance of the plan in question, and that orders had been given to equip six more ships of the line, making the naval forces for this purpose, like those of Denmark, ten ships of the line and six frigates.

Franklin to Morris, Passy, June 3, 1780:

Everything here in Europe continues to wear a new face.   Russia, Sweden, Denmark, and Holland are raising a strong naval force to establish the free navigation for neutral ships and of all their cargoes, though belonging to enemies, except contraband—that is, military stores.   France and Spain have approved of it, and it is likely to become henceforth the law of nations that *free ships make free goods.*   England does not like this confederacy.[4]

Adams to the President of Congress.   Paris, June 10, 1780:

. . . Sweden arms ten ships (of the line) and six frigates.   She will send out at first but four of the former; the six others will remain at Karlskrona, but in a condition to sail at the first signal.[5]

Adams writes again on July 15—giving facts to prove his statements—that the northern powers were proceeding in earnest to protect their confederacy against any violations of the rights of neutrality.[6]   Sweden appointed Henry de Trolle as "admiral-general" of her fleet.   Hamburg announced on June 23 that on the 18th of that month a Danish man-of-war and three frigates with *seventy-eight* merchant ships of different nations, under convoy, sailed from the Sound—which illustrates the significance of the venture.

On August 22, Adams transmits France's answer, of August 4, 1780, to Sweden's declaration which had been sent to the bellig-

---

[1] The text says *six,* but this is a mistake.   See next paragraph.
[2] *Ibid.,* III, 698.
[3] *Ibid.,* III, 704.
[4] *Ibid.,* III, 761.
[5] *Ibid.,* III, 774.
[6] *Ibid.,* III, 858.

erent powers. France expresses pleasure and satisfaction in seeing Sweden's intention to take more vigorous steps to accomplish what she had already begun, by acting in concert with other nations, and especially with the Empress of Russia. The answer asserts, diplomatically, that "there is no Frenchman who is ignorant of the alliance and friendship which has so long subsisted between the two crowns."[1]—This statement contained more truth than fiction.

Carmichael to the Committee of Foreign Affairs, St. Ildefonso, September 9, 1780:

. . . The treaty for an armed neutrality was signed by Sweden (in Sweden) the 4th of August; Denmark had not signed it the 8th of the same month, but there is no doubt they will. The English party in Holland opposed and retarded it there as long as possible, and finally clogged it with such conditions as they hope will frustrate the negotiation.[2]

Dumas reports to Franklin, from The Hague, October 3, 1780, that Russia and Sweden had given orders "to fit out immediately for new sea fleets equal to those they had already fitted out," and then deems it important to add:

The King of Sweden, in his passage here, as well as his whole journey, discovered very little regard for the English. A good deal of pains was taken to induce him to accept an invitation to sup with Sir Joseph Yorke. He supped twice with the French ambassador, who entertained him twice with a play, which was acted at a theatre fitted up for the purpose.[3]

On February 1, 1781—and in the meantime the Netherlands had entered the League, December, 1780—Adams transmits a copy in full of the Russia-Denmark marine agreement to Congress, giving the slight difference between that and the Swedish convention pact, and declaring that the signing of this treaty was "one of the most brilliant events which has yet been produced by the American Revolution."[4]   Inasmuch as at first only three countries joined hands: Sweden, Denmark, and Russia, the Scandinavian kings were duly considered the "principal contracting parties." Prussia joined in May, 1781, and others followed. Catherine's proclamation had already been adopted in principle by France, Spain, United States, and of course the Scandinavian

---

[1] *Ibid.*, IV, 36.
[2] *Ibid.*, IV, 53.
[3] *Ibid.*, IV, 77.
[4] *Ibid.*, IV, 244.

countries. Ships were to pass unmolested anywhere and carry anything except ammunition. Now, if Danish, Swedish, or Russian ships were seized by the cruisers of any belligerent power, a strict retaliation would be made by the allied marines of those three countries. John Adams applauded the justice, wisdom, and humanity of an association of maritime powers against violence and outrages at sea.

Sweden took throughout a courageous initiative in this international dilemma; yet she could obviously do less alone than united with the others, and Russia's name added force to the pact. In this connection a letter from the American representative, Dana, at St. Petersburg, to Ellery, dated January 17, 1782, is sensible and illuminating. Speaking of the various European nations, he says:

Notwithstanding the material change which our Revolution has wrought in their old system, which is felt somehow by all the politicians of Europe, yet they seem some of them not to be sufficiently acquainted with the real nature of it. Hence that strange fluctuation or indecision in some cabinets; at least this is the best apology I can make for it. *Sweden, it appears to me acts as consistent part as any power. She maintains her rights as a neutral nation by constantly convoying her trade,[1] and is besides wisely reaping the benefits of the American commerce by silently and gradually admitting our vessels into her ports and permitting our countrymen to purchase there everything they want and to depart when and where they please.* If this country (Russia) would adopt the same system in every respect they would soon see the happiest effects from it. At present Sweden is making considerable profits by being the depot of Russian manufacturers for our use.[2]

---

[1] Italics by present writer.
[2] *Ibid.*, V, 116-117.

English writers are exceedingly bitter toward the policies of Holland and Denmark in the Armed Neutrality. Says Brown: "There can be no doubt that English hauteur and English prejudice had a powerful tendency to mature that antipathy which paved the way for the accession of Denmark, in 1780, to the armed neutrality of the Northern Powers." (*Op. cit.*, I, 218-219.) But, the Danish court, says Brown, protected Dutch commerce by allowing them to carry goods under the Danish flag. Nominal firms were established in Copenhagen and other places. De Coninck, the Dutch agent, carried on a trade which was of "vile nature." Perjuries, laughter at the sanctity of oaths, violations of neutrality, etc., were the order of the day. Count Bernstorff sanctioned this "polluted traffic." Denmark became rich on "protection money." This "secret bias" made the Danish minister Bernstorff the idol of the Dutch merchants, the protector of neutral flags. "As the flames of war extended from America to Europe, the greater was the mass of Dutch, French, and Spanish commerce thrown into the hands of pseudo-neutrals. Neutral papers and neutral flags were publicly advertised for sale in the ports of Holland, France, and Spain." (p. 229.) Hence the captures and detentions, says John Brown. The laws of nations were annihilated, and the maritime rights of Britain, "founded on public law and essential to her safety, were trampled on and set at nought. The Danes became exasperated against England for interrupting a trade alike lucrative, illegal and immoral. In all the ports of Europe gigantic preparations were seen for preparing the vaunted armament that was to execute vengeance of Europe, destroy the navy of Great Britain, and restore the liberty of the seas!" (pp. 229-230.)

Brown points out, however, that England might well have suffered a mortal wound in consequence, if the contracting parties had permanently stuck together.

Brown does not seem to harbor the same bitterness toward Sweden, possibly because Sweden's methods in the minds of Englishmen were more open and above-board. Sweden admitted anything American to enter or find refuge in Swedish harbors—which is more than Denmark would allow—but she seems to have openly proclaimed that she intended so to do. In this respect she treated all belligerents alike, and it did not cause the same hostile feeling, even though America was admitted on a par with other nations. Possibly, too, England underestimated the amount of damage Sweden could do; that is, the amount of trading Sweden could carry on with America and her allies.

And as for the political attitude of the Swedish king, at least one Britisher believes that "Gustavus preserved a strict neutrality during these complications. His sympathies were with Austria as against Prussia, and with France as against England, but his correspondence with Creutz shows how entirely he could separate his personal sympathies from his political principles." R. Nisbet Bain, *Gustavus III and his Contemporaries*, I, 209.

CHAPTER III

SWEDISH COMMERCIAL RELATIONS WITH AMERICA DURING THE
REVOLUTION.   TREATY OF AMITY AND COMMERCE

An armed neutrality for the protection of trade presupposes
the existence not only of a danger to commerce but also of something tangible to protect.   Did Sweden have anything to protect
of interest to America?   What relation could a comparatively
small nation—though the number of its inhabitants at the time
was about equal to that of our white population—far off in the
north of Europe have with the American colonists at a time when,
despite all precautionary measures, any maritime venture involved
an almost prohibitive economic risk and personal peril.   Even
Prussia dared not expose her merchants to a direct intercourse
with America—whatever trade relations it had were for the most
part carried on indirectly through the ports of Brittany—at least
up to the time when it was tolerably certain which way the
Revolution was to end.   Frederick the Great felt that commerce
with the American colonies was impossible without a formidable
fleet.   Silas Deane had advanced plans to Prussia for direct trade
relations, but the proposals had been rejected.   Frederick hesitated and refused support.   Prussia did not join the armed
neutrality until May, 1781, as we have seen.   The extreme caution of the King of Prussia prevented a commercial treaty of his
country with the United States until 1785, the last public act, it
is said, that he did.

We know that the apprehensions of the Prussian monarch,
and others, were well founded.   The belligerents in 1778 followed
their own selfish interests, as belligerents always do, and made
arbitrary interpretations of maritime laws.   England especially
took advantage of the lack of definite understanding of the term
contraband, and made it include all ordinary ship material, such
as timber, tar, and iron, which constituted Sweden's most important exports.   And there was danger to neutrals from the allied
as well as from the English privateers.   "In the beginning of
1780 more than twenty Swedish vessels had been detained or
confiscated by Spain alone."[1]   It was not until May of that same

---

[1] Odhner, II, 83.

year, that Franklin instructed Congress—after designating the
pending Armed Neutrality as "a great stroke against England"—
that no more neutral ships could be brought in by American privateers. For instance, the *Alliance,* Captain Landais,[1] had taken
"two Swedes in coming hither (to Paris), who demand of us
for damages," according to one report, from Franklin himself,
and he did not know what to do about the matter, asking Congress
for instructions on future policy. The initial lukewarmness of
other neutrals besides Prussia toward the Armed Neutrality, for
practical reasons—danger to trade and political complications—
we have previously noted.

Yet, the colonists, in order to wage war effectively, were forced
to preserve or open up trade relations with the Continent, and
Franklin, before 1776, had had the several European governments
sounded "by means of their ambassadors at The Hague, as to any
assistance they might be disposed to afford America, in case of
her eventually breaking off all connections with Britain, and
declaring herself an independent nation."[2] This assistance, of
whatever nature, depended first of all on ships, supplies, and
ports, i. e., on trade relations. As early as 1769 Franklin had
written to Samuel Cooper of Boston, that "all Europe, except
Britain," appeared to be on the American side. Still, secret moral
support was one thing, and active open encouragement on the
high seas during a state of belligerency was another. The result
had been watchfulness, fear and procrastination. United States
had sent agents soliciting aid from Russia, Prussia, Austria, Spain,
and the United Netherlands, and finally turned to the Scandinavian
countries for whatever help could be secured.

"In the spring of 1777 the American envoys turned their
attention to other courts.—Carmichael had sounded the Swedish
minister at The Hague on the possibility of getting stores from
Sweden, but had been discouraged from undertaking a journey to

---

[1] Cf. Letter of Franklin to Jay, President of Congress, date at Passy,
October 4, 1779, for report of one of these seizures: . . . "The Swedish
ambassador complains of the taking of a ship of his nation by Captain
Landais, the master of which lays his damages at sixty thousand livres.
I understand it was his own fault that he was stopped, as he did not show
his papers. Perhaps this, if proved, may enable us to avoid damages."
Wharton, III, 365.

[2] *Memoirs of Benjamin Franklin* (1834), I, 136.

42   *Sweden and the American Revolution*

Stockholm."[1]   On December 30, 1777, A. P. Bernstorff wrote to
Reventlou that Stephen Sayre was in Copenhagen at the time to
propose "un plan de commerce avec l'Amérique." Says a French
source: United States before 1782 had tried to get commercial
relations with "Amsterdam, Cadix and Sweden," but the distance
and danger of this navigation discouraged even the most intrepid
enterprisers.[2]

But we have noted in a Franklin letter[3] that an American deputy
did go to Stockholm, in the beginning of 1779, and that the "disposition of the Swedish court" at that time was "very agreeable."
We have just learned also[4] that American vessels were "gradually"
admitted into Swedish ports *during the war,* that Americans purchased there whatever they wanted, going and coming at their
pleasure, and that Sweden acted as a depot for Russian goods.
We know, too, from her part in the armed neutrality, that her
relatively large navy, her determination, her skillful king, and
her ability to construct good ships, had restored Sweden to a
place of greater influence both in the political and in the commercial world; and her finances were in excellent shape. She
convoyed her merchant vessels at an early date, defying England
herself. There were, then, some favorable factors, both potential
and kinetic, for trading with America, even during the Revolution.

Before the Revolutionary war Colonial trade with the Scandinavian countries was mainly of an indirect character. Denmark probably did some business via her own colonies in the
West Indies, and now and then a Swedish ship, as in early colonial
times, touched our shores. But the major portion of our direct
trade with the European continent was with southern Europe, and
we know now that there was an appreciable amount of such trade,
directly or indirectly, clandestine or otherwise. Our illicit traffic
in *exports* was apparently a very small item, but the secret *imports* were much larger.[5] Smuggling was quite extensive. Navigation acts were "largely evaded." "Notwithstanding our custom
house officers, New England, New York, and Philadelphia carried

---

[1] Smyth's *The Life and Writings of Benjamin Franklin,* X, 314.
[2] Noailles, *Marins et Soldats Français en Amérique,* 289.
[3] Cf. chap. I, p. 15.
[4] Cf. chap. II, last paragraph.
[5] A. M. Schlesinger, *The Colonial Merchants and the American Revolution, 1763-1776,* p. 41.

on an almost open foreign trade with Holland, Hamburg, France, etc., bringing home East India goods, sail cloth, Russian and German linens, wines, etc."[1] Though the illegitimate trade was small at first in proportion to the total amount, "toward the close of the colonial period the Americans secured nearly forty per cent of their imports and sold about forty-five per cent of their exports by trading directly with sections other than Great Britain."[2] Yet England had, of course, remained the natural emporium and distributing point of American goods for Europe.

Now Sweden, whose colonists had showed themselves vigorous intercolonial traders in America, during the seventeenth century, carried on commerce with almost all civilized countries of the globe, and an extensive one with Holland, Hamburg, France, Spain, and Great Britain—the countries that traded directly with America. The British colonies in the American Carolinas had not for a long time been able to compete with Sweden in the production of lumber; and England, which had formerly been almost entirely dependent on Sweden and Norway for her supply of naval stores, had kept up for a considerable period of time the importation of Swedish lumber. In return she re-exported "inferior varieties" of American tobacco and other goods to Sweden, as well as to Holland and Germany. So the Colonial trade with Sweden and other northern lands, before 1776, was prevailingly indirect. Besides, Americans had but few articles to send to Sweden and points north, so that there was slight incentive for direct traffic.[3]

But the American Revolution changed the situation. During the period of hostilities, the States could in the main trade only with Continental Europe; new trade routes had to be opened up from sheer necessity; and under conditions fraught alike with danger and opportunity Sweden entered the field of operations. It is doubtful whether any northern European nation, or southern either for that matter, saw the commercial potentialities of trading with the new American republic clearer than Sweden. Whether Gustavus III personally believed in the divine right of kings or

---

[1] E. R. Johnson and Collaborators, *History of Domestic and Foreign Commerce of the United States,* 51.

[2] *Ibid.,* 91.

[3] Cf. *Ibid.,* p. 126.

not, whether he inwardly favored or did not favor the American colonists, he saw early, with unusual foresight, the practical advantages of opening up direct relations with the new nation, and for the sake of ultimate profit his subjects were anxious to start such relations, even at some temporary peril and sacrifice.— Also, "the success which followed the opening up of trade relations with the East Indies," says Odhner, "encouraged the (Swedish) government to try something similar in the West, to take advantage of the war and establish the Swedish trade in West Indian and American waters. A beginning was made by granting two years storage-tax exemption (nederlagsfrihet) for goods brought home on Swedish vessels from America and the West Indies (1782), and in addition, the following year, the import duty on such goods was reduced by one third. Simultaneously a treaty of commerce was made with the new free states in North America, and a West Indian Colony was sought as a base for the Swedish trade."[1] While this work is not intended to give the statistical magnitude of the American Revolutionary trade with Sweden, if this were possible, it is meant to prove, however, by specific examples, in addition to what has already been noted, that there actually was such a trade between the two countries— a factor which in view of the circumstances is worth a passing notice.

At first, no doubt, this trade was carried on almost exclusively in American bottoms and at American risk. American ships must have been received in Swedish harbors not long after our alliance with France had been announced and maybe earlier. We know that Colonial vessels were in the ports of Gothenburg and Marstrand in the fall of 1779, and that these got safely back to America, despite the English fleet, and before the time of full coöperation of the northern powers under the provisions of the Armed Neutrality. The Providence *Gazette* of January 8, 1780, reports that the foreign news printed on that day had been furnished by "Captain Claghan, who is arrived at Boston from Gottenburg (in Sweden) after a passage of forty-two days." He had brought "fresh Advices" which were given commensurate space. On February 19, 1780, the same newspaper announces that "Wednesday last Capt. Gideon Crawford, in the Sloop Nancy, of this

---

[1] *Op. cit.*, II, 122-123.

Port (Providence), arrived in the River from Gottenburg, in Sweden, after a tedious passage of 106 Days. He sailed from Sweden in Company with Capt. Claghan, who arrived at Boston last of December." After printing some brief facts about the Swedish ports of Gothenburg and Marstrand, the *Gazette* makes public the "Extract of a letter from a principal merchant at Gottenburg, dated October 15, 1779, received by Capt. Crawford," which deserves reprinting here:

By an American Vessel lately arrived at the neighboring Port of Marstrand, I have been favored with the Firm of your House, in consequence of which I take the Liberty of addressing you this Letter, and make you a Tender of my best Services in this Port of the World.—The extending of Commerce, which every Merchant must have in View, and the Immense Field for Speculation which the glorious Independence of America opens at present, makes me bold to presume, that commercial Business might be transacted between your Country and this to mutual Advantage. Being a Native of Sweden, I think myself equally a judge thereof, as I hope to have in my Power to effectuate whatever Plan may be struck out to promote it, and at the same time to deserve the Confidence of those who may think proper to honor me with their Friendship and Correspondence.—Permit me to suggest to you a few Observations for your Government: Sweden consumes large Quantities of Tobacco, Indigo, Rice, etc., which hitherto have been imported directly from England. Swedish Exports which would answer for an American market, in my Opinion, are, Iron in Bars, wrought ditto, wrought brass and Copper, Steel, Wire, Nails, Sail-Cloth, and Cordage, all kinds of India Goods, particularly Tea, China, Silks, etc. What other European Goods might be wanted, could easily be collected at Marstrand from the neighboring countries. The Port of Marstrand is conveniently situated for distributing the Products of America, to Sweden, the Baltic, Germany, Holland and England, and the providing of the Products of all these Countries to furnish Returns to America. Ships can sail from Marstrand at all Seasons of the Year. This Town (Gothenburg) is situated only 12 English miles from Marstrand and no Place in Europe is preferable to it for purchasing of Teas, both with respect to Price and Quality.

By 1780, then, direct business relations had been established between Sweden and the United States, and the prospects for the future looked promising.

On May 6, 1780, we learn from the same newspaper source that Russia, Denmark, and Sweden were "making the greatest preparations for war," *working night and day to fit out seaports* and ships of war (to convoy their merchant marine). On November 16, 1780, the *Independent Chronicle and the Universal*

Advertiser (Boston) reports: "Tuesday last arrived in this harbor the letter of marque brig Amsterdam, Capt. Magee, in forty-four days from Gottenburgh, in Sweden. On his passage from hence to that port, he took a British vessel and carried her to Gottenburgh, where the prize was sold." The same number announces the arrival at Beverly, Mass., of the ship *Rambler,* Capt. Lovet, in forty-eight days from Gothenburg. We learn also that the northern powers had conveyed "a large quantity of stores to France," and that Great Britain had suffered a "no inconsiderable blow" to her trade in the northern seas. Newport reports on November 30, 1780, in true belligerent style with name of vessel omitted, to the *Gazette* of December 6, that "Monday evening arrived here the brig ———, Capt. Benjamin Pearce, in 8 weeks from Gottenburg in Sweden." On December 30, New York sends a letter of marine intelligence, reprinted in the same paper on February 10, 1781, to the effect that "Sweden had opened its ports to the United States along with France, Spain, Holland, Russia, and Hamburgh." This was, as we have seen, but a belated publication of a condition which had in reality existed for several months, so far as Sweden was concerned. On February 1, 1783, to give another example, it is reported in Providence from Boston that "Monday last Capt. Joseph Cooke, in a Brig from this Port, arrived at Boston from Gottenburg, in Sweden."[1] In the *Gazette* of June 14, 1783, we learn definitely that the Swedish flag is flying from the mast of a merchant vessel in Boston harbor.

The Swedish goods best known in America seem to have been tar, pitch, iron and steel. On August 21, 1777, a Boston auctioneer advertised for sale in public auction, among other goods, "a few barrels of Stockholm Tarr and pitch." In October, 1780, the store of Paschal N. Smith sold "Swede Iron suitable for Waggon and Chaise Tier." Robert Taylor of Providence advertised in March, 1781, that, besides "a few Puncheons of choice old Rum, and the best Holland *Geneva,* by the case," he was also anxious to sell "a quantity of Swedish Iron." The Newport *Mercury*[2] announced about the same time that one, Nathan Bebee,

---

[1] The marine reports still deemed it imperative to designate that Gothenburg (Göteborg) was situated in Sweden.

[2] The following coincident fact may be of interest here in connection with the *Mercury:* During the American Revolution, as it happens, one of the battle plays of the conflict was the Englishman Brooke's *Gustavus Vasa,*

sold "exceedingly cheap for cash," German, English and *Swedish* steel. Two years later Swedish iron had become plentiful. Not only does Julien David of Rhode Island have the "best Swedish iron" for sale, but Josiah Gifford, in September, 1783, sells the "best Swedish Iron by the Ton." Obviously, the export product which the Swedes had most in mind when they formulated their commercial treaty with America was iron. They hoped to furnish in the future a large share of the iron formerly sold to America by Great Britain, and we see that they had already made a good beginning by the time the Treaty of Peace was signed.[1]

Not only did American vessels, then, sail to Sweden and back during the Revolutionary period, but Swedish ships began to appear in American harbors, and Swedish goods, primarily iron products, were kept for sale in our markets. We may assume that Americans purchased many valuable supplies which they needed for war purposes, except actual ammunition. How much contraband, if any, they were able to smuggle through will never be known, nor the exact quantity of any goods purchased.

On November 7, 1782, Franklin writes an informal letter to R. R. Livingston, recommending "a Swedish gentleman of distinction," Baron de Hermelin,[2] who wished to study the natural

---

based on the Swedish patriot and liberator of the sixteenth century, of the same name. The Newport *Mercury* printed regularly on its title-page the following motto from this play: "Whene'er our Country calls—Friends, Sons, and Sires should yield their treasures up, nor own a sense beyond the Public Safety." Thus, the Swedish king became indirectly a kind of model for American heroism and freedom.

[1] Cf. Odhner, II, 119.

[2] Spelled *Kermelin* in the American source.

Odhner writes: "The mining engineer, Baron S. G. Hermelin, was sent to America with instructions to investigate the economic and political conditions of the American states. He was first to appear as a private citizen and scientist, but as one who might later be accredited as the first Swedish minister to America. This plan was not realized, but Hermelin sent home from America some interesting accounts, not only of the trade and mining industry in the new states but also of their constitution and political condition."—His American letters and official report were published by B. Taube (see bibliography) in 1894. Odhner, II, p. 117 and note.

Upon examining Hermelin's original report, we learn that the Swedish government had followed the events of the American Revolution with great interest, and that the Swedish authorities had realized that sooner or later the American colonies would be victorious. "And," says the report, "one

productions and commerce of the United States.   Franklin asked
to have him—who was a worthy man—introduced to the President
of Congress and other prominent Americans.—The Swedes were
beginning in earnest to investigate the possibilities of Sweden-
America trade relations.

The Treaty of Amity and Commerce with Sweden[1]

At the Gothenburg Tercentennial Exposition in 1923, there was
unveiled, on July 4, as the culminating feature of the Sweden-
America week, a bust statue of Gustavus III, which had been
presented by Americans to the City of Gothenburg in commemoration of the king's timely recognition of American independence.
Gustavus III had, after all, been the first European monarch to
offer the hand of friendship without special solicitation on our
part.   Our treaty of amity and commerce with Sweden was the
first treaty made with a neutral nation, and it had been suggested
by the Swedish regent.   Our previous treaties with France and
Holland[2] had been secured by earnest solicitation, and these countries were both at war with England after the Armed Neutrality

---

cherished the hope that the quite lively trade relations which had developed
between Sweden and North America after the outbreak of the war, would
after the treaty of peace increase yet more."

Baron Hermelin's report shows that iron was Sweden's most important
article of export.   Hermelin was of the opinion after the war that there
would in the future be a greater market in America for "Swedish goods
and manufactured products" than there had been before, because of the
system and stability that would inevitably follow.   Also, the contemplated
restrictions upon the importation of foreign iron products into the United
States had at least temporarily failed to materialize.   Cf. *Berättelse om
Nordamerikas Förenta Stater*.   1784.   pp. 49-50.

Hermelin (1744-1820), after spending about two years in America,
returned home late in the year 1784.   Since the United States sent no
official representative to Sweden as early as 1784, Hermelin's credentials as
Swedish minister to the United States became worthless.   He was elected
a member of The American Philosophical Society of Philadelphia and of
The American Academy of Arts and Sciences, Boston.

[1] For full text of treaty see Appendix.

[2] Cf. Providence *Gazette* for Nov. 2, 1782: "Some of the States of
Holland have *consented* to the treaty of amity and commerce *proposed to
them by Mr. Adams*. Another Northern Power (Sweden) *has solicited
the Friendship and Trade of the United States;* and a similar treaty may
be expected soon to take place there."   The italics are not in the original.

had gone into effect. Exactly five months prior to the
of the treaty between the United States and Great Britain, .
treaty between Sweden and America had been concluded.

On the occasion of the Gothenburg celebration, therefore, the
American Consul-General in Stockholm, D. I. Murphy, in an
address entitled "A Royal Friend of America," calls to mind that
Franklin had designated Sweden as "America's first ally" and
that "this was not said in derogation of the splendid part played
by France in the American Revolution. . . . It was a little more
than one hundred and forty years ago, to be exact, it was the
third day of April in the year of Our Lord 1783, that a treaty of
amity and commerce was signed at Paris between the King of
Sweden and the United States of America. The signers of that
historic document were Count Gustav Filip Creutz, the Swedish
ambassador at the Court of Versailles, on behalf of Gustavus III,
and Benjamin Franklin on behalf of the United States."

"The French government—which was always kindly disposed
toward Sweden, though not always satisfied with its politics—
desired to compensate in some measure Gustavus III and Scheffer
for the disappointments that they had suffered during the war.
This compensation was to consist in a West Indian colony and
in a treaty with the American states. As soon as the English Parliament had expressed itself in favor of peace with the seceded
colonies, Gustavus III could without impropriety enter into negotiations with them for that purpose and instructed Creutz to turn
to Franklin, who was still in France. The first meeting seems
to have taken place through Lafayette's mediation, in April, 1782;
the proposal was very well received by Franklin and immediately
forwarded to Congress. The greatest secrecy was maintained,
for Gustavus III did not wish to expose his neutrality to suspicion.
The negotiations therefore came to a standstill for a time, but
were resumed again in the fall, when Vergennes, because of the
approaching treaty of peace, urged greater speed; and by that
time the diplomats had received their official letters of authority.
Sweden was thoroughly prepared for such a treaty, since it became
more and more obvious that she would not obtain any direct
advantage from the pending peace, and so was anxious to derive
all possible profit from the American Treaty."[1]

---

[1] Odhner, *op. cit.*, II, 117.

This is an objective Swedish version of the negotiations and politics of and reasons for the treaty.

Franklin's diary contains the following item, dated at Passy, May 24, 1782:

All the Northern Princes are not ashamed of a little Civility committed towards an American. The King of Denmark traveling in England under an assumed Name, sent me a Card expressing in strong terms his Esteem for me, and inviting me to dinner with him at St. James's. And the Ambassador from the King of Sweden lately ask'd me, whether I had Powers to make a Treaty of Commerce with their Kingdom, for he said, his Majesty was desirous of such a Treaty with the United States, had directed him to ask me the Question, and had charg'd him to tell me, that it would flatter him greatly to make it with a Person whose Character he so much esteem'd, etc.[1]

Only five days later, the Swedish minister told Franklin he expected orders from his court relative to a treaty, and on June 25 Franklin writes to Robert R. Livingston, our Secretary of Foreign Affairs:

The ambassador from Sweden to this court applied to me lately to know if I had powers that would authorize my making a treaty with his master in the United States. Recollecting a general power that was formerly given to me with the other commissioners, I answered in the affirmative. He seemed much pleased, and said the King had directed him to ask the question . . In case it should be thought fit to employ me in that business, it will be well to send a more particular power, and proper instructions. The ambassador added, that it was a pleasure for him to think—and he hoped it would be remembered—that *Sweden was the first power in Europe which had voluntarily offered its friendship to the United*

---

[1] Franklin's popularity in Sweden was very great. Repeated attempts were made later to induce the United States to send Franklin's grandson as the first United States minister to Sweden. Baron de Staël, the new Swedish ambassador to France, wrote to Franklin, June 13, 1783: "Permit me, Sir, on this occasion to repeat the request which the ambassador (de Creutz) made to you respecting Mr. Franklin, your grandson. He had the honor to tell you that it would afford the King a pleasure to have a person residing with him in the capacity of the minister of Congress who bears your name in conjunction with such estimable qualifications as young Mr. Franklin possesses. He charged me before he departed to repeat to you the same assurances, and you will allow me to add, on my part, my best wishes for the success of this matter."

But the request was unheeded. In 1784, while on a visit to southern Europe, Gustavus III brought back to Sweden a bust of Benjamin Franklin, along with one of Diderot.

Traité d'Amitié et de Commerce conclu entre Sa Majesté le Roi de Suede et les Etats Unis de l'Amerique Septentrionale. ———

Le Roi de Suede des Gothes et des Vandales &c. &c. &c. Et les Treize Etats Unis de l'Amerique Septentrionale, sçavoir New-Hampshire, Massachusett Bay, Rhode Island, Connecticut, New-York, New-Jersey, Pensylvanie, les Comtés de New-Castle, de Kent et de Sussex sur le Delaware, Maryland, Virginie, Caroline Septentrionale, Caroline Meridionale et Georgie, desirant d'établir d'une maniere stable et permanente les regles qui doivent être suivies relativement à la Correspondance et au Commerce que les deux Parties ont jugé necessaire de fixer entre leurs Pays, Etats et Sujets respectifs, Sa Majesté et les Etats Unis ont cru ne pouvoir mieux remplir ce but qu'en posant pour base de leurs Arrangemens, l'Utilité et l'avantage reciproques des deux Nations, en évitant toutes les Preferences onereuses qui sont ordinairement une Source de discussions, d'embarras et de mécontentemens; et en laissant à chaque Partie la Liberté de faire au Sujet du Commerce et de la Navigation, les reglemens intérieurs qui seront à Sa Convenance.

Dans

OUR FIRST TREATY WITH SWEDEN, 1783.

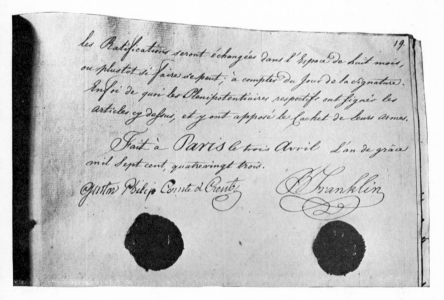

TREATY OF AMITY AND COMMERCE WITH SWEDEN, SHOWING SIGNATURES OF
BENJAMIN FRANKLIN AND COUNT DE CREUTZ.

States without being solicited. This affair should be talked of as little as possible till completed.[1]

Substantially the same facts are communicated with much satisfaction by Adams to Livingston on December 14th: "The King of Sweden has done the United States great honor in his commission to his minister here to treat with them, by inserting that he had a great desire to form a connexion with the States which had so fully established their independence and by their wise and gallant conduct so well deserved it." On the same day Franklin—and in the meantime both representatives had received their official instructions—enthuses over the polite expressions in the Swedish ambassador's commission, "to wit, 'that his Majesty thought it for the good of his subjects to enter into a treaty of amity and commerce with the United States of America, who had established their independence, so justly merited, by their courage and constancy'; or to that effect." On Christmas Eve, 1782, Franklin reports that full powers had been exchanged with Count de Creutz, that conferences had been held concerning the proposed plan, and that the Swedish minister had "dispatched a courier for further instructions respecting some of the articles."[2]

It was quoted above that the Treaty was signed on April 3, 1783. This is the date generally given; yet the following communication by Franklin to Livingston is dated at Passy on *March 7, 1783*: "Sir; I but this moment hear of this opportunity by which I can only send you a line to acquaint you that I have concluded the treaty with Sweden, *which was signed on Wednesday last.*"[3] This would fix the date a month earlier. However, we know, on April 15, that the treaty is definitively concluded, and that Franklin on that date sent a second copy of the same to Livingston, expressing the hope that the ratification by the States would soon be forthcoming. Also, "the King," wrote Franklin, "as the ambassador informs me, is now employed in examining the duties payable in his ports, with a view of lowering them in favor of America, and thereby encouraging and facilitating our mutual commerce."

By June 12, the Swedish ratification of the Treaty had arrived

---

[1] Wharton, *Dip. Corr.,* V, 512.
[2] *Ibid.,* VI, 163.
[3] *Ibid.,* VI, 276. I have been unable to account for the discrepancy. Either Franklin or some copyist or printer made a mistake of a month.

in France; on November 1, 1783, our own ratification appeared; and in March, 1784, the final exchange of ratifications took place. On July 10, 1784, Franklin dined at Grand's in Paris with some Swedish gentlemen, including Mr. Rosenstein, Secretary of the Swedish Embassy, and discussed further conditions "relating to the commerce possible between our two countries."[1]

The treaty and the minutes of the transaction leading thereto are printed in French in the Report for the United States in Congress Assembled, July 29, 1783, occupying seventeen pages, and was soon thereafter reprinted in English in the American press. Franklin's power to negotiate the treaty is dated September 8, 1782:

> The treaty is framed in such a form as to avoid, in the introductory words of the document, "all onerous preferences, which are ordinarily a source of discussion, embarrassment, and discontent." It makes careful provisions both for times of peace and war, and seems to cover every imaginable problem in international navigation, from the disposal of deceased seamen to the stipulation that the harbors of one country are to serve as places of refuge and shelter for the other, from storms, enemies, and pirates. The most striking characteristic of the whole treaty is its unequivocal spirit of good-will and friendliness.[2]

For example, the Treaty provides that:

> There shall be a firm, inviolable, and universal peace, and a true and sincere friendship between the King of Sweden, his heirs and successors, and the United States of America, and the subjects of his Majesty and those of the said States, and between the countries, islands, cities, and towns situated under the jurisdiction of the King and of the said States, without any exception of persons and places; and the conditions agreed to in this present treaty shall be perpetual between the King, his heirs and successors, and the said United States.
>
> The King and the United States engage mutually not to grant hereafter any particular favor to other nations in respect to commerce and navigation which shall not immediately become common to the other party, who shall enjoy the same favor freely, if the concession was freely made, or allow the same compensation, if the concession was conditional.
>
> The subjects of the respective and high contracting parties shall pay no higher duties on imports than the most favored nations and shall enjoy all the privileges and advantages in the respective countries.
>
> There shall be granted full, perfect, and entire liberty of conscience to the inhabitants and subjects of each party. They shall have all rights and

---

[1] Diary of July 10, 1784; Smyth, X, 353-354.
[2] A. B. Benson, *Our First Unsolicited Treaty, American-Scandinavian Review*, VII, 48 ff.

privileges and protection of the laws of the citizens of the respective countries.[1]

Cronholm calls attention to what he terms infringements of the United States upon rights as set forth in this treaty, and to the subsequent indifference on the part of Sweden. Also, it appears, that the United States adopted an Englished version of the document made by an ignorant and wholly incompetent translator, who rendered the French "fonds et biens" by "goods and effects," excluding instead of including real estate.[2] Inherited realty in Sweden owned by United States citizens are sold and the proceeds forwarded to the United States, but not vice versa, it is claimed, as originally intended.

It is doubtful, however, whether the alleged infringements by the United States of the treaty provisions, or the alleged translation blunder, ever led to any serious dissatisfaction. Practically, there has been little or no injustice done. Possibly because of sheer ignorance, it is certain that little *feeling* of wrong resulted. In most cases, I believe, foreign claims of inheritance have been settled justly irrespective of the wording or literal interpretations of the treaty. Most assuredly the *spirit* of the treaty as a whole was, in 1783, vastly more important than the literal enforcement of certain details. At least this seems a sensible view of the matter.

"On August 12, 1782, while negotiating the treaty, Dr. Franklin wrote to his government about the Swedes: 'All ranks of this nation appear to be in good humor with us, and our reputation rises throughout Europe. I understand from the Swedish ambassador that their treaty with us will go on as soon as ours with Holland is finished; our treaty with France, with such improvements as that with Holland may suggest, being intended as a basis.' This treaty has remained unbroken and is still in force."[3]

It is not strictly true, however, that this treaty is still in force, although several of its articles have been incorporated in subsequent Swedish treaties with the United States.[4] The original

---

[1] Neander N. Cronholm, *A History of Sweden,* II, 151-152.

[2] *Ibid.,* pp. 154-155. So far as the translation goes, however, the English word "effects" is to-day sometimes used to include real estate. (See Webster's Unabridged Dictionary.)

[3] *Ibid.,* p. 155.

[4] Cf. Appendix, p. 182, note.

of 1783, is now, except by historians, almost forgotten. Its main function was the official inaugurating of trade with America, and the implied recognition of our independence, which in view of Sweden's position at the time had a marked psychological influence on the other courts of Europe. Whether there was ever occasion to test in commercial practice all the detailed provisos of the treaty is at least open to doubt; and as the United States grew rapidly and conditions changed, the circumstances, though not always the articles, of the original became dimmer and dimmer and finally the whole treaty became a matter of history only, so far as conscious application was concerned. New conditions modified the commercial relations accordingly, and new problems or new interpretation of old problems took care of themselves more or less automatically, and gave birth to new treaties, while the sympathetic attitude which permeated the first formal agreement constantly prevailed. Then, also, with respect to literal enforcement either of separate clauses or the treaty as a whole, it must be remembered that all our early treaties with foreign powers were seriously restricted in their application, and could only be of slight benefit for future operations. The power of regulating commerce, as other writers have pointed out, lay with the individual States, not with Congress, hence much of the intended effect was on paper only.

Nevertheless, in 1782 and 1783 the moral effect of the Swedish treaty, and the pioneer work involved on the part of Sweden in starting negotiations long before the treaty of peace, deserves all the space given to it here. We have noted that the form of the Swedish treaty was in a measure based on those with the belligerent France and Holland. The Swedish treaty then in turn became the model for treaties with other nations and soon Denmark and Portugal entered into negotiations for similar trade agreements. Franklin writes to Livingston on June 12, 1783,— Denmark having in the interim expressed a desire to effect a treaty—that "the treaty with Denmark is going on, and will probably be ready before the commission for signing it arrives from Congress. It is on the plan of that proposed by Congress for Sweden."

In other words, aside from whatever intrinsic value the treaty articles may have had, they prompted an even greater advantage for America through their influence upon other nations to do likewise. As in the case of the Armed Neutrality it was a case of initiative and chronology. It dispelled many last vestiges of doubt; it emphasized and crystallized the European conviction that had been gradually forming since the victory of Yorktown, that the independence of the States had actually been established. Now other European powers gradually followed Sweden's example, and we find on record in the *Secret Journals* that Congress on May 7, 1784, resolved that it would be "advantageous to the United States to conclude such treaties with Russia, the Court of Vienna, Prussia, Denmark, Saxony, Hamburg, Great Britain, Spain, Portugal, Genoa, Tuscany, Rome, Naples, Venice, Sardinia, and the Ottoman ports."[1]

---

[1] *Secret Journals*, III, 222 ff.

CHAPTER IV

On May 21, 1764, Voltaire wrote to Marmontel:

I was not able to keep Count de Creutz more than one day. I should have liked to spend my whole life with him. We seldom send such ministers to foreign lands.

On the same day Voltaire wrote to Mme. de Geoffrin:

Count de Creutz is worthy of being known by you. He deserves all the compliments that you have written to me about him. If there were an Emperor Julianus in the world, Count de Creutz should be sent as ambassador to *him,* but not to a people who stage autos-da-fé and kiss the hem of monks' garments. The Swedish government must have been tipsy not to let a man of his calibre remain in France. There he would have been of some service, but that is impossible in Spain.

This impression written by the literary dictator of Europe at Ferney—where Creutz visited when on his way to enter upon his duties as minister to Spain, his first diplomatic position—will serve as an introduction to a biographical résumé of that Swedish poet who during the American Revolution, as noted, directed Swedish interests in France, and who, directly or indirectly, through his tact, culture, knowledge, sympathies, convictions, and influence, contributed to a favorable conclusion of that conflict much more perhaps than we can readily conceive. At the suggestion of a friend, this chapter, based in part on my own studies and in part on the more recent investigations by Swedish and Finnish scholars, has been written for the benefit of those who desire to know more about the personal side of Count de Creutz, and something about his more delicate activities during the French participation in the American war. My chief source, outside of both published and unpublished letters by Count de Creutz, has been the excellent monograph, *Gustav Philip Creutz* (1917), by Gunnar Castrén of Helsingfors.

Descended from a prominent Swedish family in Finland, Creutz was born in 1731, and received his education at Åbo Academy. While still very young he lost both of his parents and was educated by his uncles. He became a good scholar in the classical languages, learned several modern tongues, and always read foreign works in the original. It is no exaggeration to declare of

GUSTAV PHILIP CREUTZ.
(From the painting by Roslin.)

him that he soon spoke French like a Frenchman. And he
studied the sciences also. When in France Marmontel was deeply
impressed by the scientific erudition of young Creutz, whose
knowledge of chemistry and natural history earned for him the
undeserved reputation of being a pupil of Linné. But Creutz
was not a scientist, except in so far as it entered into the requisites
of an enlightened materialistic "philosopher" of his time. He
mastered all phases of fashionable culture. His models in literature and criticism became Boileau, Pope, and Voltaire; he studied
the French encyclopedists; he adopted French manners in society,
a French style of writing, and a French taste in his appreciation
of the arts. He developed into what has been called an "enthusiastic irreligious idealist," with a liberal mind, no prejudices, and
with an absolute faith in the great men and ideals of his age. At
twenty Creutz was a man of the world with a patriotic Swedish
heart, but with a culture and sympathy that were externally
French.

In 1751 Creutz accepted a modest position as clerk in a government office; but in 1756 he was chosen cavalier-tutor to the Duke
of Östergötland, the youngest of the three royal princes, a responsibility requiring both learning and caution, for the policy to be
followed in educating a prince was the source of constant irrita-
tion and debate between the King and his Council. Creutz succeeded, however, in keeping his position—apparently with entire
satisfaction to the royal family—until he left for Spain in 1763.
The tutorship gave the young nobleman plenty of opportunity to
study life at the court, in a period when French actresses and
dancers frequented the Swedish capital, when sensual enjoyment
was the order of the day, and when the wife of the Spanish
ambassador claimed she knew only three women in Stockholm
whose characters were beyond reproach. We have no evidence,
it seems, that Creutz himself ever became the subject of a court
scandal, though he learned to play the "mode dandy" on occasions
demanding it, and he took a certain platonic delight in epicurean
manifestations. Creutz showed, however, an unusual strength of
mind and determination in his mode of life. While a tutor he
made many friends at court and was a frequent visitor at the
residence of the French ambassador, d'Havrincourt.

The name of Gustav Philip Creutz would be known to-day, of
course, even if he had never seen southern Europe and made a

lasting impression in diplomatic circles. During the decade from
1753 to 1763 he won an undisputed place as a Swedish poet of the
French school. He belonged to the intimate circle of Queen
Louisa Ulrika, in which the Swedish language and literature
were studied. His poetry was hailed as a "spring-song" by his
contemporaries, as the first real "ice-breaking" in Swedish letters,
indicating the approach of a warmer season on the Swedish Par-
nassus. Creutz was the most popular writer of that illustrious
literary trio, of whom Hedvig Charlotta Nordenflycht and Georg
Fredrik Gyllenborg were the other two members. He eulogized
the summer à la Thompson, for he much preferred this season
to the cold northern winter; he wrote fables with new grace and
elegance; and he created pastorals, such as *Atis and Camilla,*
evincing good imagination, genuine sentiment, and a dazzling,
idyllic picturesqueness. Love was the supreme feeling, and a
refined erotic happiness life's greatest delight. But this was only
a *predilection d'artiste;* the author was no militant sensualist or
revolutionist in social affairs. There was, also, much of heaven,
spring, and flowers in Creutz's poetry. Occasionally a little
French "hoar-frost" effected a slight chill upon the reader, and
rhetorical affectation was not wanting; but the poet possessed a
remarkable power of language and verse-making, and his alex-
andrines were the most melodious in the Swedish tongue. His
descriptions of nature suggested something living and luxuriant:
they had both substance and form.

It is of importance here to note that Creutz from his early
youth followed the political developments of the day. He was
interested in politics, but detested its briberies and intrigues. To
him it seemed as though at court and in the council chamber it
were more a question of *who* should govern than of *how* to govern.
As a result the young poet wrote, besides sentimental pastorals, a
stinging satire on *The Defence of Lying*—possibly suggested by
Swift's *The Art of Political Lying*—in which Creutz lashed the
political tendencies of his environment.

The abilities, manners, and character of Count de Creutz gradually attracted the attention of the Swedish government and
resulted in his appoinment as envoyé to Madrid, his literary career
ending with this appointment. He left home late in August,
1763, but did not arrive in the Spanish capital until Midsummer
Day of the following year. On the way he visited his cousin,

Carl Johan Creutz, Swedish minister to Holland; renewed his acquaintance with d'Havrincourt, now French minister at The Hague, and to him stressed the importance of continuing the old alliance between Sweden and France with payment of the subsidies to Sweden therein prescribed. In Brussels he had another opportunity to say a friendly word for his own country. He met Prince Charles of Lorraine, who praised the bravery of the Swedes but regretted their lack of wealth. "If we had that," said Creutz, in substance, "we should not be so brave; it is moderate wealth and moderate comfort which create good morals and that courage which faces danger and death with indifference." In November Creutz arrived in Paris.

Creutz remained in the French capital much longer than he had intended, partly because of his delicate health. He did not leave Paris until May 12, 1764. But his physical condition permitted him to observe during the winter all that Paris had to offer in art and society. He met Choiseul, d'Alembert, Marmontel, Mme. Geoffrin, Mme. d'Aiguillon, and members of the foreign diplomatic corps. Paris fascinated him and he was loath to leave. His above-mentioned visit to Voltaire, near the Swiss border, was a reverent homage to the man who more than anyone else in the world had molded his *Weltanschauung,* his religion. On July 1, 1764, Count de Creutz was finally, under elaborate ceremonies, officially presented in Madrid to Carlos III of Spain.

Sweden had little in common with Spain except some commercial relations and a joint friendship for France. But, as Gunnar Castrén has pointed out, it was in Madrid that de Creutz learned to follow the intricate labyrinths of European politics and diplomacy. He listened to the conversations of other diplomats and watched the political clouds that appeared on the horizon. As a product of the Enlightenment, Creutz found much to criticise unfavorably in Spain—the contrast with France was too obvious— and his letters to Marmontel describing Spanish conditions and culture were so sensible, so keenly analytical, that his friend read them before the French Academy. But Creutz spent most of his time with the foreign ambassadors, among whom gambling seemed to be the most frequent, necessary, and disastrous pastime—and once he participated in a French play, where, among others, Caron de Beaumarchais (later the adventurous helper of the American colonists, who had come to Madrid at this time to straighten out his sister's love affairs with Clavigo) played a leading rôle.

Creutz was a poor man, and the living expenses for a foreign minister in Spain enormous. He soon longed for a change. Besides, he suffered from the oppressive "heat, monk rule, obscurantism, and the lack of refined society and cultural interests." Fortunately the merits and genius of the young diplomat were recognized in Sweden, even by the political faction opposed to him, and in 1766 Creutz was transferred to Paris. Here he was at once confronted with a task of seemingly insurmountable proportions.

Sweden had changed her government and foreign policies and made friendly overtures to England and Russia. In fact, a treaty had been consummated with England. France was bitterly offended, and there was little chance for Sweden to obtain the subsidies due her, subsidies which, according to previous agreements, France had agreed to pay Sweden in return for her good will, political concessions, and help in time of possible need. It became the delicate task of Creutz to smoothen out this international wrinkle, and, eventually, to obtain promise of resumption of subsidy payments. To this end, by extraordinary tact, social polish, and perseverance, he made friends with all men and women of either actual or potential influence, including Madame du Barry; and his efforts were finally crowned with success. Paris sang the praises of Count de Creutz, his king (Gustavus III, who in the meantime had visited Paris), and his country. Voltaire sent a poem, *Jeune et digue héritier du grand nom de Gustave.* As a reward, Creutz was raised to the rank of full ambassador, and the realization of having restored friendly relations with France, which he loved, became to him a source of unspeakable happiness. In 1774 Louis XV died; but Creutz had the ability to win over Louis XVI and his ministers as well, and succeeded in bringing about a renewal of former agreements, though in a slightly modified form.

The American Revolution put Creutz's diplomatic powers to a severe test, especially after France had declared war against England. Both Gustavus III and Creutz regretted at first the official French participation in the war, for although Creutz had full faith in an ultimate victory for the allied arms, he felt that the French finances and strength would be seriously affected no matter how the war came out, and a ruining of French credit would under the circumstances be detrimental to Sweden. France might not be able to pay her subsidies, and, being busy elsewhere, could give no aid in the North if, for example, Sweden were attacked by Russia. Being more or less isolated by the war, Gustavus III tried seriously, therefore, to be as neutral as he could, and in the negotiations with Russia concerning the proposed armed neutrality, instead of spurning all advances, adopted, externally at least, a friendly attitude toward his eastern neighbor. This displeased France of course, and Creutz again had to placate the French authorities. It was by no means smooth sailing for Count de Creutz in 1779, for instance. France bought ship supplies in Sweden. England declared these contraband of war; and despite his customary boldness toward Great Britain, Gustavus III feared secretly at times that Sweden would through her persistent policy of furnishing naval supplies to France be drawn into the conflict; and the Swedish king wished to avoid war with England if possible. So once in May, 1779, he instructed Vergennes not to purchase contraband of war in Sweden. This was an unexpectedly chilly attitude toward France, and it was Creutz again who had to act as mediator and keep the Swedish-French alliance intact. Gustavus III hesitated occasionally in his actions and sympathies— and we can understand why—but Creutz never did. The Swedish envoyé was the constant, reliable friend of both France and Sweden, a fact which, incidentally, redounded to the advantage of the American colonists.

In spite of the fact that Creutz was at first opposed to French participation in the American war, he does not seem to have shared his king's viewpoint in regard to the alleged lack of justification of the "American rebels" in taking up arms against their lawful sovereign. In theory Creutz agreed with Gustavus III, for he loved law and order, and he did not sanction disregard for authority; but in this case the king's attitude "seemed insignificant in comparison with the act of freedom which France was to perform" (Castrén, *op. cit.*, 271). And the trend of his thoughts and sympathies was naturally anti-English. "All nations," wrote Creutz on October 8, 1778, "will be grateful to France for having prevented a part of the world from keeping another part under the yoke, and for destroying despotism on the sea, a despotism practised by a power which up to now has neither

respected peoples' rights nor the sanctity of agreements, and which
has treated as an enemy every nation that has any trade or manufactured goods." This was Creutz's conviction based on a life
of observation. So he watched the progress of the war, as we
have seen, with keen interest and gave counsel, it seems, whenever he thought it would aid the Allied cause. Time and again
he complained that the French were not prosecuting the war with
the necessary vigor.

In the course of this monograph we shall see what Count de
Creutz did for the sixty or more Swedish officers who fought
with the French in the American war of independence. To the
Swedish volunteers he was a friend, sponsor, and father; and
what he did for them, he did for Sweden, for France, and, as it
happened, for America. And Creutz wished to see America win,
if for no other reason than that she was an ally of France. In
general, too, he could not bear to see any nation subjected against
its will by another.

What little benefits Sweden obtained from the war were in a
large degree procured by Creutz. He fostered, directed in part,
and reported conscientiously the progress of the negotiations for
the armed neutrality, from which Sweden derived some temporary
advantages; the little island of Saint Barthélemy in the West
Indies, which was ceded by France to Sweden at the end of the
war, can be attributed largely to Creutz's efforts, though the island
itself proved afterwards more a source of expense than anything
else. The only positive advantage gained by Sweden from the
conflict was the training and experience of some of its naval
officers—for whom Creutz, naturally, acted as the employment
agent—and the treaty of amity and commerce with the United
States made by Creutz and Benjamin Franklin. The last was a
positive result for the countries concerned.

Just how valuable for the United States the relations between
Creutz and Franklin were we shall perhaps never know; but that
their mutual friendship, through the vogue and influence of
Creutz in many circles, resulted in some advantage for the American colonists is certain. That the Swedish envoyé took a respect-
ful, not to say enthusiastic interest in Franklin personally we do
know, and he sent a careful, compelling description of him to
Sweden. "Never has a more curious figure appeared in society,"
Creutz wrote home on January 5, 1777. "He wore a fur-cap

which looked like a muff and went down to his eyes, and wore
on his nose enormous spectacles. He is very quiet and answers
in [brief] sentences." But Creutz liked the strange American;
he admired his simplicity and basic qualities, and we have, as noted,
copious evidence in Franklin's correspondence that the Northern
diplomats were not afraid of showing "civility" to the American
agents. That the Swedes appreciated the homely virtues and
personality of Franklin as well as the significance of the relation
between him and Creutz may be seen perhaps in the poetic reference to them in Carl Michael Franzén's prize-honored *Sång
Öfver Grefve Gustaf Filip Creutz,* written in 1797:

> On foreign soil what figure bid thee stay?—
> A man of wisdom, rich in years, forsooth,
> Whose every wrinkle tinged with silver-gray
> From hoary locks spoke boldly but of truth.
> Nobly stood this man of lowly birth
> 'Mong men of high. No vice, no tyrant's mirth
> Endured his searching glances without fear.
> This was Franklin. Mute, frivolity
> Beheld this virtue, pure, from 'cross the sea.
> Creutz! He offered you his hand,
> This Prince of Amity from freedom's land.

> Rejoicing at these greetings, thou turned North, etc.

Creutz returned home in 1783, a hoary bachelor at fifty-two,
having served his country for twenty years as foreign representative, of which seventeen had been spent in Paris. He was succeeded in France by Baron de Staël, whose name became more
universally known through his talented wife, Mme. de Staël.
Upon his return to Stockholm Creutz was made a *riksråd* and
chancellor, as successor to Ulrik Scheffer, and, as he had done
before at Spa and Aachen, he accompanied his king on a diplomatic journey, this time on a visit to the Empress of Russia
at Fredrikshavn. He was one of those who directed the affairs of
Sweden during Gustavus III's visit to Italy in 1784, and was
elected chairman of various important committees and depart-
ments. He was made a member of the Royal Swedish Academy
of Sciences, and chancellor of "Uppsala Academy," where he did
excellent service. He established new chairs of instruction and

made notable additions to the library. Creutz died in 1785 at
Tivoli near the pleasure palace of Ulriksdal, in the conviction that
he had done his best for his sovereign and fatherland and had
never intentionally injured a soul.

It is not easy for us to judge the magnitude of the task and
temptation of a diplomat of one hundred and fifty years ago,
when rivalry in bribing foreign representatives was the fashion.
The present writer has been unable, however, to discover anything
disgraceful in Creutz's conduct and character. He never stooped
to a low action, and his shortcomings were in no small degree
the consequential result of his position. He sometimes made rash
promises which he could not keep; he was perhaps unnecessarily
obsequious and officious; and in his desire to represent his country as magnificently as possible, he accumulated personal debts
that he could never pay. He was a poor financier, but his motives
were primarily unselfish, and more than one Swede stranded in
Paris was aided by Creutz to an extent that far exceeded his
official and necessary duty. He was uncommonly open-minded,
and open-hearted, and considerate of the failings of others. His
reports to Sweden about the Swedish officers in French service,
for instance, emphasizes only the favorable sides of their ability
and conduct. Creutz was an incessant worker, and his duties
were manifold, arduous, and intricate. Sometimes his secretaries
—among whom was the gifted but unmanageable Bengt Lidner—
gave him trouble, and often he had to attend to the work of
his office alone. But he seldom complained. He never aired his
personal difficulties in public, preferring to keep his troubles and
sorrows to himself. Ordinarily of a quiet, dreamy, melancholy
nature, and distracted mind, he often made interesting little blunders, and the stories of his absentmindedness are many.

Above all, Count de Creutz was the alert conciliator. Whenever the Swedish king was displeased with the French minister
Vergennes, or vice versa, it was Creutz, the peacemaker, who
could pour oil on the ruffled diplomatic waters to good effect and
prevent serious consequences. He was able to do this because of
his vogue in all circles of the French capital. It was not merely
a case of tact. He was not only an acknowledged poet of high
rank, but also a patron of letters, art, and music. He had his
own large library and art gallery. Moreover, he was the personal friend of artists, musicians, and litterateurs, in Paris, such

Gustav Philip Creutz 65

as Roslin and Wertmüller (both Swedish), Taraval, d'Alembert, Helvétius, Grimm, Diderot, and Grétry. Mme. d'Egmont was an intimate friend of both Creutz and his king. In 1778 the friends of Marie Antoinette dined once a week with the Swedish ambassador at his legation home, Hôtel de Bonac, before an open court of which Creutz "let on big illumination days fountains spout wine to the delight of the populace," showing how far he was willing to go to preserve French favor. And another factor which enhanced the popularity of the Swedish host was the fact that he never made any serious social mistakes at his ambassadorial soirées. Knowing everybody, he knew when, how, and whom to invite, and could always arrange his guests in groups of compatible tastes and interests. It would seem as though here were at last a poet with some practical qualifications.

In theories of government Creutz believed in the principle of benevolent despotism; but he advocated greater freedom whenever it could be put into practice without a collapse of authority and the social order. He welcomed the Swedish act of religious freedom of 1779, and in general extolled to Gustavus III the principles of greater liberty. No nation could live, he asserted, whose government was not based on freedom and benevolence. Liberty of action, was, moreover, the only economic basis for prosperity and productive wealth. While Creutz was no friend of radical views such as culminated in the French Revolution, he abhorred oppression in a degree which was quite modern. He was a gentleman diplomatic enough to agree with his king, or to yield to him, on most vital questions of government policy, but seldom without giving his own viewpoint both gently and firmly. In bringing this biographical summary to a close, it may be well for us to recall that Count de Creutz tried arduously to persuade Gustavus III to let Count von Fersen and Baron Curt von Stedingk display their orders of the Cincinnatus won in republican America.

CHAPTER V

DESCENDANTS OF THE DELAWARE SWEDES IN THE STRUGGLE FOR INDEPENDENCE. JOHN HANSON AND JOHN MORTON

To-day history and science pay much attention to race and inherited characteristics, and genealogists are solicitously occupied in tracing the ancestry of our American families, with the object of determining their various contributions to our freedom and democracy. It will not be amiss, therefore, if we devote a few pages here to the character and history of the Swedish Delaware descendants, representing as they do, incidentally, the most homogeneous branch of the Nordic stock with whatever that implies.

No nation has a monopoly on the desire of being independent; everybody wants to be free provided he may adopt his own interpretation of freedom. Yet, it is independence in the American sense which is the very alpha and omega of the existence of a Scandinavian. Not a little of the Colonial love of liberty and hatred of all forms of tyranny was imparted to the more immediate American forefathers by Viking and Norman ancestors, and the Northmen were presumably the first Europeans to see our continent. Fondness for perilous adventure, the crossing of seas with subsequent discoveries and colonizations, and the principles of empire-making, are common to all Northern peoples. And the spirit of independence is the very bone, marrow, blood— all, of the Swede. His is not a servile race, and his land has never been conquered by a foreign power.

Thus it was a real, spontaneous outburst when the passionate Swedish poet, Bengt Lidner, for a time secretary, as noted, to the Swedish ambassador de Creutz in Paris, expressed his joy over American independence in his *The Year 1783;* it was a wholehearted outpouring of his soul when Bishop Carl Michael Franzén paid his brief tribute to Benjamin Franklin in *The Song on Creutz;* and a genuine enthusiasm when the Swedish archbishop and hymnodist, Johan Olof Wallin, later cheered the father of America in his spirited dithyramb, *George Washington*. Similarly, it was this inborn sense of freedom and justice, and a remembrance of what her own kin had achieved on the American shores, which in

1902 prompted Mathilda Malling, a noted Swedish writer, to localize a novel, *Daybreak* (Daggryning), at the dawn of American independence, among the descendants of the Swedish settlers on the Delaware. Here it was but the intuitive pride of the authoress to recall that members of her own race had done something to help establish the American republic.

We may assume, then, on tested principles, that the pre-Revolutionary Americans of Swedish descent were true to their northern heritage; and if racial qualities are actually transmitted, there should be by mere instinct as large or larger proportion of pro-independents among their groups than among those of any other nationality. And we have no reason to doubt this assumption from any facts discovered so far. The problem of determining in the American Revolution the Swedish colonial portion of participation, therefore, becomes largely a problem of ascertaining proportionate numbers, and it is the purpose of this chapter to direct attention to certain factors in calculating the magnitude of the Swedish element before and at the time of the Revolution. Obviously, infallible statistical numbers for the various nationalities which comprised the United States in 1776 can not be obtained; and it must be admitted that the matter is not of any great consequence. Nevertheless, since many Americans are interested in pre-Revolutionary ancestors, since ethnical traits *are* of some importance in shaping the destiny of a nation, and it has become the fashion to estimate the contributions of the different peoples to our independence, it becomes almost a matter of duty to indicate certain lines of procedure that must be followed in any attempt to establish facts about the Swedish proportion. The results of any such endeavor, however, can only be approximate at best.

In spite of several Swedish expeditions to the Delaware colony, the settlement was never very extensive, and the number of colonists was relatively small. Yet the Swedes were an industrious, prolific, and peaceful people who sought to live on friendly terms with their neighbors, the Indians, and except for an occasional individual conflict, escaped the decimating massacres of New England, New Amsterdam, and Virginia. Contemporaries describe them as living in comfort and sobriety, with their houses full of fine children. We may believe the latter at least. As to the absolute number of members of the colony technically belonging to it as such, "they did not much exceed seven hundred souls," says Bancroft,[1] at the time of the surrender to the Dutch, in 1655. This figure is probably a little high, for Amandus Johnson[2] reports a total of less than four hundred people, including some Hollanders, for the years 1654-1655. On the other hand, some Swedes had deserted and made their homes in other colonies before this count was made; and in the fall of 1654 a number of Swedish settlers—we do not know exactly how many—who came on the *Haj* captured by the Dutch, "were persuaded by every means to settle in New Amsterdam so that most of them remained there."[3]

These were of course not included in the official list of New Sweden members. In 1663, "some thirty Swedes" arrived in South River, landed by Skipper Peter Luckassen. "In the beginning of 1669 a report reached the Swedish government that there were five hundred families in New Sweden forsaken and left to themselves."[4] Some writers have estimated the number of Swedish colonists at the end of the seventeenth century to about a thousand—a figure which is undoubtedly too small—and Bancroft opines that "The descendants of the (Swedish) colonists, in the course of a generation, widely scattered, and blended with emigrants of other lineage, constituted, perhaps, more than one part in two hundred[5] of the population of our country in the early part of the nineteenth century."[6] This estimate of a little more than one half of one per cent may be considered a fair minimum for the basis of computation, for, although Bancroft's original figure is high, he probably did not take into full consideration some factors which have been further investigated during the last twenty years, and which would presumably increase rather than decrease this percentage; for instance, the number of new settlers between

---

[1] *History of the United States* (1890), I, 510.

[2] *The Swedish Settlements on the Delaware*, II, 514.

[3] *Ibid.*, II, 590.

[4] *Ibid.*, II, 655. No doubt this figure was intentionally made as high as possible for effect.

[5] The statement by Johnson in *Contributions by Swedes to American Progress*, p. 15, allegedly based on Bancroft, and according to which "about six per cent of the population in the United States are descendants of the early Swedes on the Delaware," is obviously a misprint for six tenths of one per cent.

[6] *Op. cit.*, 509-510.

1655 and 1700. Between 1660 and 1700, Pennsylvania contained "Swedes, Dutch, and some Germans," says an up-to-date authority,[1] evidently enumerating the contemporaneous non-Anglo-Saxon nationalities in the order of their numerical importance. Philadelphia, the very soil of which had belonged to "three brothers of the Swedes, by name of Swensson, who also lived thereon,"[2] developed rapidly, to a large extent because of the pioneer work thereabouts by the preponderant Swedes. It is safe to assume, also, that after the Swedish and Dutch colonies had been absorbed by the English, and there was no more energy wasted in quarrelling with the neighbors or attempting to preserve their own identity as separate colonies, life became even more peaceful and prosperous than before and the rate of increase of population among the Swedes and Dutch increased.

The problem of calculating the number of descendants of the Swedish colonists is not simple; yet we can make a reasonable estimate. The number of Hollanders in the Swedish colony when the Dutch took it over probably did not exceed the number of Swedes who had deserted to other colonies. Hence we may accept Johnson's figure of 368 to be exact—another authority quoted by Johnson says 370—for the year 1655. We may assume that these under Dutch rule increased to 400 by 1665. In the interim, thirty more had arrived, as we have noted, and several had settled in New Amsterdam. A total of five hundred permanent Swedish settlers in America in 1665 is then a conservative figure, and below Bancroft's estimate of 700 for the year 1655. Now, under normal colonial conditions—which then obtained among the Swedes—the population, according to the estimate advanced by some students of the problem, would double in about twenty-three years,[3] the rate of increase being three per cent per annum, compounded of course. This would give a minimum of about 16,000 direct descendants of the original

---

[1] E. R. Johnson and Collaborators, *History of Domestic and Foreign Commerce of the United States,* 67.

[2] Pehr Kalm, *Resa,* diary for Sept. 15, 1748.

[3] Cf. A. B. Faust, *The German Element in the United States,* I, 283 and II, 17. While this estimate accepted by Faust seems a reasonable one for basis of computation and the Swedes probably increased in numbers as rapidly as the Germans and the Dutch, the results must obviously be considered as approximate only. No incontestable rate of increase of Colonial

Swedish settlers, in 1780, when the Revolution was at its height, or 15,000 at the outbreak of hostilities, not counting the immigrants or their descendants that came between 1665 and 1775. This would seem to tally with Bancroft's percentage basis of a "little more than one part in two hundred," or about six tenths of one per cent, which would bring the total of Swedish descendants in 1790, with an estimated white population of 3,172,444 to 19,035. This is unquestionably conservative, however, and probably does not take full cognizance of the subsequent immigration, which during a period of over a century, though small, amounted to a sum that can not be ignored. There may have been in the neighborhood of twenty thousand colonists of Swedish blood at the height of the Revolution.

During the eighteenth century, before the Revolution, occasional small groups of Scandinavians landed on our shores, and the Gloria Dei Church in Philadelphia had a Swedish pastor until 1831, showing some direct and continuous relations with the mother country. Among individual Swedish immigrants had been some men of note, whose nationality and life here can easily be traced. We have referred above to Gustav Hesselius, the portrait painter, who arrived here in 1711. One, Bothvid Elof Stjernstolpe, a nobleman and officer of artillery, born in 1748, went early to America, never to return. He left at least one child, a daughter. Adolph Benzelius, ennobled Benzilstjerna, 1718-1775, was a Swedish fortification officer in English service in America, in 1761, and an intendant of forests in the Crown Point district, when he died. He had married the daughter of the Swedish pastor in Racoon, N. J. Swedish people were quite common on the Atlantic seaboard, especially in the harbors, during this century. Names like Anderson, Johnson, Hanson, and Peterson occur with some frequency in 1750; and when we learn, for instance, that Jonas Lynd of Little Compton, R. I., in 1715, had a daughter, *Ingeborg,* we need not search long for the nationality of the parent.

population can be established; and any rate suggested would be subject to infinite variations by locality and conditions.

Baron Hermelin in his report on America (*op. cit.,* 19-20) comments in general on the relatively high increase of population in the colonies. It had been higher than in other lands, he said, because of the better economic conditions.

When the Swedish botanist, Pehr Kalm, in 1748 visited Racoon,
N. J., a parish inhabited largely by Swedes, he met a man of
Swedish ancestry, Måns Keen, near seventy years of age, who
alone had forty-five living descendants, which causes Kalm to
expatiate in his diary for December 7, on the economic reasons
for prolificness in America. This Måns Keen was a descendant
of Göran Kyn of New Sweden, the number of whose descendants born before the Revolution—though he himself had a small
family—was about four hundred.[1] This is not an unreasonable
example of the rate of increase and diffusion among the Swedish
colonists, and might be taken as a rough index of multiplication.
Even after making due allowance for incidental decimation, the
final estimate of the total number of descendants of these northern
pioneers must be a sum appreciably larger than that given by
some recent writers. Bachelorhood and race suicide were not
popular in those days, and families were large, though infant and
maternal mortality was high. On May 5, 1749, Pehr Kalm finds
the "very large town" of Rapaapo, N. J., inhabited *solely* by
Swedes, where the Swedish language was purest and least mixed
with English idioms.

In view of the above, we are a little astonished to see reproduced in *Our Foreigners,* 1920,[2] the avowedly vulnerable com-
putations regarding the proportion of nationalities of America
based on the imperfect census of 1790. The author admits that
the estimates are unscientific, but the extent of their inaccuracy
is much greater than Mr. Orth[3] realizes. It is obvious that the
compilers of the 1790 census and the estimators of the figures

[1] See Gregory B. Keen, *The Descendants of Göran Kyn of New Sweden.*
The total number of his descendants up to 1913, with names of those
intermarried with them, though not including those "more remotely con-
nected," and with no pretension to completeness except for the first six
generations, is about two thousand. "It is published," says that author,
"not merely as a record of a particular family but also as a striking
example of the wide diffusion of the blood of an early Swedish settler on
the Delaware through descendants of other surnames and other races
residing both in the United States and Europe." (Foreword.)

[2] *Chronicles of America,* vol. 35, by Samuel P. Orth. New Haven, Yale
University Press.

[3] Since this was written Mr. Orth has died, but I feel sure that if he
were living he would accept what follows in the same spirit in which it
was written.

for Delaware, Georgia, and New Jersey, the composition of whose
population was based on the 1800 census, had but little acquaintance with Swedish characteristics, language, or proper names.
Purporting to base their estimates of nationality largely on the
character of the surnames, the famous census and computation for
1790 concluded that of the real Americans in the United States at
that time only 10,664 were of other nationality than British, Dutch,
German, and French. "All others," including Hebrews, Swedes,
Danes, Finns, and Welsh, made up a little more than ten thousand.
This is of course ridiculous! Only 185 souls listed under the
caption "all others" in Delaware for 1790! Even if we make
liberal discounts for changes of residence and boundaries, and
other factors, it is absurd to imagine that the state settled by the
Swedes should have only a fraction of 185 left seven years after
the end of the Revolution, when one colonist alone, elsewhere,
had at one time, before the Revolution, forty-five living descendants. If we assume that the Swedish colonists had moved elsewhere, then they must be found in the lists of other states. But
what do we find? Maryland, whose Swedish descendants did
much for the Revolutionary cause, is listed with 209 of these
nondescripts, not including the Hebrews, however. In Pennsylvania the Swedes, if I am rightly informed, settled, among
other scattered places, virtually a whole county, the famous Up-
land (now Chester) county; yet the census of 1790 finds in all,
in the whole state, 194 individuals that are credited to this combination of Swedes, Finns, Danes, and Welsh. The figures for
New Jersey are nearer right: 5,255; but these lose their force
also when we include the Hebrews, and remember that one single
"very large town" in 1749 was inhabited entirely by Swedes, not
to mention Racoon, which seems to have been an unusual stronghold for the Swedes.

Most startling of all is the impressive total of *seven* (7) Scandinavian and Welsh souls in Rhode Island, in 1790! Before the
writer lies a list of family names of Rhode Island for 1774.
Among them are twenty-seven, representing, let us say, a hundred people, which could easily be, and probably were, Swedish
or Danish, especially *Alverson, Anderson, Benson, Clasen, Holver-
son, Johnson, Lind, Lindquist, Matteson* (dozens of them), *Olin,*
and *Peterson.* And in the following names there is at least a chance
that their bearers were of Scandinavian origin: *Bly, Braman,*

Croping, Helme, Jepson, Lasell, Norman, Overson, Sax, Shedal, and *Tallman.* Again, before 1790, as we have seen, commercial relations between Rhode Island and Sweden were by no means insignificant—if the Marine Intelligence in the contemporaneous press is worth anything—and we may assume that a small number of permanent Rhode Island residents resulted from this trade. Also, if before 1790, the Scandinavians had moved elsewhere, they should be found elsewhere, but they are not.

An index of the unreliability of the census figures for Rhode Island may be found in the estimate of the Hebrew descendants. It has been generally maintained that there were three hundred Jewish families in Rhode Island before the Revolution. We know that the Jews had a synagogue in Newport during the Revolution, and that there is a special old Hebrew cemetery in that city. Yet—the census of 1790 records but nine (9) Hebrew individuals in the state of Rhode Island! To a thoughtful reader this needs no explanation, perhaps; but it does indicate strongly that there is no necessary connection between race and surname.

Where is the principal key to the difficulty in this absurd compilation, so far as the Swedes are concerned?

As individuals, to-day, the Scandinavians are, I believe, less clannish than any other constituent of our American melting-pot, any contrary opinion being due to the fact that a large proportion of the Swedes, Norwegians and Danes are so thoroughly and rapidly Americanized that the immigrants are not recognized as such. The Swedes have a hard time even to agree on supporting a certain political candidate of their own nationality at election time, though the Norwegians exhibit greater unity in this respect. The Scandinavians fuse faster with the Anglo-Saxon than anyone else, not excepting the German, and this is only natural. They fuse rapidly to the point of extinction *as foreigners.* They instinctively yearn to be Americans; they possess an unusual degree of adaptability to new environment; and after a very short time the younger immigrants can not be distinguished by or from the stock-American. Of this we may see abundant proof. The writer has met native Americans who have worked and lived with foreign-born Scandinavians, not once knowing or thinking from either name, accent, or demeanor, that they were naturalized citizens. Mr. Orth has, I fear, unknowingly been misled in the same way, for he treats mostly of those Scandinavians who have

furnished the "rugged commonplace" of our American institu-
tions—those that furnish "strength . . . if not grace."[1]

The Swedes, for better or worse, are the most conspicuous
examples—one might be inclined to say *sinners*—of this Scandinavian type. They often foolishly sacrifice their mother tongue
entirely to be American; prefer to speak English exclusively,
even in their homes;[2] and Anglicize their names beyond recognition. Often the names *have* to be changed. Added to this is
the aristocratic Swede's partiality for things foreign—despite his
national pride—which in another land tends to make him obliter-
ate himself as an alien, and often at home leads him to adopt a
foreign name, especially if he is a military man. He is an
internationalist, who, so far as we are concerned, becomes an
Anglo-Saxon to all intents and purposes.

The Colonial Swede had of course the same assimilation traits
and tendencies, and was besides subjected to an effective external
process of nominal extinction because of circumstantial pressure.
He intermarried quickly with other colonists; his own family
name gradually and naturally took on an English character, by
intuition, environment and necessity; and by 1790 you could
seldom tell him or his name from an English-American. The
Swedish Colonial names were Anglicized to an extent unknown
of any other race. *Mårten* or *Morten* became *Morton; Kyn,
Keen; Hvijler, Wheeler; Stidden, Stidham;* and *Stålkofta.
Stalcop.* Similarly, we may assume that Hijden within a century
became *Hiden* or *Hidden; Forsman, Forseman; Symonssen,
Simmons; Mathiasson, Mathewson; Andriasson, Andrewson* or
Andrews; Thomasson, Thompson; Höök, Hawk; Fysk, Fiske;

---

[1] Cf. *Our Foreigners*, p. 159.

[2] My own experience is that the amount of Swedish spoken in American
homes of Swedish antecedents is to-day regrettably small. Germans,
French, Italians, and others use their mother tongue in the home incom-
parably more than the Swedes; the Swedish parents speak English as
soon as they are able to, which is generally very soon. And the children
always speak English. One may even address a Swedish immigrant who
came here in middle life, in Swedish, and he will answer you in some form
of English. Of course in the larger Scandinavian settlements in the
Middle West the situation is a little different, but even there the English
takes care of itself, while it requires a strenuous conscious effort to retain
the mother tongue.

Kock, Cooke; Stål and *Stille, Steele; Clementsson, Clements; Månsson, Munson; Ulf, Wolf; Ackesson, Acheson; Hindricksson, Hinderson* or *Henderson; Lorans, Laurens* or *Lawrence;* and *Smed* of course *Smith*. The number of Colonials whose cognomens were lost in the non-distinctive, all-absorbing *Johnson* also formed, as to-day, a respectable group. The "omnipresent" *Rambo* remained. So did *Swan* and *Brandt*. Several names ending in -*son* or, less often, -*sen* retained the ending and gradually changed the stem, viz: *Thorsson, Toreson;* and *Bengtsson, Benson*, a process of simplification which is constantly going on to-day in America. Then, too, there were some Swedish skilled mechanics among the Colonists whose patronymics had either been lost or disregarded, and were known wholly by their trade, such as *Nils Mjölnare* (miller), *Nils Snickare* (carpenter), and *Nils Skräddare* (tailor). These undoubtedly came to be known, in a colonial environment, if not as *Nelsons* (from the first name, following a characteristic Swedish method of forming surnames among the peasantry), then as *Miller, Carpenter,* and *Taylor,* respectively. Names like *Göransson* (later *Jurgensen*), *Eskilsson, Marcusson,* and *Påfvelsson* have just naturally disappeared as such; but their bearers didn't. I should expect also, *a priori,* that some modern American *Skinner,* if his genealogy could be traced accurately, would find his paternal antecedent to be *Olofsson Skinnare* of the Swedish colony. Names like *Sprint, Kling, Larsson, Hansson,* and *Swensson* or *Swansson* retained their identity, sometimes with slight modifications; but the several *Olofssons* were lost as such by the time of the Revolution, and there are three chances to one that the descendants of *Jonas Skog* (wood) became disguised under the translation, *Wood* or *Woods.*

The method of transforming names by literal translation or modification was of course a common practice among other nationalities as well, and it is common knowledge that this was done. Americans of German descent have made pretentious claims of German blood because of this custom—and probably rightly so; yet the extent to which the Swedish cognomens naturally lend themselves to Anglicization, and the extent to which the Swedish names were, and now are, being literally translated, and modified, has never been fully realized by the non-Scandinavian. We need not be profound scholars to detect this practice in such literal though perhaps necessary translations as *Starbranch (Stjernquist)* and *Seashore* (*Sjöstrand*). But it is not so easy maybe to see *Hjort* in *Hart,* and the writer knows of one instance where a *Hjort* became a *York* by an obvious phonetic similarity.

Yet the greatest source of mistaken identification is not, after all, the *dis*similarity between Swedish and English names, but the *similarity.* The Swedish cognomens are not by any means always "characteristically different from the British," as Professor Orth contends.[1] Many of them coming from the same source originally, it requires often but a single vowel, an accent, or a consonant to change the Swedish patronymic to a form that will baffle the expert. *Andersson* becomes *Anderson; Jonsson* or *Jonson, Johnson; Nilson, Nelson; Persson, Pierson* or *Pearson; Allén, Allen; Blom, Bloom; Holms, Holmes; Friman, Freeman; Davidsson, Davidson; Pettersson* (sometimes), *Patterson; Larsson, Lawson; Sten, Stone;* etc. All these in their second form could be either English or Swedish-American. Again, several British names are absolutely identical with Swedish names that are not uncommon. Such are: *Alexander, Hall* (mentioned before), *Hill, Holt, Love, Lyman, Lund,[2] Palmer, Swan, Wall* and several others mentioned above in the Introduction. The writer has known or heard of bona fide Swedes and Swedish-Americans—to use the hyphenated expression for the sake of a certain definiteness—by the name of *Allen, Allison, Andrews, Bennett, Blees, Brink, Cassell, Chester, Colson, Cornell, Franklin, Gometz, Hague* (Hägg), *Holmes, Jackson, Levine, Lincoln, Menton, Miller, Nestor, Norton, Osborn* (Esbjörn), *Randolph, Reading, Russell, Sandner, Willard, Williams, Wilson,* and *Winfield;* and proper names like *Stark* may be either Swedish, German, or English. Those ending in *-berg* are common in Sweden and Germany, and the ending *-holm* in modern names generally denotes Scandinavian origin.

The problem, then, is far more complicated than appears on the surface; it requires specialistic knowledge, historical instinct, and imagination to solve the puzzles. Often a far safer index of nationality is the Christian name. *Anderson* or *Johnson* does not necessarily tell us anything, but if it is *Olof Anderson,* it is a different story. Ethnical and linguistic ignorance here will inevitably lead to historical absurdities.

---

[1] *Op. cit.,* p. 30.
[2] Washington had a relative, Lund Washington.

In the above analysis, with a few exceptions, the writer has purposely restricted himself, for obvious reasons, to surnames that occur in Colonial history before and during the Revolution. The names of the Swedish colonists have been taken from Dr. Johnson's exhaustive work on the *Settlements of the Delaware*, and these have been compared with the names in Heitman's *Historical Register of Officers of the Continental Army, 1775- 1783*. The latter, among others, contains 29 *Alexanders;* 59 *Allens;* 12 *Allisons;* 35 *Andersons;* 4 *Bensons;* 9 *Davidsons;* 25 *Hills, Holts,* and *Holmes;* 3 *Jansens;* 48 *Johnsons,* including 4 *John Johnsons;* 6 *Lawsons;* 5 *Lorings;* 5 *Loves;* 8 *Lymans;* 11 *Mortons;* 4 *Munsons* and one *Manson;* 2 *Neilsons;* 16 *Nelsons,* including 7 *John Nelsons,* from Va., Pa., Md., N. J., and N. C.; 14 *Palmers;* 4 *Pearsons;* 3 *Petersons;* 5 *Piersons;* innumerable *Smiths* (15 columns of them); several *Starks, Steeles, Stones,* and *Swans;* dozens of *Thompsons,* and 2 *Walls.*

So far as *possibility* goes, these names could all be Swedish. But we assume they are not. We may be certain that the majority of officers represented by these cognomens are British. Yet in view of what has been pointed out, there should still be a respectable balance for the Swedes, even after making the most drastic allowances for the Anglo-Saxon side, and names like *Hanson* and *Peterson* may be claimed at once, and almost exclusively,[1] for the Swedish side of the ledger. I dare say a large proportion of the *Mortons* were of Swedish descent. John Morton, who signed the Declaration of Independence, was one. Then there were several officers like Captain Archibald *Denholm* of Virginia, John and Thomas *Huling* of Pennsylvania, John *Kring* of New York, Adam and Arthur *Lind* of Virginia, John *Lund* of New Hampshire, Chaplain John *Lynd* of Pennsylvania, Eneas *Manson* of Connecticut, Abel *Moslander* of North Carolina, Major Anthony *Selin* of Pennsylvania, and John *Wandin* of Georgia whose names suggest Scandinavian extraction.

The British racial element predominates of course before and during the Revolution. Nevertheless, it is not as large as we have formerly thought; many factors hitherto ignored, or not sufficiently emphasized, complicate the problem of exact proportions; and the absolute number of Americans in 1776 of Swedish descent, for instance, is larger, and the percentage considerably

---

[1] Hanson is also an English name, however.

larger, than the superficial census of 1790 would seem to indicate. From the sheer numerical magnitude, therefore,—using the names of officers as a rough number index of the rank and file—the contribution of the Swedish Colonial constituent to our independence must have been of appreciable moment, though detailed information on the subject is still wanting. Here we shall mention only two of the more illustrious Colonial Swedes.

John Hanson

In the Revolutionary struggle the descendants of the early Swedes proved a brave, patriotic element. The writer has yet to discover an unmistakably Swedish name in the lists of deserters published so frequently in the newspapers during the Revolution.

The Swedes along the Delaware were subjected to great hardships and untold suffering by the English troops for their loyalty to the Revolutionary cause. They fought in large numbers in the ranks, and they furnished some of the most brilliant officers and leaders in the struggle. John Hanson, John Morton, Thomas Sinnixon, are names that need no eulogy; they are enrolled among the founders of the Republic. But not only as soldiers did they contribute to the victory of the Revolution. Rev. Nils Collin did notable service with his pen . . . .[1]

One of the most notable Maryland patriots of Swedish descent was John Hanson, "President of the United States in Congress Assembled," for one year, from November 5, 1781. It became the duty of Hanson to express the official felicitations to General Washington upon his first visit to Congress, November 28, 1781, shortly after the surrender of the British at Yorktown. Local historians believe he was "not only a man of conspicuous ability, but one who possessed great firmness and energy of character," one who "probably contributed more than any other individual to vivify and strengthen the Revolutionary cause in western Maryland."[2]

"Born in Charles County in the first quarter of the eighteenth century (1715), he was chosen when a young man as a member of the Assembly, where he at once made his ability felt. In the year 1773 he removed to Frederick County, the bar of which became famous for its brilliant galaxy of legal lights. He was a signer of the Non-Importation Act (1769), and was elected chairman of the committee to stop importations from

---

[1] Amandus Johnson, *Contributions,* 51.
[2] J. Thomas Scharf, *History of Western Maryland,* I, 450.

JOHN HANSON.
(From the original in the National Capitol.)

Great Britain and the West Indies until the relief of Boston," which had been blockaded as a result of the famous Boston Tea Party. "As chairman of the Committee of Observation he rendered important service to Frederick County . . . . Indeed, the services of this Marylander, whose memory has been perpetuated in the national capitol, would fill a volume by themselves."[1]

It seems that John Hanson, like the sons of many other well-to-do Colonial families, was educated in England. Upon his return he represented his native county in the House of Delegates in almost every session for twenty years, and later served in the same capacity for Frederick County. He was also elected treasurer of the latter county, and in 1775 was commissioned by the Maryland Convention to establish a gun-lock factory for protection of the province. On October 9, 1776, he was made member of a commission empowered to appoint officers, reorganize troops, and encourage reinlistment of the Maryland militia or of the regular soldiers whose term of service in the Continental army were expiring. Hanson always took an active part in all agitation against arbitrary legislation of the British Parliament, and as a recognized leader held positions on various important patriotic committees. In addition to those mentioned we may note especially the Provincial Committee of Correspondence, a kind of secret service among the Colonists, and the committee for building a military jail or barracks at Frederick, where a large number of prisoners of war were confined. It was during his chairmanship of the Committee of Observation that the formidable Tory conspiracy of Lord Dunmore and White Eyes, an Indian chief, was discovered and frustrated.[2]

John Hanson was three times representative from Maryland to the Continental Congress.

Perhaps the most influential act of Hanson from a historical, constitutional viewpoint was the signing by him and Daniel Carroll of the Articles of Confederation, March 1, 1781, and as Maryland was the last to sign the Articles, they immediately went into effect. The ratification of the Articles had been held up by the great contest over western lands, until Maryland won out, a contest in which John Hanson had taken a conspicuous part both in Maryland and in Congress, and which had lasted about three years. Participation in this contest was one of the big things in Hanson's career. The signing of the Articles whereby they became operative was the culmination. The fact that the states having western claims were obliged to cede them to the United States made possible the future organization of the Northwest and Southwest territories and finally the admission of Ohio, Michigan, Wisconsin, Indiana, Illinois, Tennessee,

---

[1] Hester Dorsey Richardson, *Side-Lights on Maryland History* II, 118-119.

[2] George H. Ryden and Adolph B. Benson, *John Hanson, American Patriot, American-Scandinavian Review,* VIII, July, 1920, p. 527.

Alabama, and Mississippi on an equal footing with the thirteen original states.[1]

John Hanson died on November 22, 1783, living long enough to see the crowning result to which he had contributed so abundantly.[2]

The Hon. Alexander Contee Hanson, Chancellor of Maryland, and son of the President, was assistant private secretary to General Washington during his early manhood.

JOHN MORTON

No American patriot of Scandinavian extraction could better typify the character of the Swedish Colonial contribution to our freedom than John Morton, Signer of the Declaration of Independence.[3]

Surveyor, legislator, and justice, he was finally called upon, under circumstances of unprecedented responsibility, it seems, to cast the deciding vote for the Pennsylvania delegation, and thereby, practically decide the whole momentous question of declaration, so far as that memorable session in July, 1776, is concerned. Morton knew that this meant the sacrifice of personal ties and friendships of those who favored rejection or postponement of the proposed radical measure. But with courage, inner conviction, and clear, prophetic vision, Morton voted for the affirmative, and, some months later, won in return what came enviously close to a martyr's death.

Comparatively little is known about this simple, self-made hero, and therefore the writer deems it useful and appropriate to reprint here as a conclusion to this portion of the work, a brief character-

---

[1] *Ibid.*, p. 528. Cf. address on Hanson in the Appendix.

[2] Since Hanson died in 1783, it is obvious that he could not have installed George Washington as President of the United States, 1789, as stated in some recent publications. Apparently there is confusion here with Hanson's address to Washington of November 28, 1781.

[3] Recently a Finnish writer in one of our magazines has claimed John Morton as his own. This seems like historical quibbling; Morton was, as we now know, of Swedish ancestry, whether any of his forefathers once lived in Finland or not. Besides, Finland in the seventeenth century, when the emigration to America took place, was politically Swedish territory. We might, diplomatically, call him a Swedish Finn or a Finnish Swede. There is nothing Finnish about the name itself.

ALEXANDER CONTEE HANSON.

HANSON.

SOLA VIRTUS INVICTA

THE HANSON COAT OF ARMS.

ization of Morton's life and accomplishment by M. Atherton Leach of Philadelphia, a reliable biographer and genealogist of American families. It is reproduced with the permission of the author and the *American-Scandinavian Review* (for 1915) :[1]

In St. Paul's Churchyard in the industrial city of Chester, along the Delaware's waters in Pennsylvania, rises, serene above the din and smoke of a thousand iron throats, a plain shaft of white marble nine feet high, its four sides facing the cardinal points of the compass. Unadorned by ornamental carving, save the armorial bearings of the Commonwealth of Pennsylvania, it covers the grave of one whom Sweden, no less than Pennsylvania, may well rejoice to honor as a leader in an heroic crisis. It is the *memoria in aeterna* of John Morton, a Signer of the Declaration of Independence—that immortal document which, reaching backward to Magna Charta, carries human rights and human liberty forward to the Emancipation Proclamation.

Paternally John Morton descended from the brave company known as the Tenth Swedish Expedition, which sailed from Gothenburg, February 2, 1654, on the good ship *Örn,* bound for America under John Classon Rising, the last director of New Sweden. Three generations of his ancestors—Morton Mortonson, Morton Morton, John Morton—lived and died on Pennsylvania soil, before he, the posthumous and only child of John Morton and his wife, Mary Archer, was born in Chester County, in the year 1724. The young mother and widow, Mary Morton, was left in comfortable circumstances by her husband's will, for he, the senior John Morton, had received his proportion of his father's—Morton Morton's—grant of twelve hundred acres from William Penn, the Quaker proprietary of Pennsylvania. After a time Mary Morton married John Sketchley, an Englishman, who shared with his step-son the well-grounded education he himself had acquired, his profession as a surveyor, and the faith of the English Church, as then embodied in the practice of St. Paul's, Chester. Of this church John Sketchley had become a vestryman as early as 1742, and at his death in 1753 was succeeded by his foster son.

During his formative years and young manhood John Morton grew in the affection and confidence of his Chester County com-

---

[1] III, 226-232.

munity—a community of unusual intelligence and public spirit.
It was, therefore, no small honor that, from 1756, he should for
nineteen years be elected to represent it in the Provincial Assembly
of Pennsylvania. From 1767 he was three years high sheriff, an
office of conspicuous dignity at that period. In 1759 he became
a Provincial justice, was subsequently president judge of the
Court of General Quarter Sessions and Common Pleas of
the County, and in 1774 was appointed an associate judge of the
Supreme Court of the Province. During the two following years
he held the speakership of the Assembly. He was, too, a signer
of the Provincial currency or State bills of credit.

When John Morton began his legislative life in 1756 the
Assembly was composed of thirty-six members, and it cannot be
doubted that it represented the social and intellectual prestige of
the Province. Of this number twenty-six deputies were from the
counties of Philadelphia, Chester, and Bucks; the other ten were
sent by the Germans and Scotch-Irish of the back settlements.
The questions which agitated the public mind and its representatives were largely those arising from the endless disputes between
the Assembly and the Lieutenant-Governor; questions which
were fundamental and involved the theory as well as the fate of
that peculiar phase of Colonial government called proprietary.
The disputes covered such cardinal matters as: the right of the
Assembly to issue money for the public service on its own terms;
the claim that it alone should distribute the public burden by
imposing taxes on such commodities as it deemed best; its right
to decline to aid England in the prosecution of her foreign wars;
its right and power to establish a military force for the defence
of the Province composed of volunteers, instead of those serving
under compulsory military law; its right and duty to protect the
Indians within the Province against the rapacity of the Provincial
agents. Two strong parties were the outcome of the struggle—
that of the Proprietary, with whom the Quaker members voted,
and that of the Provincial or popular rights, led by Benjamin
Franklin, supported by the Presbyterian Scotch-Irish and the
Church people. In 1755 the Quakers and their political friends,
the Germans, were attacked for their supposed want of sympathy
with the frontier settlers exposed to the incursions of the French,
and their Indian allies, and many were not returned to the
Assembly.

John Morton's election to the Pennsylvania Assembly was, therefore, in the nature of a victory for popular rights as against the established order, and it was the arena in which he was to cultivate those qualities of faith and firmness which should eventually immortalize him. In this arena every parliamentary expedient for which there was precedent was resorted to for the maintenance of the Assembly's power, and his associates must early have recognized his constructive strength of mind and rare judgment in public affairs, since they sent him as one of Pennsylvania's four delegates to the Stamp Act Congress of 1765, convened at New York. His colleagues at this, the first American Congress, were John Dickinson, the leader of the opposition to the Stamp Act in Pennsylvania; Joseph Fox, speaker of the Assembly, and George Bryan, later vice-president of the State.

To the next Congress of the Colonies, which met at Carpenter's Hall in Philadelphia, September 5, 1774, John Morton was again a delegate. This Congress was composed of fifty-five deputies, representing all the colonies except Georgia. Historically, it is usually described as the First Continental Congress, though in reality the second, and was perhaps never excelled by any collection of men for purity of motives and disinterested patriotism. The Session lasted eight weeks, behind closed doors.

The Congress of 1775, the Second Continental Congress, so-called, met in the State House, at Philadelphia, in the eastern room on the first floor, now universally known as Independence Chamber. Its sessions were held from May 10 to August 1 and from September 5 to December 30, of that year. Its personnel was essentially that of its precursor, and John Morton, who on each successive round of the ladder measured up to the far-reaching policies of the greatest of the pre-Revolutionary leaders, was again a delegate. At this time he was also speaker of the Pennsylvania Assembly.

He was likewise a delegate to the Congress of 1776, and, at its memorable session of the 2d to 4th of July, in Independence Chamber of the State House, with an intuition reaching beyond his time, gave the casting vote of Pennsylvania in the affirmative upon the question of adopting the Declaration of Independence. The Pennsylvania vote on that day was: affirmative, Benjamin Franklin, James Wilson, John Morton; negative, Thomas Willing, Charles Humphreys. John Dickinson and Robert Morris were absent. Edward Biddle and Andrew Allen had previously resigned. Robert Morris signed later. Contrary to popular opinion, the Declaration, though signed on the fourth day of July, was not proclaimed in Philadelphia until four days later. The eminent diarist and eye-witness, Christopher Marshall, says under: "July 8th Monday. Warm sunshine morning. . . . Went in a body to the State House Yard, where, in the presence of a great concourse of people, the Declaration of Independence was read by John Nixon. The company declared their approbation by three repeated huzzas. . . . . Fine starlight, pleasant evening. There were bonfires, ringing bells with other great demonstrations of joy upon the unanimity and agreement of the declaration."

It is claimed that the vote of Congress upon the adoption of the Declaration was by colonies, each delegation voting separately, the majority deciding the colony vote. Six colonies had voted in favor of and six against the measure, leaving the Pennsylvania delegation the last to vote. The result was a tie. At this moment John Morton, as speaker of the Assembly, had been detained, entered the Hall and decided the Pennsylvania vote. It was then unanimous as to colonies but not as to delegations. It is further claimed that Morton's action gave Pennsylvania the name of the Keystone State. There seems no other sufficient reason for the appellation.

With singular ability Mr. Morton served on many important committees during his term in Congress, and was chairman of the committee of the whole on the adoption of a system of confederation, finally agreed to December 15, 1777. It may be noted that, save John Dickinson, he was the only delegate from Pennsylvania who served in all of the four great Congresses.

In the disquieting months which followed, his State was rent with internal dissensions, and he was occupied with matters of grave moment. One of his rare letters—only three are known to have been preserved—dated at Philadelphia August 16, 1776, and addressed to his friend, General Anthony Wayne, says in part:

"I received your favor of third of July, but want of opportunity to write and my engagements to make out the Commissions for our militia, who are all on their march to New Jersey to oppose Lord Howe, who is encamped on Staten Island with about 27,000

men, ... and my attendance on Congress has taken almost all
my time. I hope I shall stand excused. Our Politics here have
taken a turn which I have expected some time. The People
whom you know have all along held back joined to some others
who were the Proprietary friends . . . . became at last too heavy
to drag along, and a Convention has taken place consisting of
8 members out of each County and 8 of the City who are to
form a New Government."

Upon the abrogation of the Provincial charter of Pennsylvania
he was elected to the Convention, of which he wrote to General
Wayne, to frame a constitution for the Commonwealth. This
body, convened July 15, 1776, chose Benjamin Franklin president.
After a session of two months the Constitution was completed,
read in convention, signed by the president, committed to the
Council of Safety—then the governing body—with instructions
to present it to the Assembly of the Commonwealth at its first
meeting. Thus closed, September 26, 1776, the final act in the
great drama of proprietary government in Pennsylvania, and
again John Morton had been a constructionist.

By faith he had caught the vision of the future—the permanent,
afar off—and had enrolled his name in favor of independence,
but the anxiety incident thereto is confidently said to have acceler-
ated if, indeed, it did not cause his death, which occurred in the
anxious days of April, 1777. He was the first of the Signers to
die, hence his thoughtful countenance does not look out from
either of the really great canvases which chronicle the event he
aided to immortalize—Pine's "Congress Voting Independence"
or Trumbull's "Signing the Declaration of Independence." There
is no known authentic portrait of this man of the people, this
noble type of the best American virtues. Whatever he gained
of fame and honor came to him as the result of unflinching fidelity, boundless devotion. He was never satisfied with himself, but
pressed ever onward, sometimes toward heights beyond his power
to attain. However great his native abilities, they were over-
matched by his character.

His unpretentious home in Chester County, a stone house,
built in 1764, is still standing in Ridley Park, with the Signer's
initials, those of his wife and the date of erection cut on a circular
marble tablet set in its southern gable. So it must have been
an earlier house at Ammasland, doubtless his mother's, which

was mentioned by the Reverends Dr. Charles von Wrangel and Dr. Henry Melchoir Muhlenberg as "Squire Morton's," on the occasion of their visit to the Swedish families near and in Tinicum, in July, 1761.

By his wife, Ann Justis, who also came of the early Swedish settlers, he had three sons and five daughters to survive him. After the battle of Brandywine the successful British Army, on its march to Philadelphia despoiled the property of Mrs. Morton and her children to the extent of £365 sterling. His descendants have been numerous, many attaining distinction. One of these General Charles Lukens Davis, U. S. A., retired, is at this time (1915) president of the patriotic hereditary society, the Descendants of the Signers of the Declaration of Independence.

In 1876, a simple memorial tablet to the patriot was placed in Independence Chamber in the State House at Philadelphia by a grandson. The monument, which covers his dust in St. Paul's churchyard and elsewhere referred to, recites briefly on its four sides the salient facts of his life. The inscription on the north side reads: "John Morton, being censured by some of his friends for his boldness in giving his casting vote for the Declaration of Independence, his prophetic spirit dictated from his death-bed the following message: 'Tell them they will live to see the hour when they shall acknowledge it to have been the most glorious service I ever rendered my country.'"

Swede though he was by heredity, John Morton had remembered in her hour of need only the land of his forefather's adoption—"Land of the pilgrim's pride"—and made it possible that "From every mountain-side" freedom should ring.

CHAPTER VI

A List of Swedish Officers in the French and Colonial
Service for American Independence

In 1867 a Frenchman, surveying the relations between France
and Sweden during the American pre-revolutionary and revolutionary periods, pens this encomium:

One of the regiments designated as "foreign," which had become a part
of the French army, and which for a long time had been commanded by a
colonel and officers of the Swedish nation, had taken the name of the
Royal-Suédois.[1] From the time of its enlistment as such, almost all the
great names of the Northern noblesse had been found among its ranks;
diplomats, officers, courtiers. These young Swedes with the frank and
open countenance of their race, extremely brave in war, very enthusiastic
about France, intelligent and *spirituels*, flourished at a Versailles rejuven-
ated by the new régime . . .[2]

Thus we find Feodor Mauritz Aminoff, b. 1759, first a second
lieutenant in the Royal-Suédois, 1778, and captain in 1780; Carl
Adolph Hammarberg, a lieutenant in the same regiment, 1779;
and Herman Fleming af Liebenitz was a lieutenant in the French
army about 1780. Among the many Pipers who had served
France previously we find Carl Ulric Piper, b. 1753, employed
during the American Revolution; Gustaf Johan Staël von Holstein was an officer of French cavalry in 1781; so was Joachim
Staël von Holstein, from 1782 to 1785, in the Royal Allemagne.
Carl Jacob von Quanten, 1734-1789, attained the rank of colonel
and won the order Pour le Mérite Militaire; and dozens of
Sparres, it seems, had settled in France—some had become French
noblemen—and had obtained commands in the Royal Suédois.

Yet none of these reached America, so far as we know, nor
were they in any sense, except in a remote, potential way, volunteers for the American cause; the writer has introduced a few
names here merely to illustrate the above citation, and to show
further the variety of cognomens of these contemporary Swedish-
French officers. Moreover, the French attitude toward these
Swedish noblemen, and their reputation in higher circles, as
voiced by Geffroy, should be a favorable factor in accepting

---

[1] Cf. p. 13.
[2] A. Geffroy, *Gustave III et la Cour de France,* I, 345.

Swedes for volunteer service in America. We shall see that it was.

The old story that the number of foreign volunteers in French or American service from 1776 to 1783 will never be known has been stated elsewhere. It is said that 120 foreign volunteers took part in the battle of Grenada. There was "a large number of alien officers in the squadron of de Guichen," says Noailles.[1] and enumerates a few. There is said to have been a whole corps of them in Duc de Lauzun's legion. We know there were several Swedes in Count d'Estaing's expedition which sailed from Toulon in April, 1778, and some Swedish officers on the frigate *Junon*,[2] which captured the *Ardent* in 1779. Noailles, again, claims there were ten foreign officers on *L'Annibal* alone on the 18th of December, 1779,[3] among whom were "de Carné et de Ville-Vieille, lieutenants de Vaisseau; de Champagny, enseigne de vaisseau; Coffort et Criher, enseignes danois." The latter two are un-questionably meant to be Koefoed and Krieger, Danish naval officers, whose names we have seen before;[4] but the names of the others are Frenchified to a point that defies positive identification. Some of the other eight were undoubtedly Swedish. The majority of the alien naval officers came from the North. The Swiss, Irish, German, and Italian contributions to French warfare were confined, with possible insignificant exceptions, to the army; and the Dutch and Spaniards needed their own men. There may have been a few Prussians, but certainly not many. The Swedes, however, took part in the naval battles against the English from the very opening of hostilities by France, having been accepted, as we shall see, in comparatively large numbers. Of those Swedish officers, also, who in the very beginning of the war had sought experience in the English navy, the large majority, with or without the advice of Gustavus III, transferred their services, in 1778, to France.

But, for the French expeditionary *army* to America, not all Swedish volunteers could be accepted. Göran Magnus Sprengt-porten (1740-1819) had secured leave of absence from the

---

[1] *Marins et Soldats Français en Amérique*, p. 119.
[2] Cf. p. 21.
[3] *Op. cit.*, p. 105, note.
[4] Cf. p. 9, note.

Swedish service in 1779 and gone to Paris, where he remained for a period of two years, hoping to get a suitable commission in the auxiliary army, but he never reached America. Baron de Staël von Holstein, Swedish ambassador to France in 1783, and eventually husband of the renowned Madame de Staël, had wanted to start for America in 1776, it is reported; and "even the famous General Sandels" of Swedish-Finnish-Russian fame, whose father had been a pastor in Philadelphia, prepared to go to America, but was turned back at Paris.[1]

Thirty years ago, the eminent Swedish historian C. T. Odhner, whose work I have already quoted several times, wrote the following summary about the Swedish officers in the French-American service. It will serve here as an enlightening part of our introduction to the list of officers:

When the war broke out between France and England, several of the Swedish officers of the English fleet entered the French service, and after the French government had declared that it would gladly accept Swedish naval officers in its employ during the war, it decided to make a more extensive use of this opportunity. His Royal Swedish Majesty granted to fifteen officers of the admiralty and thirteen of the army fleet a traveling allowance of one hundred rixdollars apiece, and let them keep this allowance during the years immediately following. They were also given other advantages, such as receiving two years' pay in advance (if necessary), without bonds, and at the end of the war were permitted to enjoy the allowance privilege for another two years, so as to be able to pay off the debts contracted in foreign lands.[2] The offer had the desired effect, and during the following years a large number of Swedish officers went to France, not only naval officers but also army men, who sought positions among the troops that were leaving for America and the West Indies. The number of candidates for enlistment became so large that Creutz complained about it.[3] Some of them became a burden to him, got into debt and dire straits in general. On the whole they did well in the war; they served for the most part as lieutenants or ensignes de vaisseau; several distinguished themselves and were decorated with the order pour les mérites militaires; and some were granted French pensions. Creutz mentions in 1780, as the more important ones, O. H. Nordenskjöld, Klas Wachtmeister, G. K. de Frese, G. Rehbinder, V. v. Stedingk, M. v. Rosenstein, H. Nauckhoff, J. Puke, A. Pettersen, D. Blessing, Kasten Feif, S. v.

---

[1] Amandus Johnson, *Contributions by Swedes to American Progress*, pp. 50-51.

[2] A free translation of the main text combined with accompanying foot notes.

[3] Cf. p. 6.

Rajalin, S. Gyllenskepp, Z. Schultén. We may also mention M. Palmquist, K. J. v. Hohenhausen, A. F. Brummer and Kr. Grubbe. Among the land officers the more prominent ones are Kurt v. Stedingk, Axel v. Fersen, P. U. Liljehorn, J. H. Hamilton, G. v. Döbeln, B. v. Fock. Swedish officers are mentioned in almost all the more important events of this war, in the East and West Indies, in North America, at Senegal and Gibraltar. When Count d'Estaing in 1779 captured Grenada in the West Indies, several Swedes took part in the battle with distinction, both on land and on sea. Colonel Stedingk contributed materially both to the victory at Grenada and to the successful retreat at Savannah not long thereafter. At the capture of Pensacola in 1781, lieutenant Pettersen-Rosensvärd displayed an extraordinary bravery; he saved the company he commanded from annihilation, and was carried wounded on the shoulders of the officers to the general's tent. He was rewarded both with orders and the rank of nobility. In the naval battle near Guadeloupe, 1782, which was so disastrous to the French, several Swedes were wounded and captured, and Nauckhoff contributed not a little to the preservation of the ship on which he served. In the siege of Yorktown Fersen and Fock performed heroic service. At the attack on Gibraltar, 1782, Captain E. L. Armfelt was the last one to leave the floating battery, where he was in command, before it exploded. His lieutenant, an engineer Myrin, although wounded in the leg and with one arm shot off, had himself carried up on deck where he continued to direct the fire. Myrin died. At least eight other Swedes (i. e. Swedish officers), among them the much-eulogized Rehbinder, suffered the same fate during this war. The number of Swedish officers who participated in the struggle amounts to about seventy, most of them in French service.

Sweden has, therefore, by the side of France, made a contribution, however modest, of energy and blood to that great war which liberated America. Though of some military importance for Sweden in the training of officers, "the participation in the conflict has had no such political significance for Sweden as it has had for France."[1]

An examination of the "tres humbles apostilles" (that is, recommendatory letters) by Ambassador de Creutz to Gustavus III, which constituted Odhner's chief source, reveals an ardent sympathy for the Swedish officers in the war and a watchful interest in their personal life and all their official activities. With great care and pride, he reports to the king the abilities and achievements of his countrymen, as soon as reliable details about a certain campaign have come in, and recommends this or that honor or promotion. We can see that it is not an easy, lucrative position to serve as a French officer, for, ordinarily, he has to live way beyond his means, and rank and riches do not always

---

[1] Odhner, *op. cit.* II, pp. 103-105.

go together. Sometimes the Swede in foreign service has rela-
tives dependent on his support who must be cared for, and Creutz
calls His Majesty's attention to the case. Everything is confided
to the king. The number of citations for distinguished service is
very large, and these are communicated at once to the sovereign.
Several Swedish officers are wounded; some die of disease; and
others are killed. Creutz, ever courteous but firm and insistent,
is very assiduous in advocating higher commissions for the men
who have shown talent and knowledge, and points out the possible advantage to his own country of the experience of the
officers in the event of a war in the North.[1] The following letter
of February 6, 1780—a time when information about the progress
of the war could be given by returning officers—gives us some
specific facts to date about the work of not less than twenty-five
Swedish officers. The letter, obviously used by Odhner,[2] illustrates the type of a Creutz message. I am reproducing it in full:

Through the information which I have received from Monsieur d'Estaing,
the Viscount de Noailles, Monsieur de Stedingk and various naval commanders both in Europe and in America, I am now in a position to transmit
for Your Majesty's specific knowledge the judgment formed here concerning the talents of the various Swedes who are serving in the French navy.
All have distinguished themselves by their zeal and application; but there
is a difference in their gifts, which only the war has been able to bring
out, and it will be advantageous to Your Majesty's fleet, and the success of
the first war that you may have to endure, to advance in rank beforehand
those who have proved their ability. They should not languish with
inferior grades but be given important commissions at once and placed in
positions of command.

Count *Wachtmeister* is already known in France for the nobility and

---

[1] Swedish naval officers who had received training in the American war
had an opportunity to turn their experience to excellent advantage in the
war of 1788-1790.

[2] The present writer had independently compiled a list of fifty-four
Swedish officers before his attention was called to the work by Odhner,
based on Creutz, which added a few more names.

In Amandus Johnson's *Contributions* (p. 51), and in some subsequent
publications based thereon, the number of Swedish officers participating
in the American Revolution is given as fourteen (14), which the author
tells me is a typist's error for "41," Dr. Johnson not having had the opportunity of correcting the error by reading the proofs of his widely circulated
booklet. After my own investigation was completed, I learned from Dr.
Johnson that he had made a similar investigation a few years ago, but that
his manuscript had been destroyed in a fire.

loftiness of his sentiments. He is intent, alert, ardent, and ready to under-
take anything. He is beloved by all his comrades and inferiors. He will
inspire obedience by both attachment and severity; he has now a wide
experience on sea, a valor which joins daring with presence of mind, and
a sensitive instinct which is suitable for qualities of command. He has
perhaps less theoretical knowledge and training than the others, but he
will not be a poorer general on that account.

But those who have exhibited superior faculties in this war, and who are
really considered as extraordinary men in their class, are *Nordenskjöld,
Frese, Rehbinder,* and *Stedingk.* Monsieur d'Estaing and Viscount de
Noailles have told me that one could entrust the most difficult expedition
to them and be certain of success.

Monsieur de *Rosenstein* is of the same type. (As yet) he has only
served in Europe, but he has a marvellous training, a profound sense of
application, and his talent is of the best. *Nauckhoff* has had much instruction, but he is better suited for the head of a training school in our navy
than for a commander.

Among the lieutenants who show gifts, I must first mention *Pettersen,
Blessing Puke, Feiff* the Elder, *Rayalin,* who was present at the capture
of the *Ardent, Schultén,* and *Gyllenskepp,* who have distinguished themselves in America and who have been advanced to the rank of lieutenant de
vaisseau.

Rayalin the Younger, *Grubbe, Sjöstierna, Brummer, Ulfklo, Feiff* the
Younger, and *Lannerstierna* need another campaign to show their ability.

Palmquist, Raab, and *Staré* have shown great application and promise.

Ankarloo had received orders to return to Sweden; but he had already
embarked on the *Solitaire,* for India, and he had been given three months
pay in advance with which he had paid his debts. It would have been
necessary to return this money (had he complied with the orders), to
obtain some other funds for his return to Sweden at this season when
there was no boat, and to write to the minister (of naval affairs) to obtain
his discharge at the moment of departure, which would have injured the
reputation of the Swedes here. And so I beg Your Majesty to permit
him to remain in the service here during the campaign to India. His
conduct is much better; he has paid his debts and we believe he has ability.
I have the honor to enclose a letter to Your Majesty in his behalf.

Gustav Creutz[1]

Another message, dealing with the plight of many Swedish
survivors of the war, some of whom had lost all their effects in
naval disasters, and written by Creutz just before his return to
Sweden, may be inserted at this point because of its bearing on

---

[1] Translated from a copy of the French original. The following letter
is translated from the Swedish. Creutz uses both languages in his official
reports.

the group of Swedish naval officers as a whole. It is dated in Paris, April 27, 1783:

Before I leave this place I hope Your Royal Majesty will permit me in all humility to request a mark of Your Royal favor on behalf of the Swedish naval officers who during the last war have served under the French flag. I have nothing to add to the recent reports that I have made from time to time about their status. I can declare without exaggeration that they have done great honor to the Swedish nation and served to revive and establish the current opinion about this nation's bravery and skill in war operations. Now they are returning to their fatherland, and for advancement in the service need no other spokesmen from an enlightened and just king than the experience and competence they have acquired. But . . . they are in a condition which gives them more concern than their promotion, since their honor depends on it. The majority of them without means, they have through unusual expense and accompanying misfortune contracted debts, the payment of which, as I have recently mentioned, concerns not only their own name but that of the Swedish name in general. The good opinion about the Swedes—which has been not a little strengthened by their good behavior—has procured for them a confidence which has exceeded that enjoyed by other nations, and it would be very regrettable if a disappointment in this line should impair the impression which the Swedish officers have made here. Their own resources are the more limited, since their hope of receiving traveling expenses from this court has been frustrated . . . .

In the remainder of the letter Creutz requests his king to continue the war allowance until "their debts, which are not very large, can be paid." We have seen from Odhner's summary that the request was granted.

Other Creutz dispatches will be introduced below under the names of the individuals most concerned.

List of Swedish Officers

The following Swedish officers, arranged alphabetically, took active part in our war of independence, the first group comprising those who saw service under the French or American flag, either on American soil or in American waters. The identification is not complete in every case—often the family could be identified but not the individual—yet there is no doubt about the existence of an officer with the given patronymic in each instance. For the sake of those interested in verification, the French spellings, when different from the original, are given in parentheses.

GROUP I

1. BJELKE, NILS   (de Bielke, de Bielche)

Born June 5, 1763, of a very old and prominent family of the Swedish nobility. He was first a member of the Royal Body Guard, and became a lieutenant in the Swedish navy in 1778. Soon thereafter he entered the French naval service, and is mentioned as one of the Swedish officers who were rewarded after the capture of Pensacola, Florida, in May, 1781. He then held the rank of a supernumerary lieutenant de vaisseau. Later he served in East Indian waters and was killed in a naval action against the English on April 12, 1782, under de Suffren, the English commander being Admiral Hughes. Bjelke's fellow-countryman Lannerstjerna was killed in the same battle.[1]

2. BLESSING, DAVID GUSTAF   (Blessingane)

Blessing was fourth officer on *Le Conquérant,* which left Brest on May 2, 1780, and was still on the same vessel, as officer in the naval army of the Marquis de Vaudreuil, in May, 1782. Noailles gives his rank as lieutenant de vaisseau. He was so seriously wounded in the naval battle of Dominica, April 12, 1782, that he seems to have suffered from the effects of it the rest of his life. "All the Swedish officers distinguished themselves in an extraordinary degree on that fatal day, the 12th of April," writes Creutz, and makes special mention of Blessing. The French minister de Castries wrote to Creutz, on December 14, 1782: "I have called the attention of the king to the praiseworthy conduct which Messrs. Nauckhoff (which see) and Blessing, Swedish officers, displayed in the last campaign in America, and particularly on the 12th of April, when both were wounded. His majesty wishing to give them some proof of his satisfaction over their devotion to his service, has granted a pension of three hundred (francs) to de Blessing whose wound is causing grievous trouble." He had, previously, in December, 1781, been awarded the Croix du Mérite for bravery in action under the command

---

[1] Cf. Kerguelen-Trémarec, *Histoire des Evénements des Guerres Maritimes entre La France et L'Angleterre,* etc., p. 268.

This battle is not to be confused with the naval action near Dominica in the western waters fought on the same date. Both were of paramount importance. The French victory in the East neutralized to some extent the effect of the English victory in the West. See p. 8.

of de la Perouse. Upon Blessing's return to France, he and Nauckhoff were obliged to go to a watering-place for their health, and on October 24, 1782, Creutz informs his king that the gratuity which they had received from France, eight hundred francs, was not sufficient to defray their expenses, and implores Gustavus III to help them out. Later Creutz writes to the Swedish Admiralty asking them to support his request for a "gratification" on behalf of Blessing and Nauckhoff. In 1811, in an application for leave of absence to visit a health resort, Blessing can still use the wounds "received in the royal French service" as a potent argument for granting a subsequent request.

References to this officer are found in several French sources.

3. DU BORDIEU (de Bordieux)

This officer is mentioned by Noailles in *Marins et Soldats Français en Amérique* as an ensign of *Le Sceptre* in the naval army of de Vaudreuil at St. Domingo, May 30, 1782. In a message of October 24, 1782, Baron de Creutz writes to Gustavus III: "I have the honor to enclose a letter which I have just received from Monsieur de la Perouse, who has devastated the English possessions in Hudson Bay. He solicits Your Majesty's gracious attention on behalf of Mr. Du Bordieu, who conducted himself in a superior manner during that expedition. Since he is very poor and has had no gratuity during the whole time that he has served here, Your Majesty's kindness would relieve his misery. He will be made lieutenant de vaisseau here, but he cannot yet have the croix du mérite; *that* will in all probability be the reward of a new expedition which de la Perouse intends to make."

Castries had written to Creutz about du Bordieu: "I have called the king's attention to the testimony which Monsieur de la Perouse gives concerning the courage displayed by Mr. du Bordieux, Swedish officer, in the expedition to Hudson Bay; and I have the pleasure to announce to Your Excellency that His French Majesty, satisfied with the zeal of this officer, has wished to indicate this satisfaction by awarding him the rank of supernumerary lieutenant in the navy."

4. BRUMMER, A. F. (De Brumer, de Brummer, de Bromer)

Of old Livonian-Swedish nobility. Mentioned by Geffroy[1] as

---

[1] *Op. cit.*, I, p. 347.

Swedish officer in French service. According to Noailles,[1] he was first an ensign in the squadron of Admiral de Guichen, and later, lieutenant de vaisseau in naval army of de Vaudreuil, on *Le Palmier*, 1782. Wounded in naval action off Saint Lucia on May 15, 1780, and again on October 20, 1782, near the Straits of Gibraltar.[2] In a message to Gustavus III, dated at Paris, March 23, 1783, Creutz recommends a gratuity for Brummer, because he had lost all his personal effects when *Le Palmier* sank, 1782.

5. CEDERSTRÖM, OLOF   (Cedestrom, Le Baron de Sederstrom)
                      (Possibly Olof Rudolf, b. 1764)

Born 1758. Ensign in Swedish navy, 1778. Lieutenant-colonel 1812. Died at Ilingetorp, Kalmar Län, 1831. Knight of the Swedish Order of the Sword, and Chevalier of the French Order Pour le Mérite Militaire. Served as ensign on *L'Auguste* in the squadron of Count de Grasse, 1781, and later, according to Noailles on *Le Sceptre*, under Vaudreuil, in the same capacity. His brother Sven, was an officer in the Royal Suédois during the American Revolution, but was probably not in America. Their father, Gustav Cederström (1727—about 1768), was an officer of infantry and a warm advocate of the free press.

6. DE FRESE, GEORG K.

Creutz writes on October 24, 1779, that, among other Swedish officers, "Capitaine Frese" had won honors at the capture of Grenada. On February 3, the following year, the Swedish minister informs his king that in France "Messrs Nordenskjöld (which see) and De Frese are regarded as real geniuses, as men of superior merit." De Frese was one of the few Swedes who may have profited financially from his naval adventures. Creutz, on May 17, 1781, in announcing the arrival at Brest of Monsieur de la Motte-Piquet—with all his prizes captured from the English—refers to De Frese as follows: "I have the honor to enclose a letter from Monsieur Frese employed on *L'Invincible* which describes the cruise of M. de la Motte-Piquet. He will receive between sixteen and twenty thousand francs as his share (of the

---

[1] *Op. cit.*, p. 119.

[2] Kerguelen-Trémarec, *Historie des Événements des Guerres Maritimes*, etc., pp. 321 and 325.

prize money). There were two other Swedes on the squadron. De Frese is an excellent officer who two years ago, through his presence of mind, saved the vessel *Le Fier*." French records refer to this officer as De Frese of *Le Fier*. On March 7, 1783, Georg De Frese was recommended by the Swedish admiralty to receive "captain's pay in the Swedish squadron." He was decorated by both Sweden and France.

7. FEIF, GUSTAF CASTEN   (Feiff, Feiffe, de Seiff)

Feif came from a distinguished family of Swedish naval officers, who traced their ancestry back to Jakob Fyf of Scotland, a merchant who in the preceding century, had settled in Stockholm. Born on July 16, 1755; was first lieutenant in Swedish navy and finally captain and major.[1] Decorated with the Order of the Sword and Pour le Mérite Militaire. Perished on July 3, 1790, when *Enigheten*, which he commanded, blew up in Wiborg Bay. He was (in the American war) a lieutenant de vaisseau on *L'Engageante* in Admiral de Guichen's squadron, mentioned in letter above by Creutz, and by Noailles as "de Seiff (aîné)" to distinguish him from his younger brother.

8. FEIF, CARL DONAT   (de Seiff (cadet))

Born the 8th of December, 1759,[2] and died as a retired lieutenant-colonel in the Swedish navy, 1808. Was ensign first in Swedish, then, from December, 1778, in French service. Finally promoted to be a lieutenant and decorated with the same French and Swedish orders as his brother. Their father was a vice-admiral in the Swedish navy. Feif, the younger, was first assigned to *L'Alexandre*, which together with other ships of the allied fleet did duty in the English Channel and the Bay of Biscay. In 1780 he was transferred to *L'Hercule* in Count de Guichen's fleet, and on this vessel took part in three battles (in the West Indies) against Admiral Rodney. The following year he sailed on *Le Sagittaire* in an expedition to Boston. Advanced to lieutenant de vaisseau, he was transferred again, to *L'Engageant,* and returned to Europe. In 1782 he was ordered to the East Indian

---

[1] It will be seen that names of grades in the Swedish navy were different from ours.

[2] This is date of birth according to Anrep. Another source gives 1760 as the year of his birth.

colonies on the *Pégase*, but after an encounter with a superior English squadron, Feif was taken prisoner and remained so for three months, losing all his personal goods, wherefore Creutz in his communication to Gustavus III, March 23, 1783, calls attention to the plight of this Swedish officer. Feif, the younger, served for a time in 1782 and 1783 on *Le Conquérant* on an expedition to Cadiz and the Mediterranean.

9. FERSEN, HANS AXEL VON
(See special chapter)

10. FOCK (ROBECK), JOHAN HENRIC, BARON VON
The son of Jacob Constantine, Baron Fock, of the Swedish nobility. He participated in our war under the name of Fock, but was later, upon becoming a resident of England, obliged to change his name. Fock was born May 21, 1753; was first an officer in the Swedish army; became a captain of Schomberg's dragoons in France, 1779; and soon thereafter adjutant of Duc de Lauzun, who commanded the vanguard of the French Army in America, 1781. He was a Knight of the Order of the Sword. "He fought with great bravery during the American war of independence and received an annual French pension of 1500 livres," says Anrep. He died in England, September 22, 1817.

Baron Fock was one of the Swedish army officers who did honor to the Swedish name at Yorktown. When the Duke de Lauzun returned to France, in November, 1781, bearing the great news of the surrender of Cornwallis—reported to the king of Sweden by Creutz on November 23—he had some very pleasant things to say about Fersen and Fock. "He has also great praise for Monsieur de Fock," writes Creutz to his Swedish majesty on November 25, referring to Lauzun's verbal report on the baron. "In a cavalry attack where Lauzun's hussars repulsed a furious charge by English dragoons, Fock exhibited an extraordinary valor and intelligence. He (Lauzun) has asked me to solicit from Your Majesty the Cross of the Order of the Sword for Messrs Fersen and Fock. Monsieur de Rochambeau will demand the same kind of favor for them here."

11. GRUBBE, KRISTOFFER (Christoffer)
Born 1762; entered Swedish army, 1774; eventually a major, and lieutenant-colonel in the Swedish navy; died September 25,

1811, in Karlskrona. Grubbe descended from an old noble family whose original name was Larsson. Chronology and circumstances of French decoration with the Order Pour le Mérite Militaire indicate that this is the Grubbe to whom Geffroy refers in *Gustav III et la Cour de France*.[1] The circumstance of Geffroy's reference indicates service in America. The Swedish king also made him a Knight of the Order of the Sword.

Grubbe is mentioned, above, by both Creutz and Odhner. On November 25, and more particularly on December 2, 1781, Creutz requests a gratuity from his sovereign for Ensign Grubbe, who had "lost all his possessions" when the vessel on which he served, *L'Intrépide,* burned and blew up. "Such aid," says Creutz, "in addition to what he will receive in France, will make it possible for the officer to buy new equipment."

12. GYLLENSKEPP, S.

A Swedish lieutenant mentioned by Noailles[2] as serving in de Guichen's squadron early in the American war. According to a letter by Creutz, dated October 24, 1779, Lieutenant Gyllenskepp distinguished himself at Grenada, along with the Swedes De Frese, Stedingk, and Rehbinder. Having received an honoring testimony about his skill and ability from his commander de Choisy, chief of squadron, later in the war, Creutz in a letter of March 15, 1782, makes a comment of his own: Gyllenskepp "is really an officer of 'infinite merit,' with a sense of application and bravery which no obstacle can disturb."

13. HOHENHAUSEN, CARL JOHAN VON (Logenhausen, De Houguenousem, M. Hoguen-Houzen)

Born March 8, 1755; first an ensign in the Swedish army fleet; entered French service and eventually decorated by both France and Sweden with the same orders as Feif, Grubbe, and others. Ennobled and made captain in the Swedish service, 1786; killed at the battle of Svensksund, August 24, 1789. Mentioned by Noailles,[3] as a Swedish naval officer in French service in America. Says Anrep: "During his French service he participated in the war against England and fought in nine major battles with extra-

---

[1] I, 347.
[2] *Op. cit.,* 119.
[3] *Op. cit.*

ordinary bravery."[1]   First an ensign, he was later promoted to a
lieutenant de vaisseau on *L'Auguste* in de Vaudreuil's squadron,
being fourth in command of the vessel.   Wounded in the naval
battle of September 5, 1781, and extolled by Bougainville for
distinguished service, he was cited by the French as a Swedish
officer who would bring back to his native land "the most conspicuous knowledge" and give to it "the very best ideas of French
training." He was a man, says Creutz, who deserved special
encouragement and advancement, because his zeal and modesty
replaced all personal pretentions. Hohenhausen covered himself
with glory in Count de Guichen's naval encounter with Admiral
Rodney. "He commanded," writes Creutz on November 9, 1780,
"the second battery of the vessel *St. Michel* which by its running
fire did so much damage to the *Sandwich* commanded by Admiral
Rodney. Chevalier Aymar who commanded the *St. Michel,* and
who lost an arm in this battle, gave a most glorifying eulogy of
Mr. de Hohenhausen, and, as a recompense for the loss of his
own arm, demanded the croix du mérite for him . . . ." December 2, 1781, Creutz writes again: "I must add that Herr Hohenhausen who was wounded in the beginning of Count de Grasse's
battle with the English fleet (off the American coast on September 5), did not leave the deck to have his wound dressed, but
despite the pain that he suffered in consequence continued his
command for a period of four hours, and through his example
and bravery encouraged the others to do their duty."

14. JÄGERSKJÖLD, CARL LUDVIG (Iegrcheud, Idgernold)
   Born February 25, 1758, the son of rear-admiral in the Swedish
navy. First a lieutenant in the Swedish navy; eventually a major
in French service; decorated by Sweden and France; d. October
11, 1811. Mentioned in *Les Combattants Français de la Guerre
Américaine 1778-1783* as an enseigne de vaisseau on *La Blanche,*
1778-1779, and reported by Kerguelen (see bibliography) as
wounded in the "combat de la Praya ile de Saint-Yago," under de
Suffren, April 16, 1781.

15. JÖNSSON, ONNERT
   A Swedish naval officer who served in West Indian waters during the latter part of the war. He had once held a commission

[1] II, 285.

in the English navy. In French service he had the rank of an "enseigne surnuméraire." On March 23 and 31, 1783, Creutz applies to the Swedish authorities for some honor and financial aid on behalf of Jönsson, whose conduct was exemplary, who had the respect of his superiors, but who, together with Schützercrantz (which see), had lost all his worldly goods when he was captured from off the *Solitaire* in a battle in the West Indies. Creutz hopes his king will grant him the Order of the Sword, since he came to France too late to receive any decoration there. Jönsson himself in a communication of July 9, 1785, directs an application for help to the Swedish admiralty, motivating his request by the argument that other comrades in the same situation had received some form of assistance. He had of course been granted a gratuity from France of eight hundred livres, he said, but this was not sufficient to cover his losses.

16. LIEWEN

A young naval officer mentioned by Creutz in a message to Gustavus III, dated January 26, 1781. The Swedish minister announces Liewen's return from America, where he had participated in three battles under Count de Guichen.

17. LILLJEHORN, PEHR ULRIC (1752-1806) (Liljorn, Ligliorn, Liljehorn, Lillehorn)

Having lost his father at the age of five, Lilljehorn spent his youth near the King of Sweden, and was educated at the Swedish court. Having received permission from his monarch to enter French service, he participated in the campaigns in North America. He is mentioned by Thomas Balch in *The French in America during the War of Independence of the United States*[1] as an aide-de-camp to the King of Sweden, who came to America on *La Gloire* in 1782 to give fresh aid to American operations. Also mentioned in the memoirs of Prince de Broglie and Count de Segur, who came over on the same boat. Kerguelen reports that Lilljehorn "gave proofs of the most brilliant courage" on *La Gloire* in action against the *Hector,* September 5, 1782. Noailles refers to him as a Swedish colonel on the staff of Rochambeau's army of embarkment in the squadron of the Marquis de Vaudreuil, December, 1782, at Boston, with assignment to *Le Duc-de-Bour-*

---

[1] I, 225.

gogne. Upon his return to Sweden, he was honored with several important commissions; was made a Commander of the Order of the Sword with the Grand Cross; became a lieutenant-general, chief of Göta Garde, and an officer of the Royal Body Guard. He was buried with military honors in Storkyrkan in Stockholm. Lilljehorn represented a real volunteer for the American Revolutionary cause, and it is reported that he served for a short time in the American army.

18. MONTHELL, PETER   (de Montell, Suédois; Montet)

Born April 19, 1756, he became an ensign in the Swedish army fleet, 1777, and in 1780 received leave of absence to enter the French service, where he became an enseigne de vaisseau in July. He served first on *La Friponne,* under the command of Macnamara, and took part in various expeditions along the French and Spanish coasts, during which two frigates and six corsairs were captured. Serving on *L'Achif* in Count de Guichen's squadron the following year, he was promoted to lieutenant's rank, in February, 1782, and from then until July of the next year saw service on the fleets of Count de Grasse and the Marquis de Vaudreuil, both in South and North America. Monthell is mentioned in *Les Combattants Français* as an officer on *Le Magnifique* in the squadron of Count d'Estaing, and is mentioned by at least two other French authorities, Noailles and Kerguelen. Monthell participated in the fatal battle against Admiral Rodney near Dominica and Guadeloupe, April 9 and 12, 1782, and was slightly wounded. Upon his return to France he was decorated with the same order given to so many others of his countrymen.

19. NAUCKHOFF, HENRIC JOHAN   (Nangof, etc.)

A very prominent man in the history of the Swedish navy, eventually becoming in turn a rear-admiral, vice-admiral, and commanding admiral. Nauckhoff occupies also a high plane in the annals of the Swedish nobility. He was a descendant of an old Swedish-Esthonian family. Born September 13, 1744, he entered French service in 1778, first as lieutenant on *Alexandre* in the fleet of Count d'Orvillier, and took part in the joint cruise of the French and Spanish fleets, to compel the English fleet to give battle, 1779; left in 1780 on same vessel for South America, but the ship had to return to Brest. It is undoubtedly he who is listed in *Combattants Français* as Nangof, lieutenant de vaisseau, of *Le Conquérant* in the squadron of Count de Ternay, 1780-1781. Mentioned also by Geffroy. He took a "courageous part in the war against England," was honored by Sweden and France in consequence, was after his return to Sweden made chairman of several important commissions, and created a baron in 1813. He died February 18, 1818, in Stockholm.

In 1781 Nauckhoff was assigned to *Le Northumberland,* bound for the West Indies and convoying a merchant fleet of 200 sail. After various campaigns during which the island of Tobago was captured, he arrived in the Chesapeake Bay, August 5, 1781, and helped land 5000 troops taken on at St. Domingo for operation against Yorktown. He fought in the naval engagement of November 5, against Admiral Graves, when the latter had to turn back after having one vessel sunk and two frigates captured. He also participated in the capture of St. Eustache, after the surrender of Yorktown, on the way to Martinique; and also in the unfortunate battle of April 12, 1782, the "most severe, the longest, and most murderous of the century," where several Swedish officers bled and died, and where the English were victorious and de Grasse made a prisoner. In this battle both captains of the ·Northumberland were shot, and Nauckhoff was virtually compelled to take command of the vessel, although the nominal command had to pass to a French ensign, because of the above-mentioned French law forbidding foreigners to command French ships of war. But Nauckhoff seems to have stood by the side of the French ensign giving suggestions until the ship was saved, a fact which was attested by both naval men and land troops abroad.[1]

---

[1] Cf. p. 7.

On July 8, 1782, Creutz writes to Gustavus III:

It happened in the last battle of Count de Grasse that, when all the superior officers of the (French vessel)*Northumberland* had been killed or wounded, an ensign took command of the ship, to the detriment of Mr. Nauckhoff, lieutenant de vaisseau surnuméraire. I have filed my remonstrances with Mr. de Castries and Count de Vergennes relative to the inconveniences of a regulation so discouraging for the brave officers, who only wage war in the hope of distinguishing themselves. Besides, it is contrary to the military spirit of all other countries. The Marquis de Castries replied to me that he was aware of all the disagreeable features

In consequence, upon his return to France on *Le Conquérant*—after he had sufficiently recovered from a severe wound in the head—he received the following letter from de Castries, the French Minister of Naval Affairs, dated at Versailles December 14, 1782:

> I have not failed to notify the King, Sir, of the zeal and bravery which you have shown in all the events of the last campaign in America, and particularly in the engagement of the 12th of April, when you were wounded and where you contributed to the salvation of the vessel *Le Northumberland*. This is a service so important, a conduct so worthy of praise that His Majesty has been induced to give you a new proof of his satisfaction, and I announce to you with pleasure that he grants you a pension of four hundred livres to be drawn on his royal treasury, to count from April 12, the day when you made yourself so deserving thereof, subject, however, to your kind acceptance.
>
> I am, your most humble and obedient servant,
>
> Castries

This pension was afterwards doubled, and Nauckhoff received besides a personal gratuity from Louis XVI of 200 louis d'or. That he was profusely decorated goes without saying.

20. NORDENSKJÖLD, OTTO HENRIC, BARON (Le Sʳ Nordenvchoel)

A very prominent nobleman in Swedish naval history, who passed through the various grades and finally became vice-admiral.

(of the rule), but that he did not believe it possible to change this regulation, because it was contrary to the constitution for a foreigner who had not sworn fidelity to the king of France to command a French vessel under any circumstances. He promised me, however, to call the attention of the king to the matter, and to act in concert with Count de Vergennes for the purpose of finding out whether any measures can be taken to remedy the situation. Finally, he praised Mr. de Nauckhoff, who in spite of his embarrassing position placed himself beside the young officer in command, guided him with his advice, saved the ship, and brought it successfully to port. This young officer in his report to the Minister had the candor to confess, that without the advice and experience of Mr. Nauckhoff he would never have been able to escape . . . ."

We have seen that some modification of the regulation governing foreigners commanding French war vessels resulted from this Swedish protest.

In a message of September 8, we learn from Creutz that France was getting ready for a "terrible council of war" because of the naval disaster of April 12 in the West Indies. Some officers had already been arrested. "It is regrettable but necessary to institute examples which frighten. Without it the French will never have a navy."

"He was an extremely capable and much sought naval officer"; was a man of much originality, who in 1771 in Stockholm had held free lectures in military science, and who had made many improvements of great practical value in bomb-casting and artillery methods. He was born in March, 1747, in Finland, and studied at Åbo. He first entered the English service in 1777, but resigned and became a supernumerary naval officer in the French fleet, 1778, and was soon assigned as lieutenant to the *Amphion* in the fleet of Count d'Orvillier. The following year he was transferred to the flagship of de Vaudreuil, which participated in the capture of Senegal; and after his squadron subsequently, near Martinique, had joined the main fleet in West Indian waters, under Count d'Estaing, he took part on July 4 in the capture of Grenada. Having obtained permission from his captain to cruise beneath the fortress during the night, he bombarded it and contributed substantially to its surrender. He is known in French records as an officer of *Le Fendant*.

On the 7th of July, 1779, according to the *Biografiskt Lexicon*, he participated in the naval battle between the French and English fleets, when the British admiral Byron was defeated. After the siege of Savannah—in which he took part—had been raised, and Count d'Estaing had returned to Europe, Nordenskjöld was re-assigned to de Vaudreuil's squadron, which was ordered to Chesapeake Bay, 1779, and after the union of this squadron with de Guichen's fleet, he participated in the engagements with the English fleet under Admiral Rodney, April 17, and again on May 15 and 19. His commander gave him an honoring testimonial for his services, 1779, and the same year he was rewarded with a special recommendation by the French king to his own monarch Gustavus III. He was called home in November, 1781, to become chief of the squadron fitted out to enforce the provisions of the Armed Neutrality in the Cattegat and the North Sea. Honored with the customary decorations for similar services, he died in 1832, at the age of eighty-five, leaving behind a record of unusual bravery, firm resolution, and great presence of mind.

Few Swedish officers in French service were spoken of in more superlative terms than Baron Nordenskjöld. "The whole French navy praises his talents and ability," writes the Swedish minister on April 3, 1781. "He is really an officer of unusual merit, and with an extraordinary energy and industry." Because of his experiences and observations in both the English and the French navies, Creutz believes he would make an excellent head of a naval training school in Sweden. On May 17, of the same year, Creutz again waxes enthusiastic about Nordenskjöld, and writes to Sweden that "the officer who because of his knowledge and genius is regarded here (in France) as an astonishing man is M. de Nordenskjöld."[1] He was also an author of note on naval matters.

21. PALMQUIST, MAGNUS DANIEL (de Palmquist)

Born January 6, 1761, the son of a mathematician and fortification officer. "He took part in French service in the war against England, especially in America, 1778-1783," says one source, and another states that in the "North-American war of independence he was promoted to a lieutenant de vaisseau and distinguished himself in several engagements against the English" (*Nordisk Familjebok*). In *Combattants Français* he is assigned to *Le Magnifique* in Count d'Estaing's squadron, 1782.

Possessed of a thirst for glory, he first accepted the rank of ensign, December, 1778, and was assigned to the *Actionnaire* which was to help escort a convoy destined for the West Indies. After a rather inactive duty 1779, on the *Auguste* in the combined French and Spanish squadrons—the English fleet refusing to give battle, it is said—he had himself transferred to the frigate *Andromaque,* which left for western waters in the spring of 1780. His vessel captured the English frigate *Unicorn* outside of St. Domingo, after a violent battle. Later Palmquist contributed to the capture of the fortress at Pensacola, Florida, forcing the enemy to burn three of their own corvettes in the harbor. After cruising in the Gulf of Mexico, and joining the fleet of de Grasse, he took part in a "landing operation" at Yorktown, Virginia, just before the surrender of Cornwallis, October, 1781, and after that his boat was ordered to proceed at once to the nearest French

---

[1] For a more detailed account of Nordenskjöld's French-American service, see pages 48 to 64 of the section on Otto Henrik Nordenskjöld in *Svenska Sjöhjältar,* VI, by Arnold Munthe, a work to which the archivist Erik Naumann of Stockholm kindly called my attention. See bibliography. Nordenskjöld made a very detailed report of his experiences on the various expeditions in the French service, every report of which makes a little book, according to Munthe. He kept a very "comprehensive journal" of the campaigns of *Le Fendant.*

harbor with the news.   This port was Brest, Palmquist being then transferred to the *Couronne* and sent back to American waters. He was present at the calamitous battle on April 12, 1782, and afterward cruised on his ship outside of Boston, capturing an English convoy and chasing off the war vessel convoying it.   He was one of the many Swedish officers who received the order Pour le Mérite Militaire, which had just been established in France for meritorious service by Protestant officers.

In regard to his work in Florida's waters, the French captain Ravennel, in a report to Count de Creutz of May 16, 1781, after eulogizing the bravery of Lieutenant Pettersen, continues: "Mr de Palmquist also deserves much praise; although young he has all the capacity of an old mariner.   I am requesting the Minister to promote him to a lieutenancy . . . ."   In an undated letter by Creutz, the latter evidently asks for his promotion in Sweden also.   Baron Palmquist had distinguished himself, he points out, and "since he is quite poor, he needs some support from home."

Later Palmquist participated in the Swedish war against Russia, 1788-1790; was decorated by Sweden for distinguished service; became a member of the Swedish Academy of Military Science, and inspector of naval troops; and eventually admiral.   He died November 6, 1834, in Karlskrona.

PETTERSEN (See ROSENSVÄRD)

22. PUKE, JOHAN AF, BARON AND COUNT

One of the most interesting, romantic naval heroes of the period. Born February 27, 1751, in Karlskrona, he was first in the Dutch, then from 1770 in the English merchant service and sailed on English vessels to many ports in Europe and America.   For a time an officer in the Swedish navy, he secured royal leave of absence in 1778, as soon as France had decided to help the United States, and entered French service as an ensign on the frigate *La Gentile*, but was soon, "after many proofs of valor and difficult duties and affairs," promoted to a lieutenant de vaisseau, 1779. In 1780 *La Charmante,* on which he served, was wrecked on a rock, and of 395 men, Puke was one of 85 who escaped, naked, in a sloop, mourning the loss of the captain.   Thereupon the Minister of War wrote him a laudatory letter commending him for what he had saved.   He then sailed on the cannon boat *La Provence* in Admiral de Ternay's squadron with troops to North

America "to help the heroes of freedom against the English."
Puke once helped to save a French convoy of vessels outside of
Newport, when blockaded by a larger English fleet. In fact, he
distinguished himself on several occasions in the American war,
possessing uncommon poise in times of danger. Creutz writes
on June 4, 1781, that "in the last naval battle in America Monsieur
Puke distinguished himself in a *manière extraordinaire.*" Count
de Grasse made him lieutenant de pied on *La Provence,* a vessel
which with others covered the big convoy of ships from St.
Domingo to France. Puke continued in the service until the
treaty of peace was signed.

Upon his return to Sweden he was rewarded with a captaincy
in the Swedish navy; was everywhere considered a hero *par excellence;* was honored with many of the highest orders of the kingdom, including membership in the Council of State and Knighthood in the order of the Seraphim; received the usual distinctions
from France; and in 1809 became chief admiral in Sweden. It
was Puke who in 1784 went to the West Indies to take possession
of the island of St. Barthélemy, which had been ceded by France
to Sweden in return for general good will, friendship, political
watchfulness, belligerent aid, and certain commercial concessions
in Swedish harbors.[1] Puke died April 21, 1809, in Karlskrona.

23. RAAB, CARL   (Riaub, Rhaale, Ahaab, Haab, Raoul, Charles
        Rabb)

Born October 4, 1748. First a lieutenant in Swedish service;
then officer in the American-French fleet, where he did noble work
for which he was decorated by France with Pour le Mérite
Militaire.

Balch[2] states that this Swedish officer, "Haab or Ahaab," was
killed in the naval operations before Savannah, September 5, 1781.
At least he was fatally wounded, for Anrep reports his death as
having taken place on the following day.[3] That Charles Rabb
of *L'Annibal,* 1779-1781, and Raab of *Le Caton,* of slightly later
date, were one and the same person, is practically certain. Rank,

---

[1] See p. 23.
[2] *Op. cit.*
[3] Apropos of his regrettable death, Creutz states, November 25, 1781,
that all the Swedes in France were a credit to their nation, which was a
comfort in such a tragedy.

name, and chronology confirm this fact. No Swedish officer, except Hohenhausen perhaps, gave the French more trouble in orthography.

24. RAJALIN, CARL FREDERIC VON (Royalin)

Born November 23, 1758. After serving as naval officer on the Swedish fleet, he resigned to volunteer in the American war, and French records list him as a lieutenant de vaisseau on *Le Saint-Esprit* in the squadron of Count de Grasse. He is reported to have perished in 1782, when the French frigate *La Diane* in Admiral de Grasse's fleet was destroyed (by accident?) with all on board; but Creutz, in a letter to the Swedish king, of December 2, 1781, reports his death at that time.

25. RAJALIN, SALOMON MAURITZ, older brother of the preceding

This officer, official, and baron was born in August, 1757. Like so many other countrymen, he secured leave of absence from Sweden to enter French service against England, where in 1778, he had the rank of ensign, and from 1779 to 1782, that of lieutenant. Rajalin left France in 1781 for the West Indies with de Grasse; returned in 1782, after he had taken part among other engagements in the battle near Martinique, April 29, 1781, against Admiral Hood; that of September 5, 1781; in Count de Grasse's rather bold attack on the enemy near Saint Christopher, January 25-26, 1782; and finally in that famous disaster of April 12, 1782. He was decorated by France.

Creutz assures his king on August 30, 1782, that Salomon Rajalin is a remarkable man. "He has all the genius, talents, training of a man perfected by age and experience. He is the son of a man of rare merit, and is his sole comfort, having already lost one son (Carl Frederic) in the war . . . . Monsieur Rayalin has the potentialities of the highest success. Above all, he has a presence of mind and an eye so sharp and quick that from the farthest distance and the first moment he can judge of the character of the sail and size of a vessel on the horizon. They always consulted him on occasions demanding such judgment and he was never wrong. It is essential to advance rapidly a subject who has so many good qualities, in order that he may have opportunity to command before age weakens his spirit."

On September 8, Creutz tells of the approaching punishment

of the officers of the *Souverain,* who "conducted themselves so unworthily on April 12, 1782, when Rajalin covered himself with glory in steering his vessel to the aid of the *Bretagne.*"

But three years before this a less prejudiced critic had given his estimate of Salomon Rajalin's ability. September 2, 1779, Creutz sends to Gustavus III the following letter from de Surtine, at that time Minister of Naval Affairs: "Sir, I must inform Your Excellency about some good testimonies that have been given to me concerning Baron de Rayalin, enseigne de vaisseau in the Swedish navy, by Chevalier Bernard de Marigny, capitaine de vaisseau commanding the King's frigate the *Junon,*[1] one of those vessels which fought and captured on the seventeenth of this (?) month the English vessel the *Ardent* of sixty-four cannon in the waters of Plymouth.[2]   Chevalier de Marigny lauds highly the zeal, courage, sangfroid, and power of discernment of Baron de Rayalin, of which he gave ample proof in this engagement, and requests that he be promoted to lieutenant . . . ."

After his return to Sweden he advanced rapidly. Knight of the Order of the Sword for his services in America, he was appointed the first Swedish governor of St. Barthélemy in the West Indies, 1785-1787. He was later promoted to admiral and commanded the Swedish Archipelago Fleet in the war with Russia, 1809. For twenty years he served as administrator over the island of Gottland in the Baltic. Rajalin was a very high Free Mason. He died September 23, 1825.

26. REHBINDER, CARL GUSTAF   (Rehberimder, Rebender, Rebendes, Rebinder)

Born in 1764 on Gottröra Estate in Roslagen, Sweden; sergeant in army fleet; left Sweden in 1778, and served in the American war. *Les Combattants Français* lists "Baron de Robinder" as a supernumerary lieutenant d. v. on *Le Vengeur,* 1778-1781, of Count d'Estaing's squadron. He was present at Grenada. Later he was evidently transferred to *Le Glorieux,* 1781-1782, under de Grasse, and was killed in the famous naval engagement, the biggest of the war, near Dominica, against Admiral Rodney, April 12, 1782. Creutz's correspondence during May and June (1782,

---

[1] Cf. p. 21.

[2] Palmquist, also, helped to capture the *Ardent.*

before he had received definite reports on the battle of April 12)
reveals a special anxiety about the fate of Baron Rehbinder whom
he considered an uncommonly valuable man. Rehbinder, it seems,
had often declared that he would seek glory or death in battle for
his king to wipe out a stain upon his family name made by a
brother. He found both in the West Indies. From another,
earlier letter of March 15 of the same year, we learn that Rehbinder had participated in eight general battles, and that he had
been second in command on the *Vengeur* in de la Motte-Piquet's
famous encounter in the bay of Fort Royal, where this general
with three ships attacked fourteen and rescued the convoy of
l'Environ(?). He is commended by all well-informed officers,
says Creutz, is equally well loved in society through his amiable
qualities, and is respected because of his knowledge.

27. ROSEN, ROBERT MAGNUS VON

Born January 7, 1762; entered French service and participated
in several naval battles in the American war, under Admiral de la
Motte-Piquet, was later present at the siege of Gibraltar, 1782.
Rosen's immediate motive for going to America was to get
military education and training. After his return he was made
a captain in the Swedish navy and major in the army, and was
made a Commander of the Order of the Sword. Rosen was a
brilliant man of esprit, being known as "the witty Rosen"; was
an excellent entertainer, much like the Swedish poet Bellman,
though with better character; and was a favorite in the salon of
Queen Hedvig Elizabeth Charlotta. He became a colonel in the
army, 1790; a commissioner to Napoleon, 1809; major-general,
the same year; took part in the war of 1813-1814, and died May
20, 1825.

28. ROSÉN VON ROSENSTEIN, MAGNUS AURIVILIUS (Rosenstein,
Vosenstein, de Rosinstaing)

Born March 9, 1755, in Upsala, the son of a professor of
medicine. Was first a midshipman in English service, but
resigned in 1778 to become a captain in the Swedish navy; in
May, 1779, he joined the French navy and served until the close
of the war. He was first assigned to the *Solitaire* of the fleet of
Count d'Orvillier, which cruised for four months in the English
Channel and helped chase the English fleet of forty-four ships,

under Admiral Hardy, into their own harbors.   In January, 1780,
he left for the West Indies on the *Intrépide* in the squadron of
Count de Guichen, and participated in the engagements of April
17 and May 15 and 19 against Admiral Rodney, the *Intrépide*
serving as flagship in two of these battles. Among the officers
who distinguished themeselves in the Antilles in April and May,
1780, was Rosenstein, who was cited by the commander of *Intrépide* as a Swedish lieutenant de vaisseau and "commandant de
batterie" who "has given the best proofs of a distinguished zeal
for the service of the King and the glory of the French navy."
He may have been back in France in the fall of 1780, for on
October 27, Creutz writes that, "according to reports, innumerable Swedish officers have returned from America, above all,
Rosenstein."   After coast duty around St. Domingo, and joining
the Spanish fleet at Havana, his vessel took part in the capture
of Pensacola, Florida, 1781.   Returning with the French ships
to St. Domingo, his ship caught fire and blew up after three
hours, Rosenstein losing all his personal effects and with great
difficulty saving his life.   Being poor, and working hard to aid
his brothers in Sweden, he was recommended by Creutz for a
special gratuity to cover his loss.

Transferred to *Le Saint-Esprit,* Rosenstein left for Virginia
and was present at the successful battle of September 5 against
Admiral Graves, who was thus prevented from relieving Cornwallis at Yorktown.   Again Rosenstein was cited for bravery,
this time by Marquis de Chabert, commander of *Le Saint-Esprit,*
for his part in the engagement of that date.   It was Rosenstein
who saved the *Auguste.*   In January, 1782, he served in the
expedition to the island of St. Christopher, where 6000 troops
were landed to besiege Brimstonhill.   During the siege Admiral
Hood arrived with twenty-two ships of the line and a violent battle
took place on January 25 and 26, with the result that the besieged
received no aid and were forced to capitulate after eleven days.
Rosenstein then sailed to Martinique and transferred to the flagship *Ville de Paris,* under de Grasse, participating in the bloody
battles of Guadeloupe near Dominica, April 9-12, 1782, where the
French were defeated after twelve hours of continuous fighting.
Here Rosenstein was taken prisoner, along with the French
admiral, by his former chief, Sir Peter Parker, but was exchanged
after a short time.

Having taken part in several strenuous campaigns and battles and proved himself a man of indomitable valor, he was suitably rewarded by France and Sweden, and was eventually made a rear-admiral, 1797. He died, unmarried, in Upsala, November 4, 1801.

29. ROSENSVÄRD, ADOLPH FREDRIK (Petersen, de Petterson)

Probably the most valiant Swedish hero in the American war. Born 1753 in Karlskrona; studied at the University of Lund; took part in expeditions to the African coast and the Mediterranean; and became lieutenant in the Swedish navy. He participated first as a commoner, Peterson or Petersen, in the whole American war, and "exhibited extraordinary proofs of skill and manhood." He had entered French service in 1777, and is mentioned by both Geffroy and Noailles as a Swedish officer. Because of his work on American soil and in American waters, he was ennobled by his king and given the name Rosensvärd. A knight of Swedish and French orders, he died, as rear-admiral, in Karlskrona, 1799.

Anrep[1] says of Petersen: "He distinguished himself to such a degree in the French service that King Louis XVI wrote in 1781 a special personal message about it to Gustavus III filled with the most ample eulogy concerning his exceptional valor, much brilliance, and burning zeal and loyalty; he was severely wounded outside the fort of Pensacola, Florida (May 8, 1781), but took part in the battle until the end, despite his injuries."

Petersen served first on the frigate *L'Andromaque*, where he was alternately capitaine-en-second and lieutenant-en-pied. In the latter capacity he had charge of the economic affairs of the vessel, an office evincing great confidence in him, since the French statutes forbade a foreigner to serve in that capacity. An exception was made in the case of Lieutenant Petersen because of a special request to that effect by his commander. He first took part in some campaigns of Admiral de Guichen in American waters; then in those of Admiral Monteille, both near the French colonies and in conjunction with the Spanish fleet under Solano, near Florida. "Having arrived in this place (Florida)" says the Swedish *Biografiskt Lexicon*—to illustrate the calibre of Petersen's work—"Petersen was ordered to land with two detachments

---

[1] III, 509.

of infantry and artillery in order to join the [Spanish governor
of Louisiana] General Don [Bernardino] de Gálvez, who was
stationed outside of Pensacola, a fortress which guarded the
entrance to the harbor. This attempt was successful despite a
heavy cannon fire from the fortress and a strong resistance from
troops that were concealed in the bushes. Here Petersen was
given command over a brigade of artillery, and after a few days
received orders to capture an enemy entrenchment situated on a
height dominating the English fortress. This had been tried two
days in succession previously, but had been repulsed with great
losses. It was now accomplished by Petersen with alacrity and
heroism, and he succeeded in maintaining his position there,
although he had only two field cannons for defense and was the
target of two fortifications and one redoubt for fourteen hours,
and had to chase off the troops which were endeavoring to cut
off his retreat. During these hours he was wounded by a gun
bullet in the lower leg, by a cannon ball in the upper leg, and was
also injured in the head. Since these wounds were not very
serious, however, or deprived him of consciousness, he had himself carried about, and continued his command until he had succeeded in the evening to throw up an entrenchment from which
he received some protection. The next day trenches were dug
here and batteries set up. When this had been accomplished,
after four days, and the batteries were ready to open fire on the
English fortress, it became Petersen's turn to take command.
He had himself carried at the head of his artillery, withstood all
night an incessant fire from the fortress, and with the 300 men
which he had for defensive purposes repulsed two attacks. The
siege continued for six weeks with a constant fire from both sides,
until finally the more formidable English fortification blew up and
the smaller one was taken by storm, whereupon the city and the
other strongholds capitulated and the English army were taken
prisoners May 8, 1781. During this action Petersen served both
in the infantry and near the fortification, and more especially in
the artillery,[1] first as major and later as lieutenant-colonel. For

[1] On May 16, 1781, Captain Ravenal, writes from the *Andromaque*
in Pensacola: . . . "The brave officer ('Monsieur de Petterson') was
employed at the siege of Pensacola, started by the Spaniards, as an officer
of artillery. I gave him seventy men to command; he acquitted himself
of this duty, as of his ordinary one, with all the zeal, activity, and knowl-

this brave, coolheaded and persevering exploit, Petersen received at once letters of gratitude from General Don Gálvez and the French Minister of Naval Affairs, Castries, and later from the Swedish minister in Paris, Count de Creutz, and was awarded by the French king the order of Pour le Mérite Militaire. In a letter from Paris, dated September 1, 1781, Count de Creutz called the attention of Gustavus III to the 'exceptional valor, genius, and intelligence of Lieutenant Petersen at right severe attacks, and their contribution to the capture of this important port.' His Majesty immediately made him a Knight of the Order of the Sword and besides, on the 27th of the month, raised him to the peerage 'because of his extraordinary ability and deserving conduct during the present war in French service, whereby he had honored the good name of the Swedish people, and in the more remote foreign lands had substantiated their traditional reputation for bravery and military prowess.' In addition he was promoted to a captaincy in the (Swedish) navy on October 15 of the same year."

In the apostille of November 30, 1781, where Creutz describes Petersen's work at Pensacola, we can observe a strong personal conviction in what he relates. Sometimes a little irritated, in his strenuous duties, over the many applications for honors, promotions, financial assistance, and pensions, he was undoubtedly happy to call the king's attention to a Swedish officer of Petersen's calibre. He is an officer, says Creutz, who with an almost supernatural daring set about alone to save the corps of Irishmen whom he commanded, when it had been abandoned by the Spanish. Returning wounded, and carried by his soldiers, he was saluted by the whole army, and the officers lifted him upon their shoulders and bore him in triumph to the general's tent. It is to him alone that the Spaniards owe the capture of the place. In the combat he acted more like a general than a subordinate officer.

I implore Your Majesty in the name of the glory of the (Swedish) nation to reward this officer and not permit a merit

---

edge that one can desire. The general, knowing his merit, always kept him very busy. In one encounter with the enemy he was wounded three times . . . . His spirit did not permit him to rest but six or seven days, however; he reentered the fray when he was scarcely able to walk, and did not discontinue. He assisted me in the battle with the frigate *Unicorn* with the same ardor . . . ."

Revenal then goes on to recommend the "la croix du vrai mérite."

so rare to languish in inferior ranks. The court of Spain has written to this court on his behalf. He will receive a pension here (in France)."

Petersen, now Rosensvärd, served afterwards under Admiral Grasse in American waters, and after his return to Sweden, in 1783, he was advanced to the rank of major.

30. Schultén, Jackris

Born October 7, 1749, he began his naval training at the age of thirteen. He received leave of absence in 1778 to enter French service, and was assigned to the *Amazone,* with the rank of enseigne de vaisseau, under the command of count de la Perouse. After cruising in the waters off the British coast, his ship was united with the French squadron destined for the island of Martinique in the West Indies, and early in July, 1779, took part in the siege of Grenada. He helped to capture (on September the tenth), in single battle, the English frigate *Ariel,* and also the corsair-frigate *Tiger.* Promoted to lieutenant, his vessel joined the squadron commanded by Admiral Termées and participated in the naval encounter of June 20, 1780. Thereupon he was sent "from Rhode Island in America with dispatches to France." In December of the same year he was second in command[1] (kaptenens närmsta man) on the frigate *L'Astrée,* which sailed from Brest to Boston.

In July, 1781, he helped capture an English frigate and put a number of others to flight, and in the following year took part in the historic naval battle of April 9 and 12, near Guadeloupe.[2] He is mentioned in a note by Creutz of August 12, along with Nauckhoff, Rajalin, and Rosenstein, as having given a good

---

[1] It should be remembered that the rank of lieutenant in 1780 was, relatively, more important than it is to-day, especially in the navy. There were only a very few officers on each ship, and there was no rank between the lieutenant and the commanding captain.

[2] Creutz writes anxiously about this battle on May 30, 1782: "The (French) court has finally received some news from de Grasse, but they still keep secret the details about the encounter of April 12. It transpires, however, that this admiral was abandoned by de Bougainville, commander of one division, and that that gave the English the opportunity to surround the vessel of Monsieur de Grasse . . . . All the captains of the vessels taken were killed: I fear there were many Swedish officers who perished, for there were some on all the ships. I am impatiently waiting for news from those who survived that fatal day . . . ."

account of himself at that time. Schultén served until the end of the war, received a pension from France, and was decorated by both Sweden and France. Upon his return to Sweden he was made a captain in the navy, 1783, and his rise after that was rapid.

31. SCHÜTZERCRANTZ, JOHAN HERMAN (Schuzsleirans, Schut-
zerterantz, Schuteretants, Schultzerkrantz)

Born February 6, 1762; the son of a prominent Swedish physician who had been ennobled for his services; enlisted early in French navy for American war service and soon became a lieutenant de vaisseau on *Le Saint-Esprit*. Like Rosenstein he was cited by Admiral de Grasse, through the commander of the *Saint-Esprit*, as being worthy of special royal favor because of his part in the naval battle of September 5, 1781, in the Chesapeake Bay. He served on the *Solitaire* and was taken prisoner and lost his belongings at the same time as Jönsson. He was decorated by France, and Sweden made him a Commander of the Order of Charles XIII. After his return to Sweden, he served for a time, after 1796, as lieutenant-colonel in the Swedish army, and eventually became rear-admiral in the navy. He died March 21, 1821, in Stockholm.

32. SJÖSTJERNA, ARON (Scalierna, Scostierna, Scoslierna, Scas-
lierna)

Born 1754; son of a captain-commander in the Swedish navy. According to Faucher de Saint-Maurice and Noailles, Sjöstjerna was a supernumerary Swedish officer, apparently an enseigne, who was severely wounded in July, 1779, in the naval battle before Grenada,[1] under Count d'Estaing. Became, after the American war, a superior naval officer in the Swedish fleet. Was decorated by both Sweden and France with the usual honors awarded for meritorious service in America. Retired from active duty in 1796.

33. STEDINGK, CURT BOGISLAUS, BARON VON (See special
chapter)

34. STEDINGK, VICTOR, BARON VON

Brother of Curt Bogislaus; born November 11, 1751, in Swedish Pomerania; studied at Upsala and became an officer in

---

[1] Creutz writes to the king on September 9, that there was little hope of Sjöstjerna's recovery.

the Swedish navy; served for a time under the Spanish flag, but
like his brother enlisted in French service in November, 1778, to
fight for American independence, was assigned to the squadron
of Count de Grasse, and with the rank of lieutenant, on the
Robuste, was present at the capture of Grenada (July, 1779) and
St. Martin.

Later we find him back in France, in Brest, on *Saint-Esprit,* too
poor in health to return to America. However, in July, 1782,
his more famous brother, Curt, tells us[1] that Victor had "embarked
on *L'Amphion* with a large convoy" bound for the West Indies.
In the Spring of 1783 he served also on the *Concorde* and *Amphitrite* and participated in the battle with the English cannon boat
Argo. Besides being honored with high orders by his own
government, he was rewarded by France with the usual decoration
for Protestants, 1780, and upon his return to Sweden was granted
a gratuity of 2400 livres for his service in America. Victor
Stedingk rose later to the rank of admiral in the Swedish navy,
and filled many positions of trust in naval matters. At various
times he commanded squadrons in the Swedish fleet; again he
accompanied the Swedish kings, Gustavus III and Gustavus IV,
on important missions; and in 1793 he was special commissioner,
to St. Petersburg. Victor Stedingk enjoyed great popularity,
both in royal and commoner circles, because of his extraordinary
good temper. He died August 30, 1823, in Stockholm.

35. TILAS, BARON

A Swedish officer who is mentioned by Count de Creutz in a
letter from Paris, dated October 24, 1779. He had evidently
taken part in the siege of Grenada, either on land or on sea, for
Creutz writes to Gustavus III that as soon as "Major Stedingk"
returns he will learn the conduct (in America) of Baron Tilas.
Tilas was already in America when Count d'Estaing accepted him
for French service. He had obviously made a good name for
himself, for Creutz asks his king to reward some other Swedish
officers with the same favor that he intended to give Baron Tilas.

It has been impossible to date to identify this officer completely
with any certainty. One, Daniel Axel Tilas, born 1747, went to
America in 1788—perhaps he had been here before—and was

---

[1] H. L. v. Dardel, *Fältmarskalken von Stedingks tidigare levnadsöden,*
p. 98.

never heard from afterwards. Another, Eric Gustaf, born September 25, 1751, was a captain in the Swedish admiralty. It could be either of these, or neither.

36. TOLL, CARL FREDRIK (?) (de Toll)

Born June 11, 1758; a Swedish officer mentioned by three French sources as having taken part in the American war; he was wounded in the naval engagement off Dominica, the biggest of the war, where so many men and officers lost their lives; decorated by Sweden and France; eventually a captain in the Swedish army and major in the so-called army fleet, 1793; died December 8, 1798, in Sveaborg, Finland. (See records by St. Maurice, Noailles, Kerguelen, and Creutz [letter of June 5, 1782]).

The last member of one branch of this family, of the Swedish-Finnish nobility, has recently, 1923, it is reported, died in Finland.

37. TOTT OR THOTT

A Swedish officer of old nobility stock. Reported by Noailles as "Tot, lieutenant, (Suédois)" on *Le Destin* in the naval army of the Marquis de Vaudreuil, May 30, 1782.

It has been impossible thus far to identify the individual in Anrep or other Swedish sources available to the writer, though the family name is very common in Swedish gentry circles. It is barely possible that this officer may be the enseigne Toll above who was wounded the month before, but other circumstances make this assumption seem improbable. It is not unlikely that this officer is the "Chevalier de Tott" mentioned in the records of Dubourg and Thomas Balch as having previously fought with the Turks against the Russians—any contemporary Swede would avail himself of the opportunity to fight against Russia—and who was especially skillful in handling artillery.

38. TÖRNQUIST (de Tornquist)

An officer listed in *Les Combattants Français* as "de Tornquist, Suédois," an enseigne on *Le Vaillant* in 1781 and 1782, in the squadron of Count de Grasse. Probably a bourgeois commoner and volunteer. He served later in the naval army of de Vaudreuil, on *Le Northumberland*. May have been ennobled later and given another name.

39. ULFVENKLOU, HENRIK GUSTAF (?)   (Ulfklou)

Mentioned by Geffroy as being a Swedish officer in French service in remote America at the time of the Revolution. No details about his record here are given. Born in 1756, he served at one time as a captain in the Swedish navy. For his services under the French flag he was honored with the same decoration given to so many of his countrymen, and was appropriately rewarded by his own government. He died in 1819 in the province of Blekinge, Sweden. It would seem from the chronology, early profession, and circumstances as though he were the famous mystic and conjurer of the eighties, Henrik Gustaf Ulfvenklou.

We learn, however, from a letter by Creutz of June, 1780, that Ulfvenklou, or Ulfklo, served in the West Indies in the expedition of Count de Guichen. "Monsieur Ulfkloo, who wrote me (Creutz) from the naval roadstead of St. Pierre de la Martinique, (without going into details) gives me positive information about the expedition. He was returning from La Trinité island with the frigate *La Medée* and spent the 27th of (?) near St. Lucia, meeting the English fleet. Fortunately the latter was in such a bad condition that it was unable to give him chase, and the frigates that the fleet released were not able to catch him."

"Here," Creutz continues, "the French are very dissatisfied over the action of Monsieur de la Motte-Piquet going to St. Domingo. If he had awaited the arrival of Count de Guichen, the English admiral would not have dared to attack the French, and the superiority would have been so great that all the English Windward Islands could have been seized."

40. VIRGIN, ARVID (de Virgin)

Born August 4, 1757; a notable naval officer in Swedish history who finally attained the rank of rear-admiral. In his younger days he served in the French navy, and is mentioned by Noailles as an enseigne Suédois on *Le Languedoc* in the squadron of Marquis de Vaudreuil, in the spring of 1782, in American waters. He received the order Pour le Mérite Militaire from France. He died March 1, 1840.

41. WACHTMEISTER AF JOHANNESHUS, CLAËS ADAM

Born 1755 in Karlskrona, Sweden; member of the old Swedish-Livonian nobility; served through the grades of ensign, lieutenant, and captain in the Swedish army fleet; entered the French service in 1776, long before the other Swedish naval officers; was decorated for meritorious service by Sweden and France, 1779 and 1782, respectively; and resigned from French service, 1783. "He participated during his French service in the whole American war of independence, and was wounded off Ouezzan, July 27, 1778," under Count d'Orvillier against Admiral Keppel. One source reports that he "won honors in the French war, both in America and in the West Indies." Wachtmeister eventually became admiral and chief of the Swedish admiralty. He died June 26, 1828, on his estate Södertuna in Södermanland, Sweden.

Wachtmeister was one of the most remarkable Swedes in the French service. Responsibility and official seniority combined to make him respected and sought by everybody. During the whole war it was he, it seems, who, in times of stress, went security for Swedish debts in the French capital; he was especially solicitous about the weal of his own countrymen. In a laudatory epistle to Gustavus III, of October 3, 1781, Creutz enumerates the good qualities of Count Wachtmeister. He is a credit to the Swedish nobility, says Creutz, and very popular with all the generals without exciting the jealousy of anyone.

A brother of Claës Adam, Hans Fredrik, was in the English service and for a short time took part in the American Revolutionary War on the English side.[1]

42. ZACHAUD, DANIEL (later ennobled Zacco)

Born April 15, 1754, in Stockholm. Was first a Swedish naval officer, but entered French service in 1779, and was assigned to *l'Hercule* in the naval army of de Vaudreuil, May, 1782. Promoted and decorated for active duty in the American war, the same year; and after his return to Sweden received many honors from his native land. He became a high officer in his own country, whose services were eagerly sought on important committees, commissions, and military courts. He died of apoplexy in the Swedish capital, December 6, 1810.

---

[1] Only two other cases of a Swedish officer serving on the English side, after the French entered the conflict, have come to the attention of the writer. One, Carl Adolph Ribbing, 1760-1813, served under Admiral Rodney, and was wounded by the French-Americans in the battle of April 12, 1782; he was for a time a prisoner of the French, but subsequently entered Dutch service against the English.

GROUP II

List of Swedish officers whose activities were probably confined to European, Asiatic, or African soils and waters. Though
some of these may have served in America, and chiefly under
Bailli de Suffren, in the early part of the war, 1778-1779, it seems
likely that they helped fight our battles elsewhere. Some of these
were the most ardent and capable volunteers in the American war.

43. ANCKARLOO, FREDRIK MAGNUS   (d'Ankarloo, d'Ankarlor)

Born December 31, 1750; son of an admiral in the Swedish
navy; first naval cadet in Swedish fleet; served first as enseigne,
then as lieutenant de vaisseau in French service; was mortally
wounded on September 3, 1782, in naval action under de Suffren
against the English, and, according to Anrep, died the same year.
This naval action took place near Ceylon in Indian waters, and
Lieutenant Anckarloo while awaiting in a Ceylon hospital the fatal
outcome of his wounds was visited by a fellow-countryman, Karl
von Döbeln, another Swedish officer in French service (see
Döbeln, below), who brought back valuable reports about the
officers and campaigns in East Indian waters. Ankarloo may
have been in America during his early foreign service. He is
mentioned several times by Creutz.

It was his brother, David, who as commander of the Swedish
frigate *Illerim* became an accidental victim of the war in 1780,
in Malaga, while engaged on a mission for the Swedish king to
the King of Morocco. Europe and America made much of the
affair, and the United States counted on Swedish sympathy for
their cause in consequence.[1]

44. ARMFELT, ERIK LUDWIG   (1740-1814) (le baron d'Arnfeldt)

A Swedish infantry officer, captain in the Royal Suédois, whose
activities were probably confined to European soil and water.
Took part in the siege of Gibraltar, 1782, and was decorated by
France for bravery against the English. Knight of the Swedish
Order of the Sword with Grand Cross. Apropos of the attack
on Gibraltar, September 13, 1782, when floating batteries were
employed, Chevalier,[2] like Odhner above, reports that Baron Arm-

---

[1] See p. 35 and note.
[2] *Op. cit.*, p. 350.

felt was the last man to leave the "Talla Piedra" before its explosion. "He was presented to the Count of Artois, who granted him a pension of six hundred livres."

His more famous relative, the Finnish-born Gustaf Mauritz Armfelt, also, arrived in Paris early in the Spring of 1780, hoping to enlist in the French expeditionary force for service on American soil; but his arrival came too late. The auxiliary army left France before Armfelt could obtain a commission. Soon thereafter his interests changed and he seems to have given up the plan altogether of taking part in the war.

There had been several Armfelts in French service during the eighteenth century.

45. BILDT, CARL DANIEL (1754-1784)

First a lieutenant in the Swedish navy; then lieutenant de vaisseau in French service during the war with England. Like Anckarloo he served in the squadron of Bailli de Suffren. He died on Cape of Good Hope.

46. DE FRESE

A Swedish lieutenant in de la Marck's German regiment who is mentioned by von Döbeln as one of three Swedish victims of disease among French officers on the way to East Indian territories to fight the English, in the fall of 1782. Lieutenant De Frese died in Port Louis, Île de France (Mauritius).

47. DE FRESE, HANS

Born in 1758, the son of Paul Joachim De Frese, a lieutenant-colonel in the Swedish army. He was first an adjutant in the service of the Swedish Queen Dowager, and Anrep reports that he was killed in the East Indies, in 1780, in a naval action against the English.

48. DÖBELN, BARON GEORGE KARL VON

One of the most enthusiastic supporters of the American cause, and one of the most brilliant military men in the annals of Swedish history, but one who was fated through accidental reasons to do service outside of the western continent.

Born April 29, 1758, on Stora Torpa estate, Län of Kronoborg, Sweden. He was early destined for the ministry, and also took an examination in law, but preferred military life, and in 1780 volunteered for the American war. "The American war attracted him, and he set out for it via Paris." Count de Creutz secured for him a temporary appointment in the Royal Suédois. "After thirteen months in Paris, with a letter of recommendation from Franklin, he was to have accompanied an American privateer as commander of artillery, but accepted the suggestion of the new Swedish minister to France, Baron de Staël, to transfer to Count de la Marck's German regiment of infantry which had received orders to depart for points unknown. Döbeln first left France with the fleet of Count de Guichen, from Brest, December 11, 1781, but met the English and a storm outside and the fleet was obliged to return to port, about January 1, 1782. A part of this fleet seems to have been destined for America. He sailed again on February 11. In the meantime de la Marck's regiment had been ordered to the East Indies, and on February 25, when the American and East Indian convoys separated, Döbeln found himself on the transport *L'Amitié,* with his detachment, bound for the East. Sailing around Africa, visiting Cape Town, he arrived in Port Louis on Mauritius in July, where he later witnessed the death of several officers. So many had died on the journey that his whole detachment was reduced to a few hundred, and von Döbeln became third in rank in his own grade, though he had been the eighteenth at the start. In March, 1783, the fleet anchored on Trincomalee, on Ceylon, where he had found Lieutenant Anckarloo ill. Sailing again on the fourteenth, the detachment prepared in April for the coming battle of Cuddalore (Goudelour), on the 15th to the 20th of June, the most violent battle that up to that time had raged in those parts. Döbeln was constantly employed in reconnoitering, and after the battle was instructed to draw up maps and give account of the engagement. He was promoted to the rank of captain, and after the Treaty of Versailles was pensioned for life, a pension which was, however, withheld during the Revolution. He died in 1820, in Stockholm.

This officer is the famous von Döbeln who was immortalized by the Swedish-Finnish poet Johan Ludvig Runeberg, for his exploits in the subsequent Swedish-Finnish-Russian war, as "Döbeln vid Jutas."

49. FOCK, BARON BERNDT WILHELM   (See relative Fock in
Group I)

Born August 9, 1763, in Åbo, Finland. Was given leave of
absence in 1780 to enter French service, and was technically
appointed enseigne in the Royal Suédois for 1780 to 1782; no
details of his French service against England are given, but circumstances, chronology, and relationship to Fock-Robeck, who
served in America, seem to point to some active duty in the war.
Later Swedish governor and postmaster-general. He died April
15, 1837, in the Swedish capital.

There had been many Focks in the French service.

50. GAHN AF COLQUHOUN, CARL PONTUS

Born on March 1, 1759, in Fahlun, Sweden; prominent officer
in Swedish army, who was ennobled in 1809; entered foreign
service in 1778, first in French, and took part in three campaigns
against the English; later in Dutch and Prussian service; died
without issue, in Stockholm, May 9, 1825. Was at one time Vice-
Governor of the Military Academy at Carlberg.

51. GEDDA, GEORG

Born 1755, in Finland; studied at Upsala; entered French
service in 1770 and served more or less continuously for fifteen
years in the Royal Suédois, finally attaining the rank of captain.
He participated in the war against England in European and
African waters, at Gibraltar and elsewhere. He took part in the
joint cruise of the Spanish and French fleets under Don Louis
Cordova, and was present at the battle of October 20, 1782, at
Cape Spartel against Admiral Howe. He finally became adjutant-
general to the Swedish king, and was ennobled in 1797. He died
in 1806.

52. HAMILTON, J. H., AF HAGEBY

One of the Swedish army officers who participated in the war.
According to Odhner, as we have seen above, he served on land,
but it is not certain that he served on American soil. He was
educated in Geneva; became eventually a captain, then colonel in
the French service. He was decorated by France. In 1794 he
was a colonel in the Swedish army. He died in Stockholm on the
8th of August, 1805, from an infection resulting from a mosquito
bite.

53. LANNERSTJERNA, ADOLPH CHRISTIAN (Lannerchienna)

Born September 4, 1755; first a captain in the Swedish army's fleet; then ship lieutenant in French service; decorated by Sweden; was killed in the naval engagement off Ceylon, April 12, 1782, along with Bjelke, serving under de Suffren.[1] There is no doubt whatever about the identification.

54. MALMSKJÖLD, JOHAN GUSTAF

Born 1741 in Karlskrona; first an officer in Swedish navy, then in French; "participated, when on French fleet, in the war against England"; Knight of French Order Pour le Mérite Militaire; later lieutenant-colonel in Swedish navy; perished with the *Sophia Albertina*, 1781.

55. MYRIN

A Swedish engineer who lost his life at the siege of Gibraltar. He was a fighter, also, of the Petersen type, who continued to give orders long after he was wounded, and "with a calmness which confounded the most intrepid." Mortally wounded, he asked to be allowed to expire in the presence of his general, says Creutz in a report of October 12, 1782, and solicits His Majesty, Gustavus III, to remember his two unfortunate sisters who through their brother's death will be left without support. It is this Myrin who is mentioned above by Odhner.

56. PEIJRON, CARL (Peyron)

Born in 1757 in Stockholm. A favorite of Gustavus III, who became a captain in Count de la Marck's regiment in France in 1780. From a letter written by him from Brest on the last day of the year 1781, when the fleet carrying de la Marck's regiment was being obliged to return to Brest until a more favorable opportunity to sail should present itself, we may infer that he was still on duty and evidently participating in the activities of the war. I have thus far, however, been unable to obtain details of his service.

57. RAPPE, ALBRECHT AUGUST ARNOLD (1760-1841)

First a lieutenant of cavalry in Sweden; entered Prussian service in 1778, but resigned and entered the French, serving until

---

[1] Chevalier, *op. cit.*, p. 409.

the end of the war. He took part in the sieges of Port-Mahon on Minorca and Gibraltar. Later he became Court Marshal and major in the Swedish army and was decorated by his own government.

58. RAPPE, CLAËS ERIC (1756-1836)

Brother of the preceding; in French service from 1778 to 1784, as lieutenant and captain in the regiment of de la Marck; in 1782-3 he was ordered to Coromandel in Asia with his regiment, and participated in the battle against the English on June 13, 1783. Upon his resignation he was granted a pension by the French king. He died in Ramnåsa in Län of Kronoborg, Sweden.[1]

59. STARÉ

A Swedish officer mentioned by Creutz in February, 1780, as showing promise in the French service.[2] No details about his work have been available to the writer.

60. ULFSPARRE AF BROXVIK, JOHAN CARL

Born 1756; lieutenant in Göteborg, 1779; lieutenant in French service, 1780; "he participated during his French service in the whole war against England——." He died in 1802, murdered, it is said.

61. WREDE, GÖRAN CASIMIR

Born 1763; died in the presence of von Döbeln, September 23, 1782, on Île de France in the Indian Ocean while on the way to fight the English.

62. WREDE, HENRIK

Brother and inseparable companion of the preceding; born 1764; took part in the same disastrous expedition as his brother, and suffered the same fate, dying at the same place, two weeks later, October 7, 1782.

An older relative, Count Fabian Wrede (1760-1824), served in the French army in the Royal Suédois, and in de la Marck's regi-

---

[1] The Rappes had been waiting a long time in France for suitable commissions. See letter by Creutz to Gustavus III, of February 3, 1780.

[2] Cf. p. 92.

ment from 1779 to 1780, but so far as can be learned took no part in any expedition against the English.

ADDENDA (*Unidentified*)

63. DE FONDELIN*

Swedish lieutenant de vaisseau on *L'Éveillé*.

64. DE TROMELIN*

Swedish lieutenant de vaisseau on *L'Actionnaire*.

In addition to these Swedish officers, we have the names of at least five more which are mentioned in the official and diplomatic correspondence of the period under circumstances that would indicate the possibility of service on the French-American side. These are ensigns Diedrichs and Klick (probably Magnus Wilhelm Klick, b. 1760 and naval officer in Swedish fleet) concerning whom Creutz makes inquiries in a letter of November 21, 1779; and three officers who are recommended to the Swedish king by Henrik Trolle on February 21, 1782, to take the place in French service of three other Swedish naval officers who had either died or returned home.[1]   The young men recommended were Arvid Julius Egerström, Christer Jägerskjöld, and David Christopher Gyllenskepp, the last two having surnames that we have seen before.

---

* The nationality is not absolutely established in these two instances, but if these officers were French we should expect to find their first names also. This is almost always the case.

[1] Raab (killed in action), Nordenskjöld and Sjöstjerna.

CHAPTER VII

COUNT AXEL VON FERSEN

The best known Swedish officer of the American Revolution, and until recently the most illustrious Swede that ever came to the United States and stayed for any length of time, was Count Johan Hans Axel von Fersen, first aide-de-camp to Count Rochambeau. Now and then even American sources contain a reference to "the handsome Comte de Fersen,"[1] who was "conspicuous in this (foreign) gallaxy of officers"; who, as a trusted personal missionary so often represented the French commander in duties involving delicate diplomacy, and who at one time at least was sent by his chief to remove a cause of possible offence to General Washington.[2] Heitman,[3] though he ignores Fersen's nationality, knows him to be a colonel who distinguished himself at "York," and concedes that Fersen was "a man of great merit." Charlemagne Tower knows that Fersen was present at the historical first meeting of Rochambeau and Washington, in Hartford, Connecticut, late in September, 1780—probably on the 21st—when Lafayette and Knox also were in attendance, "for the desire to see Washington was so great that the officers who could do so eagerly availed themselves of the opportunity."[4] Asa Bird Gardiner, who compiled the biographical facts for the foreign members of the Order of the Cincinnati in France, adds a few more facts.[5] For his services at Yorktown, Fersen was, on January 27, 1782, assigned to be Mestre de Camp en second of the Regiment Royal Deux-Ponts, Infantry; and on the 21st of September, 1783, he was promoted to Mestre de Camp propriétaire of the regiment Royal-Suédois, infantry, in the French army, receiving besides a pension of twenty thousand livres. "As a further recompense for his services in the United States, he was appointed by the King of Sweden (Gustavus III) titular colonel

---

[1] Edwin M. Stone, *Our French Allies*, p. 225.

[2] *Ibid.*, p. 281.

[3] *Historical Register of Officers of the Continental Army, 1775-1783,* p. 654.

[4] *The Marquis Lafayette in the American Revolution*, II, p. 161.

[5] *The Order of the Cincinnati in France*, pp. 70-73. The first three original members of the Cincinnati here given are Rochambeau, Fersen, and Stedingk.

in the Swedish Army and lieutenant-colonel of the 9th (Adels-
Fanan) regiment of light cavalry . . . ."[1] Writers on social
matters are acquainted with "the gallant De Fersen," a "fugitive
from the love of a queen,"[2] or with "the handsome Swede" who
in 1780 entered the Newport society of "enlightened men and
modest and handsome women." Later authors have quoted
Fersen's letters to his father on his American campaign. James
Breck Perkins, who has no particular love for Fersen, quotes
his diary several times as authority, incidentally adding this bit
of personal conjecture: "Even Fersen, who did not love us, found
the inhabitants of the country prosperous without luxury or display."[3]   An American lady, Katherine Prescott Wormeley, who
over twenty years ago translated Klinckowström's *Le Comte de
Fersen et La Cour de France,* interpolates a few sympathetic
remarks about Fersen's life and work in America:

"From the beginning of the year 1779 Count Axel Fersen, liberal in
opinion through family tradition and parental example, and inspired by the
new enthusiasm then reigning in France, demanded earnestly to be allowed
to take part in the expedition of French troops to the war of independence
then going on in North America." Thanks to Gustavus III, Count de
Creutz, and family friendships, "young Fersen was appointed aide-de-camp
to the Count de Vaux, who had just been made commander of the first
expedition, which was to have sailed from Havre-de-Grâce, where the
troops assembled, but never did so.

"It was not until the spring of 1780 that young Fersen embarked at
Brest, as aide-de-camp to the Comte de Rochambeau, commanding the
expeditionary corps of the French army to aid the Americans in their
war of independence against England. His letters to his father from that
period until 1783 are of very great interest from their descriptions of three
campaigns. After taking part in the expedition to Rhode Island, Count
Fersen was present at the siege and capitulation of Yorktown . . . which
contributed in a great measure to put an end to the war. Young Fersen
had been employed by General Rochambeau, in preference to the other
aides-de-camp, during conferences with General Washington and the other
leaders of the American army, and it was he who conducted the negotiations,—a preference founded as much on his personal qualifications as on
his knowledge of the English language.[4]

[1] *Ibid.,* p. 71.
[2] Cf. F. P. North, *Newport a Hundred Years Ago,* Lippincott's Magazine,
XXVI, 351-362.
[3] *France in the American Revolution,* p. 409.
[4] Katherine Prescott Wormeley, *Diary and Correspondence of Count
Axel Fersen,* etc., pp. 19-20. Count Fersen had learned English in London
in 1778. Cf. F. F. Flach, *Grefve Hans Axel von Fersen,* p. 25, note 2.

These facts about Fersen are essentially correct, though we may
have our own ideas about the literal interpretation of his "liberal"
views, he being at heart and mind a conservative,[1] though a lover
of freedom. Born in Stockholm, 1755, the son of a minister of
state and chief of the French party in Sweden, he received his
early education at Brunswick, Turin, and Strassbourg, and made
his debut in Paris society in 1774. In 1777 he became a colonel
in the Royal Suédois, and two years later we find him exerting
his influence to become a member of the French expeditionary
corps to America. Count de Creutz, in a dispatch to the President of the Chancery, in Sweden, solicits him to interview Fersen's
father about the plan, and because of the secrecy and importance
of the expedition to America, suggests that the latter send his
reply in cipher.[2] By June 17, 1779, Creutz can report that "if
there is any possibility of sending troops to North America,
Fersen will obtain a suitable position on the expedition."[3] This
was the more remarkable because the French court, in view of
recent naval failures, had changed some of its plans and decided
to send, if any, only a small auxiliary army to America. "They
will content themselves, perhaps," writes Creutz on May 20, 1779,
"with sending two or three thousand men, under the command of
Lafayette. It will still be possible to send Count de Fersen with
them, in a manner befitting an officer in the service of France and
under conditions that follow his father's instructions." Then,
when Rochambeau, early in 1780, was chosen commander of the
American expeditionary force, Creutz personally interviewed
him on Fersen's behalf, and although the French general had

---

[1] Fersen, therefore, could not easily see how the aristocratic Virginians,
for instance, could accept a government based on perfect equality. But
many a sensible thinker and patriot at the time had the same opinion.

[2] See letter of March 21, 1779, in the *Gallica* collection of Creutz dispatches in Riksarkivet, Stockholm.

[3] Fersen was obviously anxious to get away from the French court, for
a time at least. During the summer of 1778 he had tried, it seems, to
enter the Austrian army—perhaps with some recommendation from Marie
Antoinette—but the attempt was unsuccessful. See letter by Creutz of
August 27, 1778. No French officers were permitted by the emperor,
naturally, to enter the Austrian service. Fersen then thought of possibilities
in the Prussian army, according to a message by Creutz of August 30th,
and adds: "He (Fersen) is extremely popular here (in France), both
because of his manners and his personal appearance."

made it a rule not to accept volunteers, he did accept Fersen with
pleasure as his adjutant. All that was necessary, as Creutz wrote
on March 2, was the consent of the French ministry, and he did
not expect any trouble in obtaining that approval.

Fersen embarked for America on the *Jason,* with Counts Damas
and Dumas, in April, 1780; left Brest in May; and arrived outside of Newport in the middle of July. In Rhode Island he lived
for eleven months in Newport, with Damas, at the home of
Robert Stevens in 299 New Lane (now Mary Street). As a
voluntary exile from Marie Antoinette, he had tried hard to forget the attractions of the French court (though, like some others,
he hated its gilt), and needed strenuous activity; but found much
idleness in Newport because of the season and the military circumstances. He cared little for society, it seems, but with his
physical and linguistic qualifications, and always a gentleman, we
may well imagine him to have been popular with the fair sex of
Newport. At all events, he made some good friends whom he
revisited later, when, after the Chesapeake campaign, the French
army was quartered in Providence, 1782, and Fersen lived with
Nicholas Brown "in the Main Street, this side of the (Crawford
Street) Bridge."[1]

Count von Fersen, who often knew the secret plans of a coming
campaign as soon as the leading generals, was constantly—as
might be expected of the first adjutant—being employed, not only
as a personal emissary but as an agent in missions of more
official military trust, by both Rochambeau and Washington.
For instance: on "the 15th of August, 1781, de Rochambeau
answered the letters that Count de Barras had written him (on
important military matters) and de Fersen was entrusted with
taking them (the answers) to Newport. This circumstance was
commented on, because up to that time an American dragoon had
been chosen for this duty. The other officers drew from this fact
more or less exact inferences about the projects of the general-

---

[1] "Rochambeau's aides, among them the Count de Fersen, well-known
as the friend of Queen Marie Antoinette and the driver of the royal carriage on the flight to Varennes, were lodged with Nicholas Brown in the
square three-story brick house, later the office of the Second United States
Bank, now 27-31 South Main Street."

Howard Willis Preston, *Rochambeau and the French Troops in Providence in 1780-81-82,* pp. 12-13.

THE NICHOLAS BROWN HOUSE.

The Nicholas Brown House as it appears to-day. Count von Fersen made his home here for a short time in 1782.

in-chief."[1] About the same time Fersen was sent to Newport
for the purpose of hastening the departure of the French fleet
and the shipping of the French artillery to Providence. Von
Fersen was also sent by Washington (in September) from Cape
Henry to Annapolis with ten transports of the squadron of de
Barras to hasten the arrival of troops. "He acquitted himself
of this mission with diligence, and the troops were able to embark
at the head of the Elk and at Annapolis to reach the James River
by water. He himself took the land route, and with his friend de
Damas accompanied Rochambeau, while Vauban and Laubardiere
embarked at the Elk with the troops under command of de Custine,
and while Clozen and Cromot Dubourg followed the same route
as the cavalry of Lauzun across Virginia."[2]

Washington had ordered the troops that were embarked on
the Chesapeake to halt after learning that the fleet of de Grasse
had left the Capes to fight Admiral Graves, but when he arrived
at Williamsburg and found both French fleets in the Chesapeake,
he sent Count Fersen to hurry the troops, as told above.[3] On
September 15, 1781, Washington notified Count de Grasse of this
plan, and imparted to Major-General Lincoln, from Williamsburg, the same information:

DEAR SIR:
Upon Information of the sailing of the fleet from the Chesapeake Bay,
I gave orders for the troops, who were embarked, to be stopped. Since
my arrival at this place, I am informed that Count de Grasse has been
joined by Count de Barras, and, having captured two English frigates, has
returned to his former station at the Capes. On this pleasing information
I have sent forward Count Fersen to hurry on the troops with all possible
despatch . . .

In July, 1782, Fersen passed through Virginia to Philadelphia.
Here, following an interview between Washington and Rochambeau, Fersen was charged with embarking the siege artillery which
had been left at West-Point, Va., and bringing it to Baltimore.
Since he had only one ship to accompany his convoy, Fersen had
to execute this operation with the utmost rapidity and secrecy.

Fersen writes from Philadelphia, August 8, 1782:

On the 16th of July, I was with Rochambeau, who had given "rendez-
vous" in Philadelphia to General Washington as he wished to confer with

---

[1] See Dubourg, MS. *Journal,* p. 42.
[2] Thomas Balch, *The French in America,* II, pp. 122-123.
[3] Cf. B. J. Lossing, *Pictorial Field Book of the Revolution,* II, pp. 307-308.

him as to their future plans of operations. The result of this conference was that I was sent to Yorktown in Virginia on the 19th on a mission which was secret then, but which now has become public property. I was to have our siege artillery shipped at once from West Point (eight miles higher up than Yorktown on the same river) to Baltimore by the Chesapeake Bay. This operation demanded great secrecy as well as promptness in execution, as we had only one vessel of forty guns to escort the convoy under the eyes of the English, who with two frigates would not only have prevented our sailing out of the York river, but would have seized some of our vessels besides . . . . As soon as I had everything in working order and the vessels started, I returned to report to Rochambeau who was stationed with his army at Baltimore . . . .

French sources refer to Fersen as the "excellent camarade" of de Lauzun and de Chastellux, though these two gentlemen had nothing to say in their published memoirs about their Swedish friend.[1] "It was the same Fersen," says Faucher de St.-Maurice, "who for a long time had made himself conspicuous at the court of Versailles by the nobility of his countenance and the elegance of his manners, the one who was called 'le beau Fersen' and who served as coachman for Marie Antoinette in her flight to Varennes." Although no doubt many French courtiers were happy when Fersen left Versailles—Count de Creutz, on April 10, 1779, had written to his King about the kind reception afforded Fersen by the French queen and commended him for courageously and resolutely going to America,—Captain Joachim Merlant speaks of him as the charming Swede who with ardent, chivalrous heart was devoted to Marie Antoinette. Merlant also relates the

---

[1] Cf. above, p. 4. When Duke de Lauzun returned to France, however, in the fall of 1781, he paid a verbal tribute to Fersen. Count de Creutz writes on November 25, 1781: "The Duke of Lauzun who has returned with the news (about Yorktown) has given a flattering testimony of honor about the young Count de Fersen. He told me that in all the operations where the fighting was intense, Fersen was present, now in the trenches and now in the midst of the attack, and that he exhibited the most brilliant proofs of valor." Cf. p. 98.

Count de Clozen, also, who had enjoyed Fersen's companionship for three years, speaks of his Swedish friend in his memoirs. When he arrived in Boston, late in 1782, there were two officers ready to embark whom Clozen was especially delighted to see—Counts de Deux-Ponts and von Fersen. Clozen and Fersen embarked together for France in Boston harbor at 3 P.M. on December 23, 1782. Cf. Allan Forbes and Paul F. Cadman, *France and New England,* I, p. 186, which contains a quotation from Clozen about Fersen. I have not seen the original.

famous wheelwright incident on the trip to Hartford, Connecticut, in which Fersen had an interesting part, and asserts that Fersen was the only one who in his letters gave the essential details of that notable, first Hartford conference.[1]

Americans and Europeans alike—among whom Thomas Carlyle is a conspicuous example—have been interested most of all in Fersen's relation to the unfortunate Queen on the French throne, the more so because it was obviously a relation *sans reproche.* Here was a young Swedish nobleman who in a short time had unconsciously won the place in the Queen's heart formerly held, it appears, by Lauzun. The whole court talked of the "prodigious favor" he enjoyed, both from Marie Antoinette and the Court as a whole. He was tall and well formed; his face bore the marks of nobility, melancholy, and distinction; his character was romanesque. He had more judgment than esprit, to the French mind, but concealed a "burning heart beneath a surface of ice." In 1779 he was welcomed into the intimate circles of the Queen; one talked of secret meetings and prolonged interviews. Fersen showed extraordinary modesty, reserve, and firmness for his age to overcome the attraction and decide to embark for America. He claimed he left the French shores without regrets.

His friendship for Lauzun must have occasioned some strangely dramatic moments. Both were something more than mere admirers of the French Queen, and during the long hours of enforced idleness in Newport, when there was little to do but write letters and memoirs, and attend social functions, they must have had many an opportunity to compare experiences, if this were possible, and revive memories of Versailles. Fersen wrote to his father about his ardent attachment to the Duke de Lauzun. The latter, during a moment of generosity and chivalry, thought seriously of giving up his Legion to Fersen,[2] who enthusiastically accepted the proposal, and both wrote to the Queen about the official transfer, but evidently nothing came of it.

Wharton, in the Introduction to his *Diplomatic Correspondence of the American Revolution,* after referring to Fersen's presence at the battle of Yorktown,[3] recalls the fact that the Swedish

---

[1] For a detailed description of the marches of the French army through New England, see Forbes and Cadman, *op. cit.*

[2] See letter to his father of November 13, 1780.

[3] Among the portraits in Trumbull's famous painting: *Surrender of*

colonel at the end of his service received the badge of the Cincinnati "at the hands of Washington"[1] himself. On Fersen's
return to France, in June, 1783—he had remained here, as noted,
until December, 1782, a while after the departure of Rochambeau—
"he was attached to the royal family, and his attachment to the
Queen," says Wharton, "was the subject of much republican
criticism. On June 20, 1791, he undertook to procure a carriage
for the king's escape from Paris. On this carriage he took the
place of driver . . . . Fersen, however, cannot be ranked among
the French officers who sought America under the influence of
liberal views. His position in the French court was embarrassing
from the peculiar and chivalrous admiration exhibited by him for
the queen, and for the interest which, drawn by his singular
beauty and devotion, she seems to have taken in him. His transfer to America, no doubt the consequence of this awkwardness,
was procured by Vergennes."[2]

The implications in these categorical statements seem a bit
severe and unjust to Fersen. In reality he was no narrow-minded
aristocrat. As other biographers have pointed out, he had indeed
fewer prejudices than most of his class, having been brought up
in an atmosphere of what was then considered liberal ideas. As
we have seen, the "awkwardness" mentioned by Wharton un-
questionably played some rôle in his decision to go to America;
yet, whatever the inner motives and views of Count Fersen may
have been, he gave a good account of himself in this country,
both as a soldier[3] and as a diplomat. He performed his duties
with characteristic Scandinavian seriousness, and his letters on the
American campaign (see bibliography) constitute a valuable con-

---

Lord Cornwallis, in the Capitol at Washington, is the figure on horseback
of Count de Fersen. The likeness was painted, like that of the other
French officers in the picture, from life, in Paris, 1787, at the residence of
the American minister, Mr. Jefferson.

[1] This can not be interpreted literally, however, for Fersen had embarked
for the return voyage before the Cincinnati had been established. Because
of storms and other conditions, however, it took several months to get
back home. See letter of Feb. 13, 1783, page 145. Fersen received the
badge and insignia of the American order in Naples while traveling with
his king early in 1784. Cf. Flach, *op. cit.,* p. 46.

[2] Vol. I, p. 407.

[3] During the siege of Yorktown, as we have seen, Fersen exhibited as a
soldier distinct proofs of calmness and courage. Cf. p. 134, note.

tribution to our first-hand sources about the activities and non-activities of the French expeditionary forces, because of their spontaneous frankness, their objective truthfulness. When honored by many tasks of delicate responsibility, his fellow officers accepted this as just and natural. When an alleged coolness arose between Washington and Rochambeau, it was Fersen who was sent to learn and remove the "cause of this displeasure."[1] Count de Creutz wrote to Gustavus III, on March 28, 1781: "There has been some feeling of discontent between Monsieur de Rochambeau and General Washington, probably in regard to some delays in remittances of money promised to Congress. The young Count de Fersen has been dispatched to General Washington's camp to settle this matter; that proves how much confidence is placed in the sagacity and prudence of this young officer." Fersen himself had written to his father on January 17, 1781, that he would try to carry out his diplomatic mission well, and we know now that his task was successful. At the Hartford meeting, reported as having taken place at various times between September 20 and October 1, 1780, Fersen was sent ahead to announce the arrival of the French party. In the beginning of September, 1780 (see letter of September 8), Fersen is the only aide-de-camp to accompany his General "upon the mainland." Incidentally, Fersen reports staying away two days and seeing "one of the finest regions in the world." On December 7, Fersen writes of another trip inland,—this time he was one of three companions—when the party stayed six days; but this time he is not so enthusiastic about the sights, and found the people lazy and selfish. The indecision and procrastination of colonists who did not know whether they wanted independence or not found no sympathy with Fersen on general principles; and the personal attitude of some colonials toward the French—and Fersen of course was considered a Frenchman—often left much to be desired, and may have been a cause for Fersen's less agreeable impressions of some of the people.

But Count Fersen treated everybody alike, and he is equally objective in his confidential criticism of his own commander. He writes on May 17, 1781, that he was tired of Rochambeau, who was "distrustful in a very disagreeable and sometimes insulting manner. He has more confidence in me," says Fersen, "than in

---

[1] Cf. first page of this chapter.

my comrades, but even that is paltry." Later he modified his
opinion, however, and believed Rochambeau's arrogant behavior
a necessary corollary of precaution and military discipline.

The young Swedish colonel came to America to learn and to
do something, and frankly admitted it. On October 23, 1781,
immediately after the surrender of Cornwallis, he writes from
Yorktown:

All our young colonels belonging to the French court are departing to
spend their winter in Paris. Some will return; others will stay there,
and I shall be much surprised if they are not all made brigadier-generals
after being at the siege of Yorktown; they think they have done the finest
thing in the world. I shall stay here, having no other reason to go to
Paris than my amusement and pleasure, and those I must sacrifice. My
affairs can get on without me; I should spend a great deal of money, and
I ought to be careful of it. I prefer to employ it in making another campaign here and in achieving what I have begun. When I took the resolution to come here I foresaw the annoyance I should have to put up with;
it is fair that the instruction I have acquired should cost me something.[1]

We must admit that these are the words of sense and proper
spirit; and Fersen's willingness to sacrifice his personal income
in the war for American freedom, irrespective of any selfish
element or the character of the initial impulses for enlisting in our
cause, is entitled to some recognition. As we have seen, he
remained here until his work was finished.

Upon his return to France, Fersen was called upon to accompany Gustavus III on his travels through France, Italy and other
countries, and became again the devoted admirer of the French
court, and the protector of its royalty. For his services in America
he was of course made a knight of the Order Pour le Mérite
Militaire; a commander of the Swedish Order of the Sword with
the Grand Cross; and, as we have seen, a member of the Order
of the Cincinnati, though he was forbidden to carry the emblem
of the last order,[2] especially in the presence of his king. His
defiant, hazardous, romantic protection of the French royal family

---

[1] Translation by K. P. Wormeley.

[2] Cf. p. 160. Because of the refusal of Gustavus III to permit his subjects to carry the badge of the much-coveted Cincinnati, Washington
writes from Mount Vernon, Aug. 20, 1784, to Rochambeau: "Considering
how recently the King of Sweden has changed the government of his country, it is not so much to be wondered at that his fears should get the better
of his liberality, as to anything which might have the semblance of repub-
licanism; but when it is further considered, how few of his nation had,

against the revolutionary republicans, and his subsequent attempt to save them from the pending tragedy are well known. The coachman's disguise of one of the three or four men in all Paris that could be trusted, namely Fersen, got the unfortunate king and queen out of Paris successfully; but whether because of lack of prudence in devising the original plans of escape or because of the historical indiscretion on the part of the king near the frontier, the scheme failed—after Fersen had left the driver's box—and the doom of Louis XVI and Marie Antoinette was sealed forever. A later plan by Fersen to have the king escape from the Temple failed also.

After the disastrous events of the French Revolution, Fersen lost active interest in France and returned to Sweden, where he soon became a favorite of Charles XIII. Having already been employed by Gustavus III on a secret mission, in 1791, he was promoted to major-general in 1792, the same year that witnessed the murder of Gustavus III, and soon became Grand Marshal of the Palace and chancellor of Upsala University. He served as ambassador to the Imperial Diet in 1797, and, again, to Dresden, 1803; became Lord of the Realm, 1799; Knight of the Order of the Seraphim; and was appointed chancellor of Sweden (Grand Marshal of the Realm) in 1801. Unjustly accused of being an accessory to the sudden death of the popular heir-elect to the Swedish throne, Carl August, Duke of Augustenburg, Count von Fersen was killed by a mob during an uprising in Stockholm against the titled classes on the occasion of the funeral of the Crown Prince, June 20, 1810.

---

or could have, a right to the order, I think he might have suffered his complaisance to overcome them."

It will be remembered that a foreigner must attain the rank of colonel to be considered a candidate for the Order of the Cincinnati. Since some Swedish officers, like Liljehorn, apparently accepted a lower rank in the American-French service, than they held in their own country, and since foreigners could not secure the requisite rank for the Cincinnati, that of captain, in the navy—and most Swedes were naval officers—only two Swedish officers, it seems, were honored with this American order—Fersen and Stedingk. The letter by Washington just quoted proves, however, that there were Swedish officers entitled to this honor.

Flach (*op. cit.*, p. 46) implies that Fersen, out of courtesy for General Washington and the French bearers of the Cincinnati, succeeded in winning his sovereign's consent to wear the American decoration while on active duty in the French army. He was not, however, to wear it elsewhere.

ADDITIONAL EXTRACTS FROM THE AMERICAN
LETTERS OF COUNT VON FERSEN
(*From the translation by Georgine Holmes*)[1]

Newport, September 8, 1780.

. . . The people [in Rhode Island] seem in easy circumstances
and free from any love of display or ceremony; they are satisfied
with a simple style of living, which with us is confined to persons
of inferior rank. Their dress is plain, but of the finest texture,
and their manners have not been spoiled by the luxuriousness of
Europe. Their country is bound to be a prosperous one, should
peace be theirs, and if the two parties which divide it now do
not reduce it to the state of Poland and so many other republics.
These two parties are called the Whigs and the Tories. The first
named is entirely for liberty and independence; it is composed
of people of the lowest extraction, who possess nothing in the
way of worldly goods. The Tories are nearly all country people;
they sympathize with England, that is to say, they are for peace
at any price, and do not seem to care for either freedom or
liberty. They are of a better class of people in this country, and
the only ones, in fact, who seem to have any landed property.
Some of these Tories have relations or possessions in their mother
country, England; others, wishing to keep what they have already
acquired in this country, have embraced the British side, as this
is the stronger. When the Whigs have the mastery they plunder
the others as hard as they can. This, of course, keeps up a bitter
animosity and hatred between the two sides, which will be with
difficulty overcome, and which will be the very hotbed of future
troubles. . . .

Newport, October 16, 1780.

. . . We are vegetating at the very door of the enemy, in a
most disastrous state of idleness and inactivity, all of which is
attributable to our inferior numbers, which are terribly tired out,
being obliged to be always fatiguingly on the defensive. We are
of no possible aid to our allies; we cannot leave our island without exposing our fleet to the danger of being captured or
destroyed; our fleet cannot leave port without exposing us to
the enemy, who with superior forces in the way of men and ships

---

[1] For a complete list of translations see Bibliography.

would certainly attack us and cut off our retreat to the mainland . . . Instead of helping the Americans we are a draw-back
to them; we cannot reinforce their army, we are about a twelve
days' march from them, separated by great arms of the sea which
are dangerous to cross in winter because of their huge floating
blocks of ice. We are in fact a burden to the allies, because our
victualling makes provisions scarce for them. Our paying gold
cash down, even, undervalues government paper, as this deprives
General Washington's army of the facility of using their paper
to purchase provisions—it is refused whenever offered. Our
financial is as bad as our military condition. We had brought
with us only two hundred and sixty pounds, half in specie and
half by letters of credit on Mr. Holcker, a banker in Philadelphia;
we ought of course to have brought double that amount. The
scarcity of specie here makes us use our ready money continually;
the consequence is, it enforces us to the most rigid economy, when
we ought to have been lavish and profuse in our expenditures.
This ruins our credit . . . .

About fifteen days ago I went to Hartford (some forty miles
from here) with Monsieur de Rochambeau. There were only six
of us in the party: the general, the admiral, Viscount Rochambeau (the general's son), a superior officer of the engineering
corps, and two aids-de-camp (myself included). An interview
was arranged between the generals, Washington and Rochambeau.
I was sent on slightly in advance to announce Rochambeau's
approach, and thus had an opportuntiy of studying this most
illustrious man of our century (not to say the *only one*). His
majestic, handsome countenance is stamped with an honesty and a
gentleness which correspond with his moral qualities. He looks
like a hero; he is very cold, speaks little, but is frank and courteous in manner; a tinge of melancholy affects his whole bearing,
which is not unbecoming; on the contrary it renders him, if possible, more interesting. His suite outnumbers ours; the Marquis de Lafayette; General Knox of the artillery; Monsieur de
Gouvion, a French officer of engineers; and six aids-de-camp;
besides an escort of twenty-two dragoons. Of course this latter
was indispensable, as he had to cross a country bristling with
enemies; no post-horses being procurable, the journey had to be
taken on horseback with private horses on account of the miser-
able condition of the roads. In this one instance, however, nearly

every one had come in carriages except our own aids-de-camp. It was a three days' journey for us as well as for Washington. Whilst we were journeying we heard of Rodney's arrival in New York. We continued on, however. During our stay in Hartford the two generals and the admiral were closeted together all day; the Marquis de Lafayette assisted as interpreter, as General Washington does not speak French nor understand it. They separated, quite charmed with one another, at least they said so. . . .

Newport, January 9, 1781.

(After describing the poor state of affairs in the south) . . . Ours is not much better; we are forced to be the idle spectators of the loss of a section of the country and cannot raise a finger to help them the southerners. I have traveled but little in this country. Several of our army officers are now absent on a trip; all they have seen and all the mistakes they may commit will be a guide for me. I shall await the month of March. The different American states have passed a resolution to raise a standing army of twenty thousand men for three years. The appointment has been made and public interest again has been thoroughly aroused. They hope to have all the recruits in by the first of March. I sincerely *trust* they may succeed, but I am not *sure* of it. Some of these recruits have been engaged for three years, others only for the duration of the war, but none of them will serve for love; it is only by dint of offering them high pay that the different regiments have been filled at all. Money is scarce; in fact there is none. The taxes do not suffice; there is no credit, no resources, it seems to me. This is the time or never to be of some service to them and repair our inactive and useless campaign by furnishing them with all the means and the clothing they may need. Should, however, our reinforcements from France fail to come we may be ourselves in *want* and reduced to the humiliating expedient of paying our army in paper money. You see, dear father, by these explanations, you have a truthful statement of the whole question, and how difficult it is to raise an army which can only be kept on a standing footing by money. Besides all this the spirit of patriotism is only to be found amongst the military chiefs and the principal men of the country, who do make great sacrifices; the bulk of the population, however, only look out for their own interests. Money is the prime motor of

all their actions; their only thought is how to make it. Every
one for himself, no one for the public good. The inhabitants of
the coast and the stanchest Whigs carry provisions of all kinds
to the British fleet anchored in Gardiner's Bay, and they get well
paid for their pains, they swindle us unmercifully; everything is
exorbitantly high, and whenever they have any business dealings
with us they generally treat us more like foes than friends. Their
cupidity is unequalled, for money is their god; virtue, and honor
hold no place beside the precious metal. There are, of course,
estimable people among them, people noted for their noble, generous natures—fortunately there are many such—but I am speaking of the country as a whole. I believe there is more of the
Dutch than of the English element among them. This, dear
father, is my opinion of this country, its inhabitants, and its war,
and this opinion is corroborated by all intelligent-minded persons—persons who are better able to judge the situation than I
can. With troops, with ships, and plenty of money, all this could
be remedied; but should this latter not be sent forthwith to help
us in our need and enable us to succor our allies, then nothing can
be done, and the ministry of France will have capped the climax
by its stupidity. We have just received most disastrous news;
the Pennsylvania troops, numbering some twenty-five hundred
men and recruited in the state of Pennsylvania, have passed over
to the enemy. They were, it is true, thoroughly demoralized,
being destitute of clothes, and shoes, then starved for nearly
four days. . . .

Newport, May 17, 1781.

. . . I wish something were settled for me, as I begin to weary
of being with Monsieur de Rochambeau. He seems to single me
out, to be sure, with his attention, for all of which I am grateful,
of course; but his manner is defiant, insultingly so. He seems
to have much more confidence in me than in my comrades, but
that is not saying much. He does not trust his officers either,
who are quite displeased, as are the superior army officers; but
they have the tact to hide their feelings and to work for the good
of the cause.

We push economy to such an extreme that we keep no spies in
New York because this would be an outlay of some fifty louis a
month. We have to depend therefore entirely on General Washington for all our information, leaving the Americans to provide

the spies when they can ill afford to pay them; consequently these latter have to sacrifice themselves for love of country. By these means we always have belated news. The result will be that we will some day have no news at all, for men who work for nothing will soon get tired of being hanged for nothing!

We are still preparing to march, but when we leave here for good I do not know. A part of our artillery and camp furniture is stored at Providence. The general officers are completing their military arrangements.

Our army, unfortunately, is as little disciplined as the French army always is under ordinary circumstances. Our chiefs are very strict, and not a day passes that there are not some two or three of the officers placed under arrest. I have myself seen some lamentable scenes where a whole corps of men ought to have been cashiered, but as we only number five thousand we cannot afford to lose a man. . . . .

Williamsburg, March 25, 1782.

. . . The chief product of Virginia is tobacco. This state (the largest of the thirteen) could grow other staples if she wished, but the indolence and pride of the natives are stumbling-blocks to all progressive industry. It really seems as if the Virginians belonged to a totally different race of people, for instead of personally managing their farms, or attending to the business part of it, each land-owner wants to be a lord. No white man ever labors, but the work is all done by black slaves, guarded by white men who in their turn are under an overseer or superintendent, like in the West Indies. In Virginia there are about twenty blacks to one white man. That is the reason this state sends so few soldiers to the field. Business men, of course, are looked upon and considered quite an inferior order of being by the lordly planters who, not looking on them as gentlemen, preclude them from their society. They (the planters) have mostly aristocratic tendencies; the only wonder is how they were ever induced to form part of a confederation or accept a government founded on perfect equality of rights. That same spirit, however, which prompted them to throw off the British yoke might lead them some day to other (rebellious) outbreaks, and I should not be surprised to see Virginia free herself from the other states, once peace is signed.—I am even prepared to see the American government become a perfectly aristocratic one . . .

Boston, November 30, 1782.

. . . We were quite sorry to part with Rochambeau, who was well liked by his men. They do not seem to feel that same attachment for Vioménil. I *ought* to like him, because he shows the utmost courtesy and regard. But the Baron is a quick-tempered, passionate man; he has not that precious gift of self-control which characterized Rochambeau, who was the only man fit to command here, and thoroughly capable of maintaining that perfect order and harmony which has always existed between two nations that are so different in their customs and language, and who at bottom, let it be said, do not really like each other. There has never been the slightest misunderstanding between our armies during the whole time that we have been together, though we have often had just cause of complaint. Our allies have not always acted nicely toward us, and our sojourn amongst them has neither heightened our love nor our esteem for them. Rochambeau himself has often had occasion to be vexed with them, but he never varied in his conduct toward them. His example has been a powerful check on the army, and the severe discipline he maintained has kept every one within bounds, so that even the English and the Americans who have been witnesses of his strictness could not help but admire it. The wise, prudent stand Rochambeau had taken has contributed more to conciliate America toward us than four brilliant victories could ever have done . . .

Porto Cabello, South America (on the return voyage) February 13, 1783.

I am very well, although the trip [from Boston] was long and wearisome; it reacted more on my mental than on my physical condition . . . A sailor's life is certainly a tiresome one, especially in the French navy. We lost the *Bourgoyne* carrying seventy-four guns which went down with four hundred men aboard . . . We arrived here the night of the 10th but with a scattered fleet. We have five ships here which came in four different arrivals several days apart. Three ships sought shelter in Curaçao, thirty leagues from here; they could get no farther. There are three of them heaven knows where. We have not laid eyes on them for ten days. The first convoy of thirty-two sail that left Boston with us was lost by bad steering during three heavy windstorms off the coast of America. Of a second convoy of ten sail which we took at Porto Rico, only *five* entered the harbor of Curaçao; the other five have no doubt been wrecked. They had followed in our wake till we reached the western point of this island; then when we made for this place, Porto Cabello, the wind was dead against us, so that they no doubt were obliged to go leeward. The ocean currents here are so strong that in one night we were carried some thirteen leagues from the spot we were in at sundown. It took us thirteen days to reach *terra firma* after leaving Curaçoa, only a distance of thirty-five leagues! It was just within sight of Curaçao that the *Bourgoyne* went down. We arrived here safe and sound at last, and that is saying a good deal. I could not have believed it possible, it seems so like a miracle. I do not know the reason, but the English never have the losses we do.

CHAPTER VIII

COLONEL CURT VON STEDINGK

In the early part of 1780, a proud but exceedingly affable man was slowly making his way, on crutches, through certain quarters of Paris. He was apparently well known, for many greeted him, and whenever he stopped people gathered about him to hear the stories of his adventures. In the salons and corridors of the upper classes he was especially popular. Held up as the ideal type of a soldier, he had once been represented in a theater as leading a party of soldiers to assault. The recipient of enviable royal honors from two kings, the hero had once for his exploits been praised by Louis XVI before the whole court. It was the same man on crutches who later dared aspire to the charms and brilliancy of Mlle. Necker, a personal venture, however, in which both his courage and his crutches, as a Frenchman[1] has observed, were eclipsed by his rival, the diplomatist and fellow-countryman, Baron de Staël.

The subject of all this attention and admiration was a veteran of the American war, who had become the persona gratissima at a time when the spirit and expectations of the conflict still ran high. His realistic tales of bravery on the part of the Allies, while they served to emphasize the seriousness of the struggle and the necessity for sending money and troops, had also brought optimism and encouragement to the French. As for himself, he had been one of the first volunteers to enter the scene of strife on the western continent, and having received a wound which compelled him to use crutches, he had returned in advance of the others.[2] His name was Curt von Stedingk,[3] a Swedish colonel in French service. Of that quartet of eminent Swedes who contributed so conspicuously to the social, diplomatic, political, or military life of France at various periods during the American Revolution, von Stedingk was a leading member. The others were de Creutz, de Staël, and von Fersen.

---

[1] Paul Gaulot, in *A Friend of the Queen.*
[2] *Ibid.,* I, 115.
[3] Often erroneously spelled *Steding.* Not to be confused with Capt. Steding, who was a Hessian staff officer.

Heitman's list of officers of the Continental Army, French section, contains this reference to Stedingk:

Steding, Baron de. Swede; two assaults; two landings; one siege; commanded trenches; also a column in the assault on Savannah, where he received a wound; a naval action.[1]

Bancroft, the only prominent American historian who finds any occasion to mention Stedingk, quotes from the colonel's description of the siege of Savannah and indirectly designates his allegiance by referring to his king, Gustavus III. Gardiner[2] is naturally the American who should know most about Stedingk. According to him, Count von Stedingk (he was later made a count), with the rank of lieutenant-colonel in the Royal-Suédois,

"served in 1778 under Count d'Estaing in his operations in Rhode Island, and was with the troops which were landed on Conanicut Island in Narragansett Bay.[3] He also served in 1779, under Count d'Estaing, and commanded a division at the Siege of Savannah, where he was severely wounded while leading it to assault, on the 9th of October, 1779."

Gardiner knows of Stedingk's prompt rewards from France and Sweden, and something about his later life. On July 22, 1811, the same Stedingk—now a field marshal, and apparently without crutches—was appointed to command the Swedish army of thirty thousand men which subsequently operated with the allied armies against the Emperor Napoleon's forces and entered Paris in 1814. We are likewise informed that on July 4, 1888, his great-grandson, Captain Hans Ludvig, Count von Stedingk, succeeded his distinguished great-grandfather in the Rhode Island State Society of Cincinnati.

French sources agree that Stedingk commanded the left column (out of two columns, a vanguard, and a reserve corps) at the battle of Savannah, and that in this attack he received a "forte contusion à la jambe."[4] That the expedition against Savannah

---

[1] Heitman, *Historical Register,* etc., p. 666.

[2] Cf. Chap. VII, first paragraph, note 5. Also *op. cit.,* pp. 70-73.

[3] This must be a mistake. Stedingk was in Paris throughout the year 1778. He did not leave France until early in the following spring. See pp. 153-4.

[4] Cf. Noailles, *op. cit.,* p. 101. Just what Noailles means when he states that Stedingk was third in command of the *Second division* at the battle of Savannah is not clear. But this is of little consequence: it is obvious that Stedingk was one of the three or four principal commanders of all the forces that took part in the siege.

was undertaken contrary to the advices of Stedingk, but that he did excellent work in covering the retreat after the siege was abandoned, is generally acknowledged by French writers. Geffroy[1] refers to Stedingk's popularity in France and testifies that he repeatedly distinguished himself at the head of French troops, and especially at the celebrated action on the "Ile de la Grenade," in the West Indies, where Stedingk, in July, 1779, commanded the central division in a successful attack on the fortress there.

An informative contemporaneous account of Stedingk's part in the battle of Savannah may be obtained in the two journals[2] left us by some French officers, who undoubtedly participated in the disastrous affair or had some first-hand information of the fruitless attack. Dillon and Stedingk were to lead the attacking right and left columns, respectively, and Viscount de Noailles the reserve corps, or third column. Mr. Roman, a Frenchman, who had once supposedly helped to build the defenses of Savannah, was pressed into service as guide, and the march was started.

Upon emerging from the woods M. de Steding(k) asked M. Roman (an officer in the American artillery) how far his point of attack was from the redoubt which the vanguard was to assault. Mr. Roman, who led the sixty volunteers (at the head of Stedingk's column) simply in the capacity of a guide, replied he knew nothing beyond his own command; that he was unacquainted with the surroundings of the city; that the works had been altered since the enemy had taken possession of them; and that he could act as guide not longer.[3]

In the interim Dillon's column fell back toward the left instead of moving to the right.

The column of M. de Stedingk, which moved to the left, while traversing a muddy swamp full of brambles, lost its formation and no longer preserved order. This swamp, upon which the enemy's trenches rested, formed a slope which served as a glacis to them. The firing was very lively; and, although this column was here most seriously injured, it crossed the road to Augusta that it might advance to the enemy's right which it was ordered to attack. On this spot nearly all the sixty volunteers were killed. The Baron de Stedingk was here wounded. The column of M. D'Estaing (Dillon) and the repulsed vanguard which had

---

[1] *Op. cit.*
[2] C. C. Jones, *The Siege of Savannah*, translated from the two journals of French officers. For Stedingk's part see pp. 28 ff.
[3] *Ibid.*, p. 30.

retreated to the left, arrived here as soon as the column of M. de Stedingk
and threw it into utter confusion. At this moment everything was in such
disorder that the formations were no longer preserved. The road to
Augustus was choked up . . .

When it was seen that success was impossible the General ordered
retreat.

We beat a retreat which was mainly affected across the swamp lying
to the right of the Augusta road; our forces being entirely, and at short
range, exposed to the concentrated fire of the entrenchments which constantly increased in vehemence. At this juncture the enemy showed themselves openly upon the parapets and delivered their fire with their muskets
almost touching our troops. The General here received a second shot.
Baron de Stedingk retreated without loss by following the road to Augusta
and turning the swamp by a long detour.[1]

But let us turn to the Swedish sources for a consecutive and
more detailed account of Stedingk's life and work.

Curt Bogislaus Ludvig Christoffer, Baron and Count von
Stedingk, the descendant of an old Westphalian family, was born
October 26, 1746, on the ancestral estate at Pinnau in Swedish
Pomerania. As a boy he took part in the Seven Years War;
served for a time in the King's Regiment; entered Upsala
University, where he obtained a classical education, in 1763;
and in 1766 obtained a commission in the Royal Suédois. His
rise in France was relatively rapid: he was advanced to captain
in 1770; to "captain-major," 1773; and was, besides, sometime
chamberlain to King Gustavus III. At the outbreak of the American Revolution, as we have noted, he held the rank of lieutenant-
colonel, which was advanced to colonel in March, 1779.

Thereupon Stedingk was permitted to join a French expedition
to America, and served in the campaigns mentioned above. An
excellent judge in military matters, and outside of de Creutz and
Fersen the best known Swede in France, he exerted not a little
influence on the early French operations in the West Indies and
in the southern part of the United States. Whenever his advice
was not followed, as at Savannah, the result was defeat. It was
Stedingk who suggested to France that it was better, so far as
possible, to send foreign soldiers to America; and he himself
hoped to recruit a regiment of Swedes for service across the sea,
partly in order, no doubt, to create an opportunity for his own

[1] *Ibid.*, pp. 35-36.

countrymen and a larger opening for himself, and partly because he believed he might thereby be able to accomplish more. Unfortunately this plan came to nought.

That Colonel Stedingk often is mentioned in the private letters and official messages by Count de Creutz, and especially during the autumns of 1778 and 1779, goes without saying. "I have received a letter from Marshal de Broglie," writes the Swedish envoyé on September 30, 1778, "in which he gives an extraordinary eulogy (un éloge infini) of M. de Stedingk. He told me that he was astonished at the training of this young man, and at his knowledge, whether it concerned detail or tactics in general. If there is a war on land he will employ him in the capacity of a major in the army."[1] In a letter of September 9, 1779, containing information about the part played by the Swedes in the capture of Grenada, he makes special mention of Stedingk[2] as having distinguished himself at the head of the central column of the attacking force, and encloses a note from Count d'Estaing, dated at the fortress of St. George, Grenada, July 12, 1779, which gives first-hand information about Stedingk's ability and accomplishment:

"I have a personal obligation to express to Your Excellency (de Creutz) for having created the happy opportunity which enabled me to carry on my war operations with the aid of an officer of such merit and distinction as Baron de Stedingk, colonel of infantry. Through his talent and courage he has contributed to the success of an attack as violent as it was difficult. And, again, he did not want his brother (Victor), who served on the *Robuste,* to be the only one of that name (Stedingk), who should be present at the naval battle. I have the honor to inform Your Excellency that I shall ask the Minister of the (French) King to call His Majesty's attention to what the (Brothers) Stedingk

---

[1] We have seen that he obtained a colonel's commission the following spring.

[2] In a letter to the Swedish Minister of Foreign Affairs, Scheffer, of the same date, September 9, Creutz announces "the greatest and most glorious news" of the capture of Grenada and of a naval victory against Admiral Byron. The latter was the more glorious because, in addition to the violence of the fighting, d'Estaing had the wind and water currents against him, and, besides, had only fifteen vessels available. "They chased Mr. Byron until nightfall," says Creutz, and then adds: "Monsieur de Stedingk has singularly distinguished himself in the attack."

have accomplished, and if my prayers are heeded the croix du mérite shall be offered to both.

"I have the honor," etc.

On the twenty-fourth of October, Creutz informs the Swedish king that as soon as "Major Stedingk, who is on his way home," arrives in France, he will from him obtain detailed reports about the other Swedish officers who participated in the same engagement. On December 12 we learn of the unsuccessful attack on Savannah, and that Stedingk had been dangerously wounded in the siege. On the 16th we know the character of his wound and that this had become dangerous only because Stedingk had continued to fight at the head of his column after grape-shot had pierced his leg. A few days later we hear of Stedingk's arrival at Brest, that his wound was almost healed, that his general health was better, and that "during this campaign he had won both fame and a good constitution." On December 23, Stedingk, we know, is back in Paris and has brought confirmation about the murderous character of the battle of Savannah, where sixty-three officers were killed or wounded in the second attack alone. Creutz writes further:

"Count Arthur Dillon has confided to me that it is to the valor, composure, and good disposition of Monsieur Stedingk that the troops whose retreat he covered were saved. Count d'Estaing having been seriously wounded in his leg he had turned over the command to Dillon and himself (Stedingk); and Count d'Estaing told everybody that Stedingk had covered himself with glory."

A brief history of Stedingk's early service in France, his experiences at the French court, and his enlistment and participation in the American war, is found in H. L. Dardel's recent, instructive work, *Fältmarskalken von Stedingks tidigare levnadsöden,* a book based on the colonel's letters to his Swedish friend, the governor-general Carl Sparre, which appeared in a limited edition in 1922. A few pertinent extracts translated from Dardel's compilation are here reproduced. They need no other comment than that given occasionally by the editor of the letters.

Sparre had written to Vergennes and asked him to do something for Stedingk, and on the 9th of December, 1778, Stedingk is able to announce that he, accompanied by the minister of foreign affairs, had paid a visit to the secretary of war, Prince de

Montbarey, and that at this visit the former had assured the latter that by procuring a suitable position for Stedingk he would perform a deed which would be useful to France and agreeable to the king of Sweden. The result of this interview was that the minister of war promised to obtain from his king a colonel's commission for Stedingk.

But the chances of getting into the war at an early date were nevertheless slight. "The French are going to avoid war on land as long as they can," writes Stedingk, "so as not to impair the strength of the fleet, which is the principal factor in our war operations. The fleet has been brought to such a height of perfection that France has never seen its equal, not even during its golden period; and all this has been done without additional taxation, a fact which illustrates clearly Mr. Necker's wise and resolute administration and the abundant resources of this country. If peace is made in Germany this winter, as we believe here, France, freed from anxiety in that direction, will be able to deal a heavy blow against England. Because of all these reasons I think I ought to await the development of events and prolong my stay here as long as possible."[1]

After Stedingk had received the permission of Gustavus III to accept a colonel's commission in the French service, he was appointed to that rank on March 27, 1779; but what gave him still greater joy was that he was permitted to accompany the troops that were destined for America. He writes about this on the same day to Sparre: "This advantage is all the more valuable because it has been granted to only a few, and the demand to go to America has become very great and fashionable since Lafayette received such an enthusiastic reception from the whole nation that it can be compared to nothing less than the ovation received by the Crusaders when they left for the Holy Land. Only Viscount de Noailles, Chevalier de Lameth, a nephew of Marshal de Broglie, and myself have obtained this permission; and de Maurepas has recently assured us that no others will obtain any, inasmuch as he disapproves of that fiery spirit which inflames the blood of so many young men. So far as I am concerned—I who can not, unfortunately, be counted among the latter,—it is thought and mind that have made the decision, and I shall never regret it,

[1] Pp. 73-74.

even if the outcome should prove disastrous to my health and life—something which my friends here seem to fear. I feel determined and calm, yes even glad that I can participate in the denouement of the spectacle."

"During the time that has elapsed since I left France," Stedingk writes from Grenada, the ninth of July, 1779, "so many remarkable events have happened that a whole book would be necessary to describe them in detail. Time and circumstances, however, will not permit this . . . . Our squadron arrived at Martinique on the 28th of June, after a crossing that lasted almost three months. But we may consider ourselves fortunate, since we had neither severe weather nor superior enemies to encounter, and we escaped (Admiral) Byron who had been lying in wait for us. Nevertheless the journey was very disagreeable to me. Sickness broke out among the crew, and we suffered from malignant fever. We had hoped to rest a day on Martinique, but Count d'Estaing, whom we met there with his fleet, sent out an order that only the sick might disembark, and that we should take on water, whereupon we set sail on the following day with twenty-five warships and almost three thousand marines. We steered toward Grenada and neighboring islands, which constitute the best possession that the English have in the Antilles. Three days later we effected our landing without any great resistance."[1]

"Twenty-four hours after our victory (at Grenada)," Stedingk writes in at letter to Sparre, "Admiral Byron appeared off Grenada with a fleet consisting of twenty-two[2] ships of the line and thirty transport vessels, with five thousand marines. He believed that he would still be able to save this possession. I had gone aboard the *Diadème,* a ship with seventy-seven cannon. Byron bore down upon us under full sails and began the battle before we had time to draw up a line formation, because we were lying under the lee, while he could take advantage of the wind. The cannonading began at six o'clock in the morning and continued wth undiminished violence until three o'clock in the afternoon, and was resumed from four until five . . . .

"I had desired to be present at a naval battle, but I hope with

---

[1] Pp. 76-77.

For a detailed description of the battle of Grenada see below, pp. 162 ff.

[2] In a letter to Creutz three days later, Stedingk gives the number as twenty-one. Cf. p. 163.

all my heart that I shall never have to be present at another. Whereas land troops require bravery, the personnel of the navy demands heroism. The consequences of a naval battle follow in more rapid succession and are more terrible. The firing is done at pistol range with cannon à 36. Three times I was knocked down by projectiles which crushed or injured ten or twelve men at a time, and it is no exaggeration to say that the deck of our ship was literally covered with blood, brain substance, and mutilated limbs. Under such circumstances the rôle of an infantry officer is anything but pleasant: he is exposed to the fire without being able to do any real good except to give proof of bravery and sangfroid. Six thousand shots were fired on each side; yet we lost only a thousand men, and none of our vessels were disabled. The Englishmen's losses must have been much larger. Five of their ships lost their masts and would have been captured if darkness had not come on. Byron retreated favored by the wind. We were, later, not able to make him continue the battle, and he manœuvered so skillfully that he lost only one transport ship with two hundred men. Old sailors assert that they have never taken part in such a violent and at the same time indecisive battle. The battle of Ouessant in the beginning of this war can not be compared to this one . . .

"We have returned to Grenada, but as soon as conditions have been improved we shall follow up our advantages as much as the wintering will permit.

"I believe I shall return with Count d'Estaing to France after this campaign. One can not last long in this country because of the heat, fatigue, and oppressiveness of the climate. To be sure, I have accomplished but little for my honor, but I am given credit for what little I have done. Count d'Estaing and my comrades are satisfied with me, and in his account to the court he has praised me undoubtedly more than I deserve. I shall receive the croix du mérite if my king allows me to accept it, and maybe I shall get a regiment if I decide to stay in France. But I love my King too much for that, and I shall never dispense with that handsome title 'Swedish' . . ."[1]

---

[1] Pp. 79-81.
Sometimes the colonial subject of a country is more enthusiastic about his nationality and political allegiance than a native of the mother country. This may explain, in part, Stedingk's spontaneous expression of loyalty

February 1, 1780. "Since my return to France time has past with extraordinary rapidity. It has been one long succession of trips to Versailles, reports to the Minister, and applications on behalf of individuals whom I had the honor to command (in America). Then there has been an infinite number of little social duties to attend to, so that I have hardly had time to breathe . . .

Fortunately my health has been benefitted by the satisfaction in my soul. My wound is healed, and I feel better than I have for a long time. Both the royal family and the public treat us the best way possible. Count d'Estaing is the subject of general admiration and enthusiasm, and we share a little of his honor; but it would seem as though the Ministry did not judge us so favorably. Nothing has been done for Count d'Estaing; at least the little that one intended to do was so much below his expectations that he did not consider it fitting to accept it—and it is quite certain that he will not be marshal of France. Count Dillon, second in command, will not be brigadier (general) immediately, although the queen has strongly recommended it . . . Viscount de Noailles will be treated a little better because of family connections . . . So far as I am concerned, I was offered a bonus in money, which I declined to accept as though I had already an income of a hundred thousand, since in reality the acceptance would not have improved my position. All three of us received the croix militaire; but the authorities refused to give it to old captains who under our command had had bullets pass right through their body. It was my feeling that we could not accept such tokens of honor when these brave (soldiers) did not receive them, but I was compelled to adopt the policy of the majority. The kindness which the king and queen have shown, however, repays me completely for these trivial annoyances. The king, who is not very communicative, has talked to me several times, even at his *grand couvert.* I was astonished at his memory and knowledge of the smallest details concerning the events of the war. The queen has conversed with me in the most delightful manner. She takes our part, and she does so with the warmth of friendship. Through her beauty and charm, she makes us regret that we have but one life apiece to sacrifice for her. Staël,

---

to Sweden and its monarch. Being born south of the Baltic made him doubly proud, it seems, of being a Swede. Note by present author.

Fersen,[1] and I are invited to all the little festivities and suppers which the court gives for the royal family in Versailles during the carnival, and we are the only foreigners, Austrians included, who participate. This is what brings comfort! After such kindness one gladly rushes into a rain of bullets, and if I had an income of two hundred thousand a year, I should never have anything more to do with the ministers.

As yet no plan has been made for the next campaign (in America). Mr. de Guichen has finally left with eighteen vessels and five thousand marines. This force, if it arrives in time, should be sufficient to keep our possessions, but not to take the offensive. The troops are composed almost exclusively of contingents of three or four hundred men per regiment, and without any of their own higher officers. Although I am indebted to a similar arrangement for the luck which eventually gave me the command over an army division, I am convinced that it is a poor system—different contingents mingled together in one corps, without colours, without esprit de corps.

I wish they (the French authorities) would give me four hundred men from the Royal Suédois regiment, with officers of my own choice; that they would increase the number of soldiers by an equal number of recruits, for whom I should procure Swedish officers; and I am convinced that such a corps, under the name of 'the Swedish volunteers,' or any other name one might choose to give them, would do good service. The war in America may be considered as the preliminary to one in Sweden, if we are so unfortunate as to have any. To be successful, however, I need the all-powerful protection of the king, for I expect nothing from the ministers with whom I have to deal. Moreover, I am convinced that it will be necessary to send troops to the American continent. The Americans are now weaker and the Englishmen stronger than ever before. The former are tired of the war, are ruined by it, and will soon seek some peaceful settlement. Their antipathy against the French and their sensitiveness about their independence has induced Congress to refuse the offer of a contingent of troops that was made to it. Franklin keeps saying that they (the Americans) don't need them, but either they are deceiving themselves or are speaking against their own inner convictions."[2]

---

[1] Fersen had not yet left for America.
[2] Pp. 83-86.

February 29, 1780. After telling Sparre that he has completely recovered from the effects of his wound and hopes to return soon to the field of action, Stedingk continues: "Eight regiments have been selected for embarkation. The wise decision has finally been made to send out whole regiments instead of contingents, as heretofore. We do not yet know who is to command these troops, but in all probability it will be Rochambeau. He is a man of talent, but he is systematic and will not swerve from the established regulations. I do not know him very well, and I suspect that he is one of those who criticise us a bit, consequently I have no hopes of being employed by him. . . . .

Marquis de Lafayette has to-day taken farewell of the court and returned to the insurgents. When we know what kind of people they are, we cannot help admiring his persistency and courage. Liked by everybody, worshiped by his family, rich, in (official) favor, and, because of commanding a regiment, having the opportunity to participate in the war together with his own countrymen, he yet goes off to America and exposes himself to a defeat merely to support the cause which he has once embraced, and perhaps to be buried under a structure which is about to collapse . . . . Americans ought certainly to raise a statue to Lafayette."[1]

June 18, 1780. At the Chateau de la Trousse. "Upon my return from the campaign in America I was well received (in France) and my company was much in demand. I considered that the road to honor and success had been opened to me. I was mistaken. The older generation saw in our actions more temerity than leadership, and the younger thought that in our opportunity to distinguish ourselves we had already reaped a sufficient reward. Carried away by the yearning for honor, and realizing that such could be obtained in America, a country that they had formerly looked down upon with disdain, all men wanted to be sent there, and considered it was time that we should relinquish our claims. But since they couldn't very well refuse me permission to go there, they intended to send me along as an adjutant to General Rochambeau. My friends considered this

---

[1] Pp. 87-88.

The type of people that Stedingk had met on the American mainland had not been the best; hence these words. His discouragement, however, was but temporary; in reality he himself was ready to return to America.

unsuitable for me, and the end of the matter was that I was appointed colonel en second of the Alsace regiment, which is perhaps the most handsome one in France, but which will be the last one to embark, just because of its elegance and because the nephew of the Elector is colonel (Colonel propriétaire) of the regiment."[1]

Stedingk's anticipation of returning to America was not realized. He writes on January 23, 1783, from Paris: "The peace preliminaries were signed last Monday (the 20th). The peace is honorable for France and advantageous for our allies, without being humiliating for England—all circumstances considered—and of such character that it ought to prove lasting. The whole honor of having brought this about should be given to Vergennes, whose influence on this ground has surely increased. (The Englishman) Fitz Herbert was presented to the royal family last Tuesday, and has offered his good wishes. He is a brilliant man, very supple and charming—a fitting mediator. Franklin is triumphing, but in that modest way which becomes a philosopher who knows on what insignificant causes the world events may depend."[2]

December 17, 1783. "The public festivities in celebration of the peace have been quite trivial. The king did not want any at all, and answered the deputies of the city that they ought instead to pay their debts, but custom prevailed. Some fire-works, a public ball for the people in the new hall—which was especially well illuminated—and a very simple illumination in the city are all that were arranged to celebrate this glorious peace."[3]

We have seen that upon his return from America, Stedingk accepted the order Pour le Mérite Militaire from France. To this, in the same year, 1779, his own monarch added the military Order of the Sword (with Grand Cross, 1789). At the same time that he was appointed colonel en second of the Alsatian regiment of infantry (1780), he was commissioned colonel of cavalry of a regiment of dragoons in northern Finland. It thus happened that in 1780 Stedingk, was simultaneously, the head of two regiments, in two widely separated parts of Europe. That he received the American Order of the Cincinnati has already

---

[1] P. 89.
[2] P. 101.
[3] P. 107.

been indicated. As in Fersen's case, however, he was not permitted by his king, because of its republican symbolism, to display it publicly or officially.[1]

Colonel Stedingk remained in France until 1787, returning, as ambassador from Sweden, in 1814. He had the chief command

---

[1] Stedingk's letters contain some delicate correspondence with the king on the matter, in which it appears between the lines that Stedingk was not a little astonished at the objection of his monarch. But upon second thought, of course, Stedingk graciously acknowledged the viewpoint of Gustavus III and externally sustained the objection.

Cf. p. 138, note 2. Also von Dardel, *op. cit.,* pp. 108-109. Dardel writes and quotes as follows:

"Gustavus III, who during his sojourn in Italy had learned that Swedish officers who had participated in the American war of independence and had been honored by President (!) Washington with the Order of the Cincinnati had carried this decoration in Paris, has issued an order to (the Swedish minister in Paris) de Staël forbidding them to display it. Upon Stedingk, who outside of Fersen was the only Swede who had received this distinction, this decree made a painful impression and on the 2nd of March 1784, he wrote a letter to Gustavus III, in which he sought to explain why he had neglected to ask his permission to carry the order. Stedingk treats also of this delicate subject in a letter to Sparre of the 22nd of March: 'With great impatience I am awaiting His Majesty's answer to the letter I had the honor to write to him. Only such an answer can relieve the anxiety over having aroused his displeasure because of this deuced Cincinnatus. I have always regarded this institution as a bit of childishness, which has had only one justifiable raison d'être, that of having practiced benevolence. Only the fact that I have considered it of such slight importance has prevented me from consulting the king about the affair. It would be unfortunate, indeed, if this trivialty should disturb his good opinon about me, but he is too good and just for that. Another factor which may prove embarrassing is this: When I no longer carry my Cincinnatus, other bearers of the order will be offended at my repeated distraction, for this is the reason I give (for not displaying it), since I do not like to give the real reason.'"

The answer of the king, dated March 26, 1784, shows how difficult it was for him, despite his early acknowledgement of American independence, to modify his deep-seated monarchial viewpoint. He willingly forgives Stedingk for his thoughtlessness, but feels impelled to explain his objections and refusal.

So far as Stedingk is concerned, however, we cannot help feeling that deep down in his heart he bore the emblem of the Cincinnatus with a certain pride.

For a Swedish description of the Order of the Cincinnatus, see Hermelin, *op. cit.,* pp. 36-39.

of the Swedish troops at Savolax, in the war with Russia, 1788. Because of his wide knowledge of European problems, his extreme popularity, and extraordinary tact in all matters of importance, he was in 1790 appointed Swedish ambassador to St. Petersburg. He made an excellent diplomat. He enjoyed great favor at the court of Catherine II, and at that of her successor Alexander I, and was much respected by other members of the diplomatic corps. It was Stedingk who, after Sweden's last and disastrous war with Russia—in which she lost Finland—concluded peace with that country, on April 25, 1809, whereupon he again became his country's representative in Russia for two years. He held knighthood in Russian orders, and was once dubbed by Catherine II herself.

Sweden showed further its appreciation of Stedingk by naming him Lord of the Realm in 1796, a title implying singular distinction; a Swedish nobleman, 1797; a baron, in 1800; and a count in 1809. Already a general of infantry, he became Field Marshal in 1811; and was second in command of the Swedish troops that were sent to Germany in 1813, under the Crown Prince Carl Johan (Bernadotte). When Bernadotte assumed command of the North German army, Stedingk was given full charge of the Swedish troops, and took part in the battles of Dennewitz, Gross-beeren, and Leipzig. Later he accompanied the Crown Prince to Paris and participated in the treaty of peace, May 30, 1814, to which he became a signatory. The same year he was decorated by Prussia.

Stedingk's later years were full of honor and activity. Among these was his appointment as chancellor of the military academy at Carlberg, in 1818, and his commission as special ambassador to Russia in 1826. His ninetieth birthday, ten years later, became the occasion for elaborate congratulations from all Europe, especially from the Swedish people of course; and upon his death, which occurred on January 7, 1837, in Stockholm, the whole army was ordered to take on official mourning. He left five daughters and a son, Ludvig Ernst, born 1794, who succeeded his father in the Order of the Cincinnati.

Baron von Stedingk, as he was generally known, was one of the most brilliant military and political men of his country, if not of Europe. He was prominent not only in the annals of Swedish history, but contributed to the settlement of international problems of two continents. Undoubtedly his calm temperament, his simplicity of life, and general optimism, helped to explain his

longevity. The veteran of many wars, he yet lived to see sixty
years of an independence for which he had once fought in
America. That he outlived most if not all high-rank officers of
the American Revolution is obvious.—In private life, also,
Stedingk was noted for all the good qualities of heart and mind:
modesty, delicacy, amiability, disinterestedness.

A few years after the death of Stedingk, his son-in-law, Count
Björnstjerna, general and Swedish minister to London, published
in three volumes, in French, the memoirs and correspondence of
his illustrious father-in-law (see bibliography). Since this work
seems to be but little known in this country—the present writer
finally obtained a copy from the Congressional Library,—it has
been thought advisable, as a suitable conclusion, to append here a
translation of Stedingk's letters on the two most important engagements in which he took part in his American campaign. To my
knowledge, these letters have never before been translated, in full,
into English.

From the Memoirs of Curt von Stedingk[1]
Letter from M. de Stedingk to Count de Creutz
Grenada, July 12, 1779.

We have just taken Grenada. The importance of this victory, of great
consequence in itself, is greatly intensified by the conduct of the troops.
They covered themselves with glory. Never, perhaps, was there a more
spirited or brilliant assault.

Just picture to yourself a high, steep, isolated mountain, dominating the
cone-shaped hill which surrounds it. It towers protectively over the town,
the road, and the fort, and is covered from top to bottom with a system
of triple entrenchments. On its crest is a battery imbedded in masonry,
with five 36-calibre cannons, which have to be captured before reaching
the summit. This place appeared so strong that Mylord Macartney deemed
it impregnable. Consequently he had brought his most precious effects
there for safe keeping, and the other inhabitants had followed his example.

The attack was made in three columns; we were thirteen hundred men;
and I performed the duties of a kind of major-general of this little army.
I marched with M. de Dillon at the head of the central column, the one
which was attacking the big battery and the intrenchments of the rear.
The object of attack given me by M. d'Estaing was the mouths of the
cannon of the principal battery.—I shall never in my life forget the mark
of esteem that he showed me on that occasion; I owe him the unpre-
judiced testimony that nobody could exhibit greater valor and intelligence
than he has done; and he is also worshipped by his troops.

---

[1] See *Mémoires posthumes*, I, 31-44.

After having landed on the second of the month in a little bay, out of cannon range, the troops followed some paths over rocks and mountains to a common center for the final preparations. It was impossible to use horse mounts, and very frequently we crawled on all fours in the mud and on the stones. On the third (of July) the time for the attack had arrived, and after refreshing the troops we began the assault at three o'clock in the morning. The whole mountain was afire; from the fort and the buildings in the port came an incessant stream of bullets, and cannon balls and grenades rained down upon us. We kept on marching without shooting off a gun; the palisades were torn away; the intrenchments captured, one after the other; the charge was repulsed; and still the dying cried: Long live the King!

It is difficult to conceive to what point of exaltation a soul may rise at such moments, and how far man ascends above man. Every soldier was a hero. As I was marching at the head of the advance guard, I came to a fortified battery, but found it so high that in spite of my efforts I was unable to reach the embrasure. My strength was exhausted; I begged the soldier following me to help me, and offered him my purse. "No," he said, "I want to be the first one to mount; I shall help you afterwards." Later, at the moment of mounting he was killed, and his body served as a step for me. In less than an hour the mountain stronghold was captured. The soldier for a time gave himself up to all the fury of an irritated conqueror; but I had the good fortune to save the lives of two English officers at the very moment when they were about to be stabbed, and at the risk of being disabled myself. The booty was immense, and we captured sixty buildings in the port.

The naval battle also was severe. Byron arrived at the break of day with twenty-one ships of the line. He had the wind in his favor, and came down upon us with full sails and in the best order, while we were lying still without yet having drawn up in battle line. In addition, the currents favored him; he manœuvered to perfection; and fought with a genuinely English desperation. Barrington conducted himself like a hero; three times his flag was shot down; and three times it was raised again. At the end of the action there was not a cannon left that was not put out of service; but in the absence of cannon he continued his fire (from small arms) from the quarterdeck and the mast platforms. In spite of all that the English fleet was completely defeated, and only escaped from us through the darkness of the night and the advantage of a favorable wind. M. d'Estaing owes his victory in particular to the superiority of marksmanship and skill of the cannoneers, an advantage which through the whole war will be on the side of the French.

(Interpolation by Björnstjerna) After this splendid victory of arms, Count d'Estaing sailed his fleet toward the southern part of the United States of America, where the English had accumulated war material. Aided by Americans he succeeded in landing his troops near Savannah in Georgia. The main fortress, occupied by the English, and already formidable in itself, had been strengthened still more by detached forts and abatis which had been constructed there.

Count d'Estaing, nevertheless, resolved to storm it, despite the counsel of Stedingk, who regarded the undertaking as rash and impracticable.

We shall here reproduce the letter which M. de Stedingk, upon his return to France, wrote to the King Gustavus III, and in which he narrates the story of Count d'Estaing's expedition against Savannah.

Letter of M. de Stedingk to his King
Paris, January 18, 1780.

SIRE:

I had demanded of Your Majesty the permission of giving you a few details about our last expedition, but observing that nothing was said about it in the public announcements, and suspecting the reason whch prompted the Ministry to withhold the publication of anything, I have been forced to keep silent, since, unfortunately, one does not dare to write what can not be seen and read by everybody. At last an account has appeared in the Gazette de la Cour which is true enough but much abridged. I must add that it was neither chance, unfavorable winds, nor broken steering-gear, which, in my opinion, took us to Georgia, but a prudent and well considered plan. The English apparently intend to concentrate their forces in the southern possessions of America. The retention of these provinces, richer and more beautiful though less cultivated than those of the North, is a desire nearest to their hearts. Being already masters of Florida and Georgia, all they need is to take Charlestown in order to have complete control over the two Carolinas and perhaps Virginia. They have a large supporting party in these provinces; three quarters of the inhabitants are Tories. Besides, foreseeing that they will be obliged to give up something at the treaty of peace, they prefer to cede New England, which, situated as it is beween Canada and the southern provinces, will necessarily be dependent upon them both politically and commercially. The English menaced Charlestown last summer, but finding this place in a state of defense, and being exceedingly anxious to preserve their men, they retired without further measures. Count d'Estaing foresaw that if he could destroy the little army of General Prevost before any aid from New York could arrive, the English would be done for in this part of America, where, in reality, their total strength at the time was limited to 550 men at St. Augustine. Enterprising, active, and courageous, as he is to the highest degree, he overcame all difficulties, risks, and dangers which he encountered on the way . . . The anchoring of his fleet was dangerous, the season advanced, storms frequent, and the landings accompanied by unprecedented difficulties. But, on the other hand, he counted on an effective support from the Americans, in an affair which concerned them so closely; on the valor of his troops; the good will of their commanders; and especially on the good fortune which has so often attended him. The Americans sent us scarcely two thousand men; besides they were so poorly armed, so poorly clothed, and, I dare say, so poorly commanded, that we were never able to get much help from them. We received poor service from the pilots and the natives of the country.

In general it appears as though the Americans were tired of the war. Their troops seem to be composed almost wholly of deserters and vagabonds of all nations, and even when we compare them with those of the English, who are excellent, acclimated, and well trained and fed, one is astonished that America was not subjugated a long time ago. But one has a far better opinion of English ministers (for instance) than of English generals. It took two weeks to effect a landing of all our troops. I spent three days and three nights in a sloop without being able to cross the (sand) bars, and taking in so much water that in order to make known our distress we were obliged to fire our guns continually, although at each shot we ran the risk of blowing up, several sloops having been destroyed that way. These delays, and the meagre acquaintance of the Americans with their own country, gave Prevost ample time to unite his forces in Savannah in very strong battle lines, and to mount more than 120 cannons in batteries. These lines were laid out in an alternation system, with a redoubt made and palisaded for two hundred men, and a battery, in horseshoe shape, of ten to twelve cannons in embrasures. Behind this first line, within half a gunshot, was a trench in which had been placed low batteries with stone foundations and 2-calibre guns. The troops stayed in these lines and were there protected from our cannon fire. Behind the trench were storeplaces for arms with cannons and cavalry obstructions, to which men might fall back when driven from the lines, and on the height where the town was situated there were three batteries which were pointed toward the first redoubts. The whole entrenchment was surrounded by an abatis of cedar. The strength of this position and the solidity of the works compelled us to force the entrenchment and commence a regular siege. We were much too small a number for the multifarious duties which the situation demanded, only comprising in all some six thousand men, including the Americans. Besides we were seriously short of necessary accessories and often had no bread. The ardor and boldness of the troops made up for everything. We established our camp within half a gun-shot's range from the lines, in a forest which protected us a little, but which did not guarantee protection from the bullets of the enemy.

A trench was opened at 20 fathoms away, and the first night our works were extended to within 60 fathoms of the lines. There we planted the batteries after having mounted 12- and 10-calibre cannons and balls with infinite trouble, having been obliged to pull them in the sand by hand on marine gun-carriages. Our fire soon silenced that of the enemy who had only six guns of 24-calibre, and the rest nines. In all the sorties which they attempted they were vigorously repulsed. Finally we were approaching the moment when we might expect to harvest the fruit of all our endeavors, when a frightful weather, the lack of food, and sickness which broke out in the crew, distressed our fleet considerable. The constant complaints of the officers who commanded it at last compelled Count d'Estaing to change his first plan, which he did very reluctantly, as he said. For that purpose a place was selected far removed from our trench, where the enemy had less breastworks, but where there were local difficul-

ties that were at least equally serious. During the course of our campaign
I had commanded the central division. On the day of the attack Count
d'Estaing wanted to give me the vanguard, and put me in charge of the
assault upon the redoubt which constituted the key to a successful enterprise. I dared refuse it and predict to him the outcome of the day's
events. I begged him not to put me in command of anything and to
permit me just to march beside him with a gun. This statement was not
made with the intention of pleasing anyone, and certainly not Count
d'Estaing; I expected that he would leave me without any command.
But instead of that he strengthened my column with 400 Americans and
put me in charge of one of the (two) principal attacks. Count Dillon
commanded the other; Viscount de Betisi, the advance guard; and Count
de Noailles, the reserve corps. Then, like brave men, we resolved to
conquer or perish. This is the spirit that had been infused into our troops.

We crossed a swamp where we sank in up to our waists; we made
our way between the redoubts and batteries which bombarded us with
grape-shot at exceedingly close range, the space between only allowing
six men abreast. Finally we reached the last trench, where I had the
pleasure to plant the American flag, but the enemy renewed his attack
and our people were annihilated by his cross fire. The advance guard,
having been driven from the redoubt which it had captured, fell back on
the end of the (main) columns and put them in disorder.

Then came the order to retreat, which had to take place beneath the
fire of the batteries. I returned with only twenty men, most of them
wounded. Out of 900 men of elite troops that constituted my column,
400 men and 39 officers were killed or wounded. Count Dillon lost about
as many. I had been wounded at the beginning of the assault (which
lasted only about three quarters of an hour in all), but fortunately that
did not prevent me from marching. The moment of our retreat was the
most grievous in my life; the cries of the dying pierced my heart. Up
to that point all had succeeded; my doubts had disappeared; I had believed
our attack infaillable; and—that hope had been shattered. I longed for
death, and I would have found it perhaps if it had not been necessary to
save 400 men who, being almost entirely without officers, and under the
fire of the enemy, found themselves blocked in their retreat by a destroyed
bridge. I had the good fortune to rally them and to make my retreat in
such order that the enemy who had come out to pursue us could not
catch us. I returned to camp two hours after the rest, carrying my
wounded also . . .[1]

I am, etc.
Curt v. Stedingk

---

[1] The remainder of the letter is of a more personal nature. Stedingk
indicates, however, that he might resume the narrative about the battle
of Savannah at some later date. Nothing more of importance was written
down, however, so far as we know, though there may have been reports
viva voce.

CONCLUDING REMARKS

It appears from what we have learned in the last three chapters that there were, as Odhner claimed, "about seventy" Swedish officers, most of them young noblemen, who took some part, either directly or indirectly, in the American war of independence. And what is more: there were about that number on the French and American side. Of these about two thirds saw active duty on our shores or in North American waters. In addition, there must have been some Swedish citizens whose records as French officers in American service have been lost entirely. How many there were of these is of course a matter of conjecture. The present writer does not believe that the number was very large. Including the Danes, however, we can now put the minimum number of Scandinavian officers in the joint service of America and France at seventy-five.

Most of the Swedish naval officers attained, as mentioned, as high rank as was possible for a foreigner to procure. All survivors, almost without exception, became (later in life) prominent in the history of their own country—a third of them very prominent—showing the character of the participants who got training in America. Of those who served on American soil, von Fersen and von Stedingk were awarded the order of the Cincinnati. Of all the Swedish officers at least three died of disease while on active duty, nine were killed or died of wounds received in action, and eleven more were wounded. Some were taken prisoners and several lost their personal possessions in the war. Through the Swedish king, many of his subjects in French service received financial aid from their own government to help pay the heavy traveling expenses—which served as an inducement to enlist—and there was besides a constant flow of applications for additional help. The drain on various public and individual Swedish funds was not an insignificant item, although in return Sweden could expect to derive some profit eventually from the unusual training received by its officers abroad. How much the Swedes were actuated in their participation by motives of democracy and liberalism, or love for America and its people, is of course impossible to say. That the motives were both selfish and unselfish is perhaps the nearest to the truth. Many wanted more training and better employment, though few, if any, lacked either entirely. All survivors, it seems, returned to Sweden after the war.

The achievements of the Swedish officers, while not of momentous consequences perhaps in the final result, are nevertheless worthy of some interest and recognition. They were men of valor and ability, who contributed to the American cause all that was possible under the circumstances, and far more than we have hitherto known.

BIBLIOGRAPHY

(Only sources which have contributed some positive information are included in this list.)

Unpublished Sources

CREUTZ, GUSTAF PHILIP, COUNT DE
  a. Ambassadören Greve Creutz' depecher (enskilda) 1777-1779. Excerpts in Swedish and French.
  Private and separate letters and dispatches preserved in Riksarkivet, Stockholm.
  b. Ambassadören Greve Creutz' depecher 1779-1783. Samlingen Gallica. Excerpts in Swedish and French.
  Reports and recommendatory notes.

DUBOURG, MARIE FRANÇOIS JOSEPH MAXIME, BARON CROMOT-
  MS. copy of Journal depuis mon départ de France 26 Mars 1781, jusqu'au 18 Novembre de la même année que l'Armée aux ordres de M. L. C. te de Rochambeau est entré dans ses quartiers d'hiver.
  No date. Contains list of officers' quarters in Newport. In Rider Collection of Brown University Library, Providence, Rhode Island.

MERITFÖRTECKNINGAR OCH ANSÖKNINGAR RÖRANDE SVENSKA FLOTTAN
  Extracts from applications and qualification lists, made by Erik Naumann, Stockholm; contains in chronological order, list of achievements by Swedish officers in French naval service.

TROLLE, HENRIK AF
  Various letters (memorialer) by "General-Admiral" Trolle to His Royal Majesty, Gustavus III, 1782-1784. Selected from collection in Riksarkivet.

Published Sources

ANREP, G.
  Svenska Adelns Ättar-Taflor. I,-IV, Stockholm, 1848-1864. A very valuable source of identification of Swedish officers of the nobility.

BABCOCK, KENDRIK CHARLES, PH.D.
The Scandinavian Element in the United States.   Published
by the University of Illinois, 1914.
Deals almost entirely with modern Scandinavian immigrants.

BAIN, R. NISBET
Gustavus III and his Contemporaries.   London, 2 vols., 1894.
A good work for orientation.

BAKER, WILLIAM S.
Itinerary of General Washington June 15, 1775 to December
23, 1783.   Philadelphia, 1892.

BALCH, THOMAS
The French in America during the War of Independence of
the United States, 1777-1783.   Translated by Thomas Willing Balch.   Philadelphia, 1891.   Especially Vol. II.

BALL, WILLIETTA GODDARD
Scandinavian Contributions to Early American Art.   The
American Scandinavian Review, III, 7-15, January, 1915.

BANCROFT, GEORGE
History of the United States of America from the Discovery
of the Continent.   Vol. VI, revised edition; Boston, 1876.
History of the United States.   Vol. I, New York, 1890.

BENSON, ADOLPH BURNETT
Our First Unsolicited Treaty.   The American Scandinavian
Review, VII, January-February, 1919, 43-49.
(with George H. Ryden) John Hanson, American Patriot.
Ibid., VIII, July, 1920, 525-529.
Pehr Kalm's Journey to North America.   Ibid., X, June,
1922, 350-355.

BIGELOW, JOHN
The Complete Works of Benjamin Franklin.   I-X.   New
York and London, 1887-1888.

BIOGRAPHICAL DICTIONARIES
Biografiskt Lexicon Ofver Namnkunnige svenska män.
Uppsala och Örebro, 1836-1857;   23 vols.;   Supplement,
Lund, 1836.   Then continued as:
Svenskt Biografiskt Lexicon.   Ny Följd.   Örebro och Stock-
holm, 1857-1907;   10 vols.
The National Cyclopedia of American Biography.   (Various
articles.)

BJÖRNSTJERNA, MAGNUS FREDRIK FERDINAND, COMTE DE
Mémoires posthumes du feld-maréchal comte de Stedingk, redigés sur des lettres, dépêches et autres pièces authentiques laissés à sa famille, par le géneral comte de Biornstierna. 3 vols.; Paris, 1844-1847.

BLANCHARD, CLAUDE
The Journal of Claude Blanchard, commissary of the French Auxiliary Army sent to the United States during the American Revolution. 1780-1783. Translated from a French Manuscript by William Duane, and edited by Thomas Balch. Albany, 1876.

BOËTHIUS (see Tengberg)

BOTTA, CHARLES
History of the War of Independence of the United States. I-II, Boston, 1826.
Mentions Steding(k) II, 219.

BROGLIE, PRINCE DE
Relation du voyage du Prince de Broglie en 1782 aux États-Unis d'Amérique et dans L'Amérique du Sud. No place. No date. Pamphlet, pp. 35-73.
The prince disagrees with Fersen on some personal matters, such as the beauty of Miss Hunter.

BROWN, JOHN
Original Memoirs of the Sovereigns of Sweden and Denmark from 1766 to 1818. I-II, London, 1895.
There is also a French version of these memoirs.

CALENDRIER FRANÇAIS, POUR L'ANNÉE COMMUNE 1781
De L'Imprimerie Royale. Newport, Rhode Island (?).
Gives Fersen's name at head of Rochambeau's aides-de-camp.

CARLSON, KNUTE EMIL
Relations of the United States with Sweden, University of Pennsylvania dissertation, 1921. Especially Chapter I, on negotiations during the American Revolution.
Not an exhaustive work, but valuable so far as it goes.

CASTRÉN, GUNNAR
Gustav Philip Creutz. Hälsingfors, 1917.
A splendid monograph.

CHEVALIER, E.
Histoire de la Marine Française, Paris, 1877.
Contains the names of several Swedish officers in the
French navy who took part in the American Revolution.
Casualty lists valuable.

CRONHOLM, NEANDER N.
A History of Sweden. Vols. I-II. Especially Vol. II,
Chapter XXXIV. Published for the author. Chicago, New
York and London, 1902.
Valuable, but not always reliable in details. Makes too
sweeping generalizations. Must be read with caution.

DARDEL, H. L. VON
Fältmarskalken von Stedingks tidigare levnadsöden skildrade
efter brev till Överståthållare Carl Sparre. Örebro Dag-
blads tryckeri, 1922.
Chapter II deals with Curt von Stedingk's participation
in the American war.

DEUX-PONTS, COUNT WILLIAM DE
My campaigns in America. Boston, 1868.
Comments on the fact that in 1654 the head of the main
branch of the House of Zweibrücken (Deux-Ponts) was
elected King of Sweden (Charles X Gustavus).

DONIOL, HENRY
Histoire de la Participation de la France à l'Établissement
des États-Unis d'Amérique. 5 vols. and supplement. Paris,
1886-1892.
A voluminous record containing official correspondence.

DUMAS, LIEUT.-GEN., COUNT MATHIEU
Memoirs of His Own Time; including the Revolution, the
Empire, and the Restoration. 2 vols. Philadelphia, 1839.

(LES) ÉTATS MILITAIRES POUR LES ANNÉES 1778-1784
Useful, but full of "shocking inexactitudes."

FAUST, ALBERT BERNHARD
The German Element in the United States. I-II, Boston
and New York, 1909.
The most exhaustive work on the subject; but at least
once the author makes the mistake that all people bearing
cognomens spelled like German names are German.

FERSEN, HANS AXEL, COUNT VON
The French Army in the Revolutionary War. Count de Fersen's private letters to his father, 1780-1781. Translated from the French by Georgine Holmes. In Mag. of Am. Hist., Vol. 25, January, 1891, 55-70; February, 1891, 156-175.
A good translation.
Letters by De Fersen, aid-de-camp to Rochambeau, written to his father in Sweden, 1780-1782. Translated for the magazine. Mag. of Am. Hist., Vol. 3, April, 1879, 300-309; June, 1879, 369-376; July, 1879, 437-448.
(See, also, Gurnell, Klinckowström, Lauzel, and Wormeley.)

FLACH, F. F.
Greve Hans Axel von Fersen. Minnesteckning jemte utdrag ur hans dagbok och brefvexling. Stockholm, 1896.

FORBES, ALLAN AND CADMAN, PAUL F.
France and New England. Vol. I. Boston, State Street Trust Company, 1925.
A handsome illustrated volume, with maps, giving a description of the marches of the French army through New England, with copious references to the more prominent participants, including Fersen.

FORD, WORTHINGTON CHAUNCEY
The Writings of George Washington. I-XIV. New York and London, 1889-1893 (see, also, Library of Congress).

FRANKLIN, BENJAMIN
The Life and Writings of Benjamin Franklin. Memoirs of Benjamin Franklin written by himself, and continued by his grandson and others. Philadelphia, I-II, 1834.
Contains much of his correspondence and record of diplomatic transactions. (See Wharton.)
(See, also, Bigelow, Smyth, and Sparks.)

(THE) FRENCH IN NEWPORT
See Newport Historical Magazine, Vol. 2, January, 1882, 176-178.

FRENCH MINISTRY OF FOREIGN AFFAIRS
Les Combattants Français de la Guerre Américaine, 1778-1783. Listes établies d'après les documents authentiques déposés aux Archives nationales et aux Archives du ministère

de la Guerre publiées par les soins du Ministère des Affaires
Étrangères. Paris, 1903.
A valuable source.

FRIIS, AAGE
Bernstorffsche Papiere. Ausgewählte Briefe und Aufzeich-
nungen die Familie Bernstorff betreffend aus der Zeit 1732
bis 1835.
Esp. Vol. III; Copenhagen and Christiania, 1913.
A large invaluable compilation. Preface is in German;
letters in French; and notes in Danish.

GARDENER, ASA BIRD
The Order of the Cincinnati in France. Published by the
Rhode Island State Society of the Cincinnati, 1905, in 350
copies.
Gives biographical facts about Fersen and Stedingk.

GAULOT, PAUL
A Friend of the Queen (Marie Antoinette and Count de
Fersen.) Translated by Mrs. Cashel Hoey. I-II, London,
1894.

GEFFROY, A.
Gustave III et la Cour de France. 2 vols. Esp. Chap. VI,
Vol. I. Paris, 1867.
A sympathetic, inspiring account of an interesting relation.

GEIJER, E. G.
Des Könings Gustav III nachgelassene und fünfzig Jahre
nach seinem Tode geöffnete Papiere. Uebersicht, Auszug
und Vergleichung von E. G. Geijer. Aus dem Schwed-
ischen. I-II, Hamburg, 1843.

GRASSE, COMTE DE
The Operations of the French Fleet under the Comte de
Grasse in 1781-82 as described in two contemporaneous
journals. Bradford Club Series, No. 3, New York, 1864.

GRIFFIN, APPLETON PRENTISS CLARK
List of works relating to the French Alliance in the American Revolution. U. S. Library of Congress, 1907.

GURNELL, RACHEL
The Comte de Fersen. In Gentleman's Magazine, N. S., Vol.
48, March, 1892, 295-306. Same in Living Age, Vol. 193,
May 7, 1892, 368-374.

A slightly sentimental emphasis on Fersen's relation to Marie Antoinette based on the work of Klinckowström.

HALE, E. E. AND E. E. HALE, JR.
Franklin in France, I-II. Boston, 1887-1888.

HANSON, GEORGE A., M.A.
Old Kent: The Eastern Shore of Maryland; notes illustrating the most ancient records of Kent County, Maryland, etc. Baltimore, 1876.
Gives genealogy of John Hanson.

HEITMAN, FRANCIS B.
Historical Register of Officers of the Continental Army, 1775-1783. Washington, D. C., 1914.

HERMELIN, S. G., (See Taube.)

JAMES, B. B. (See Veditz.)

JOHNSON, AMANDUS
The Swedish Settlements on the Delaware. University of Penn., Philadelphia, D. Appleton & Co., Agents, New York, I-II, 1911.
The authoritative work on the subject.
Contributions by Swedes to American Progress, 1638-1921. Pp. 1-64, Committee of the Swedish Section of America's Making, Inc., New York, 1921.

JOHNSON, E. R. AND COLLABORATORS
History of Domestic and Foreign Commerce of the United States. Washington, D. C., 1915.

JONES, C. C. (Translated from two journals written by unknown French officers)
The Siege of Savannah. Albany, 1874.
Contains an account of von Stedingk's part in the siege of Savannah.

KALM, PEHR
En resa till Norra America på Kongl. Swenska Wetenskaps Academiens befallning och Publici kostnad. Stockholm, 1753-1761, I-III. Later editions may be obtained in German, Dutch, English and French.
A record of a Swedish scientist's observations in colonial America in 1750.

KEEN, GREGORY B., LL.D.
The Descendants of Jöran Kyn of New Sweden. Philadelphia. The Swedish Colonial Society, 1913.

176   *Sweden and the American Revolution*

KEIM, DE B. RANDOLPH
Rochambeau. A Commemoration by the Congress of the
United States of America of the services of the French
auxiliary forces in the war of independence. Washington,
Government Printing Office, 1907.

KERGUELEN-TRÉMAREC, YVES-JOSEPH   (Rear-admiral)
Histoire des Événements des Guerres Maritimes entre La
France et L'Angleterre, Depuis 1778 jusqu'au 1796, an 4 de
la République.   Imprimerie de patris, 1796.

KLINCKOWSTRÖM, LE BARON R. M. DE
Le Comte de Fersen et La Cour de France. Extraits des
Papiers du Grand Marechal de Suède, comte Jean Axel de
Fersen, publiés par son petit-neveu.   I-II, Paris, 1877-1878.
Introduction and Pièces Justificatives, pp. 36-73, contain
letters in French from America. An article on Fersen,
based on this work, is found in Temple Bar, Vol. 55 for
January, 1879, 76-90, and the same article is reproduced
in Living Age, Vol. 140, February 8, 1879, 367-375.

LAFAYETTE, MARQUIS DE
Various letters.

LAUZEL, A.
Count Fersen. In Nation, Vol. 27, August 29, 1878, 128-
129; and September 5, 1878, 142-143.
Based on Klinckowström.

LEACH, M. ATHERTON
John Morton. The American Scandinavian Review, III,
226-232, July-August, 1915.
Some Account of New Sweden and Her Churches. Ibid.,
September, 1914, 16-23.

LIBRARY OF CONGRESS
List of the Benjamin Franklin Papers in the Library of Congress. Compiled by W. C. Ford. Washington, 1905.
A List of Washington Manuscripts in the Library of Congress.   Washington, 1901.

LOSSING, BENSON J.
Pictorial Field Book of the Revolution. Esp. Vol. II, 307-
308.   New York, 1860.

MALLOY, WILLIAM M.
Treaties, Conventions, International Acts, Protocols and Agreements between the United States of America and other powers 1776-1909. I-II, Washington, D. C., 1910. English text of Swedish treaty of 1783 is found in II, pp. 1725-1735.

MAUGRAS, GASTON
Le Duc de Lauzun et la Cour de Marie-Antoinette. Paris, 1895.
Based in part on letters by Fersen.

MERLANT, JOACHIM
Soldiers and Sailors in the American War for Independence. Translated by Mary Bushnell Coleman. New York, 1920.

MORÉ, COMTE DE (The Chevalier de Pontgibaud)
A French volunteer of the War of Independence. Translated by Robert B. Douglas. Paris, 1898.
Of some general interest, but has nothing about Swedish officers.

MORTON, JOHN (Biography of)
Biography of the Signers of the Declaration of Independence. Second edition, revised, Vol. III, 137-144. Philadelphia, 1828; printed at Nashville, Tenn., 1831.

MUNTHE, ARNOLD
Henrik af Trolle; Fredrik af Chapman; Otto Henrik Nordenskjöld; Gustaf III, Politiken och Flottan 1772-1784.
In series of Svenska Sjöhjältar, Vol. VI. Stockholm, 1911.
An up-to-date, valuable work. Illustrated.

NAVAL RECORDS OF THE REVOLUTION
Washington, 1906.
Record for November 8, 1780, announces registry of a Pennsylvania brigantine of eight guns and crew of twenty, named *Queen of Sweden,* showing friendly, grateful attitude.

NOAILLES, VICOMTE DE
Marins de Soldats Français en Amérique pendant la Guerre de l'Indépendance des États-Unis (1778-1783). Paris, 1903.
A very important work. Apparently as accurate as can be compiled without knowledge of the Scandinavian languages.

NEWSPAPERS:
   Providence Gazette, 1778-1784.
   Newport Mercury, 1780-1783. (Available copies)
   Independent Chronicle and the Universal Advertiser (Boston),
   1777-1781.
   Royal Gazette, New York, 1781.
   Pennsylvania Packet or the General Advertiser, 1778.

NORDISK FAMILJEBOK. KONVERSATIONS-LEXIKON OCH REALEN-
CYKLOPEDI
   I-XVIII. Stockholm, 1876-1894.
   Various articles on Swedish officers.

NORTH, FRANCES PIERREPONT
   Newport a hundred years ago. Lippincott's Magazine,
   LIX, 497.

ODHNER, C. T.
   Sveriges politiska historia under konung Gustaf III: s regering. Andra delen, 1779-1787. Stockholm, 1896.

ORTH, SAMUEL P.
   Our Foreigners. The Chronicles of America, Vol. 35. New
   Haven, Yale University Press, 1920.
        Obviously influenced by the shadows of the World War,
        but on the whole sympathetic toward the contribution of
        the Scandinavian element to the development of the United
        States.

OSTERBERG, J. S.
   Svenskarne i Rhode Island. Svea Publishing Co., Wor-
   cester, Mass., 1915.

PERKINS, JAMES BRECK
   France in the American Revolution. Boston, 1911.
        Quotes Fersen several times as authority, though there is
        no mention of Swedish officers, as such.

PRESTON, HOWARD WILLIS
   Rochambeau and the French Troops in Providence in 1780-
   1781-1782. Providence, R. I., 1924. Reprinted with additions from the Rhode Island Historical Society Collection.
        Gives exact location of Nicholas Brown House, where
        Fersen stayed while in Providence. A photo of the
        house in its present dilapidated and desecrated state is
        found opposite page 8.

PROCEEDINGS in the Senate and the House of Representatives upon the reception and acceptance from the State of Maryland of the statues of Charles Carroll of Carrollton and of John Hanson, recently erected in statuary hall of the capitol. Washington, Government Printing Office, 1903.
A series of addresses.

RAMSAY, DAVID, M.D.
The History of the American Revolution, I-II. London, 1793.

RICHARDSON, HESTER DORSEY
Side-Lights of Maryland History with Sketches of Early Maryland families. Williams and Wilkins Co., 1913.

ROCHAMBEAU, COMTE DE
Memoires militaires, historiques et politiques. Tomes I-II, Paris, 1824. (MDCCCIX)

ROSENGARTEN, J. G.
American History from German Archives with Reference to the German Soldiers in the Revolution and Franklin's Visit to Germany. Part XIII of a Narrative and Critical History prepared at request of the Pennsylvania-German Society. Lancaster, Pa., 1904.
Not always reliable. Claims Fersen and Stedingk both are Germans, though in Swedish service.

ROSENTHAL, LEWIS
America and France. New York, 1882.

RUSSELL, CHARLES HOWLAND
The French Alliance, address delivered before the Rhode Island State Society of the Cincinnati, at the State House at Newport, Rhode Island, on July 4, 1904. New York, 1904.

RYDEN, GEORGE H. (See Benson)

SAINT-MAURICE, NARCISSE HENRI EDOUARD FAUCHER DE
Notes pour servir a l'Histoire des Officiers de la Marine et de l'Armée Français qui ont fait la Guerre de l'Indépendence américaine. Quebec, 1896.

SCHARF, J. THOMAS
History of Western Maryland. Philadelphia, 2 vols., L. H. Everts, 1882.

SCHLESINGER, ARTHUR MEIER, PH.D.
The Colonial Merchants and the American Revolution, 1763-1776. New York, Columbia University Studies, Faculty of Political Science, Vol. 78, 1918.

SEGUR, LOUIS PHILIPPE, COUNT
Memoirs and Recollections.   3 vols., London, 1825.

SMYTH, ALBERT HENRY
The Life and Writings of Benjamin Franklin.   New York, The Macmillan Co., 1905-07, I-X.
Authoritative work, but poorly indexed.

SOULÉS, FRANÇOIS
Histoire des troubles de l'Amérique anglaise.   Paris, 1787. 4 volumes.
Gives the date of the first Hartford conference between Washington and Rochambeau as September 27, 1780.

SPARKS, JARED
The Works of Benjamin Franklin.   10 vols.   Boston, 1840.
The Writings of George Washington, I-XII, Boston, 1837.

STEDINGK, BARON VON   (See Björnstjerna)

STEVENS, JOHN AUSTIN
The French in Rhode Island, Mag. of Am. History, III, July, 1879, pp. 385 ff.

STONE, EDWIN M.
Our French Allies.   Providence, 1884.

TALLEYRAND, PRINCE DE   (See Broglie)

TAUBE, B.
Berättelse om Nordamerikas Förenta Stater 1784.   Bref till Kanslipresidenten af frih. S. G. Hermelin, Stockholm, 1894.

TEGNÉR, ELOF
Gustaf Mauritz Armfelt, efter Armfelts efterlemnade papper samt andra handskrifna och tryckta källor, 1-3.   Andra Upplagan, Stockholm, 1893-1894.   I, 29-30.

TENGBERG, RUDOLF OCH SIMON BOËTHIUS
Sverige under partitidehvarfvet, 1718-1809.   Part V of Sveriges Historia från äldsta Tid till våra Dagar, 1877-1881. I-VI.   Stockholm.

TONER, J. M., M.D.
The Medical Men of the Revolution.   Philadelphia, 1876.

TOWER, CHARLEMAGNE
The Marquis de Lafayette in the American Revolution. Philadelphia, 1895.

VEDITZ, C. WILLIAM A. AND BARTLETT BURLEIGH JAMES
The Revolution, constituting Vol. VI of The History of North America. Philadelphia, 1904.

VICTORY, BEATRICE MARGUERITE
Benjamin Franklin and Germany. Americana Germanica, No. 21. Publications of the University of Pennsylvania, 1915.

WASHINGTON, GEORGE
Letters, edited by Sparks and Ford (which see).

WHARTON, FRANCIS
The Revolutionary diplomatic correspondence of the United States. Vols. I-VI. Washington, 1889.

WINSOR, JUSTIN
Narrative and Critical History of America. Vol. VI, Boston, 1887.
Considers Fersen's letters very valuable.

WORMELEY, KATHERINE PRESCOTT
Diary and Correspondence of Count Axel Fersen, Grand Marshal of Sweden, relating to the Court of France. A translation of Klinckowström's Le Comte de Fersen et la Cour de France, with a few interpellations. Boston, Hardy, Pratt & Co., 1902.

APPENDIX

Treaty of amity and commerce, 1783.[1] Concluded April 3, 1783; ratified by the Continental Congress July 29, 1783; proclaimed by Congress September 25, 1783.[a]

ARTICLES

I.	(Peace and friendship)
II.	Most favored nation privileges.
III.	(Privileges to Swedish in the United States)
IV.	(Privileges to United States citizens in Sweden)
V.	Religious freedom.
VI.	Effects from deceased persons.
VII.	Commerce in case of war.
VIII.	Extent of freedom of commerce.
IX.	Contraband goods.
X.	Goods not contraband.
XI.	Ships' papers in case of war.
XII.	Navigation in time of war.
XIII.	Detention of contraband goods, etc.
XIV.	Goods on enemy's ships.
XV.	Instructions to naval vessels.
XVI.	Bond from privateers.
XVII.	Recaptured ships; embargoes.
XVIII.	Regulations for war with common enemy.
XIX.	Prizes.
XX.	(Shipwrecks)
XXI.	Asylum for ships in distress.
XXII.	Property rights in case of war.
XXIII.	Letters of marque.
XXIV.	(Shipping privileges)

---

[1]William M. Malloy, *Treaties, Conventions,* etc., II, 1725-1735.

[a] Translation from the original, which is in the French language. This treaty terminated by the limitation contained in the first separate article, *post,* fifteen years from the day of ratification, but Articles II, V, VI, VII, VIII, IX, X, XI, XII, XIII, XIV, XV, XVI, XVII, XVIII, XIX, XXI, XXII, XXIII, and XXV, as well as the separate Articles I, II, IV, and V, were revived by Article XII of the treaty of September 4, 1816, with Sweden and Norway, and were again revived by Article XVII of the treaty of July 4, 1827.

XXV. Visit of war vessels.
XXVI. (Consuls)
XXVII. Ratification.
Separate article. Duration.

SEPARATE ARTICLES

 I. Defense of ships in Sweden.
 II. Defense of ships in United States.
 III. (Mutual protection of merchant vessels)
 IV. Right to trade.
 V. Freedom of vessels from search.

The King of Sweden, of the Goths and Vandals, &c., &c., &c., and the thirteen United States of North America, to wit: New Hampshire, Massachusetts Bay, Rhode Island, Connecticut, New York, New Jersey, Pennsylvania, the counties of New Castle, Kent, and Sussex on Delaware, Maryland, Virginia, North Carolina, South Carolina, and Georgia, desiring to establish, in a stable and permanent manner, the rules which ought to be observed relative to the correspondence and commerce which the two parties have judged necessary to establish between their respective countries, states, and subjects: His Majesty and the United States have thought that they could not better accomplish that end than by taking for a basis of their arrangements the mutual interest and advantage of both nations, thereby avoiding all those burthensome preferences which are usually sources of debate, embarrassment, and discontent, and by leaving each party at liberty to make, respecting navigation and commerce, those interior regulations which shall be most convenient to itself.

With this view, His Majesty the King of Sweden has nominated and appointed for his Plenipotentiary Count Gustavus Philip de Creutz, his Ambassador Extraordinary to His Most Christian Majesty, and Knight Commander of his orders; and the United States, on their part, have fully empowered Benjamin Franklin, their Minister Plenipotentiary to His Most Christian Majesty.

The said Plenipotentiaries, after exchanging their full powers, and after mature deliberation in consequence thereof, have agreed upon, concluded, and signed the following articles:

Article I

There shall be a firm, inviolable, and universal peace, and a true and sincere friendship between the King of Sweden, his heirs and successors, and the United States of America, and the subjects of His Majesty, and those of the said States, and between the countries, islands, cities, and towns situated under the jurisdiction of the King and of the said United States, without any exception of persons or places; and the conditions agreed to in this present treaty shall be perpetual and permanent between the King, his heirs and successors, and the said United States.

Article II

The King and the United States engage mutually not to grant here-after any particular favour to other nations in respect to commerce and navigation which shall not immediately become common to the other party, who shall enjoy the same favour freely, if the concession was freely made, or on allowing the same compensation, if the concession was conditional.

Article III

The subjects of the King of Sweden shall not pay in the ports, havens, roads, countries, islands, cities, and towns of the United States, or in any of them, any other nor greater duties or imposts, of what nature soever they may be, than those which the most favoured nations are or shall be obliged to pay; and they shall all enjoy the rights, liberties, privileges, immunities and exemptions in trade, navigation and commerce which the said nations do or shall enjoy, whether in passing from one port to another of the United States, or in going to or from the same, from or to any part of the world whatever.

Article IV

The subjects and inhabitants of the said United States shall not pay in the ports, havens, roads, islands, cities, and towns under the dominion of the King of Sweden, any other or greater duties or imposts, of what nature soever they may be, or by what name soever called, than those which the most favoured nations are or shall be obliged to pay; and they shall enjoy all the rights, liberties, privileges, immunities and exemptions in trade, navigation and commerce which the said nations do or shall enjoy, whether in passing from one port to another of the dominion of His said Majesty, or in going to or from the same, from or to any part of the world whatever.

ARTICLE V

There shall be granted a full, perfect, and entire liberty of conscience to the inhabitants and subjects of each party; and no person shall be molested on account of his worship, provided he submits so far as regards the public demonstration of it to the laws of the country. Moreover, liberty shall be granted, when any of the subjects or inhabitants of either party die in the territory of the other, to bury them in convenient and decent places, which shall be assigned for the purpose; and the two contracting parties will provide, each in its jurisdiction, that the subjects and inhabitants respectively may obtain certificates of the death, in case the delivery of them is required.

ARTICLE VI

The subjects of the contracting parties in the respective States may freely dispose of their goods and effects, either by testament, donation, or otherwise, in favour of such persons as they think proper; and their heirs, in whatever place they shall reside, shall receive the succession even *ab intestato,* either in person or by their attorney, without having occasion to take out letters of naturalization. These inheritances, as well as the capitals and effects which the subjects of the two parties, in changing their dwelling, shall be desirous of removing from the place of their abode, shall be exempted from all duty called "droit de détraction" on the part of the Government of the two States, respectively. But it is at the same time agreed that nothing contained in his article shall in any manner derogate from the ordinances published in Sweden against emigrations, or which may hereafter be published, which shall remain in full force and vigor. The United States, on their part, or any of them, shall be at liberty to make, respecting this matter, such laws as they think proper.

ARTICLE VII

All and every one of the subjects and inhabitants of the Kingdom of Sweden as well as those of the United States, shall be permitted to navigate with their vessels, in all safety and freedom, and without any regard to those to whom the merchandizes and cargoes may belong, from any port whatever; and the subjects and inhabitants of the two States shall likewise be permitted to sail and trade with their vessels, and, with the same liberty and safety to frequent the places, ports, and havens of Powers enemies to both or either of the contracting parties, without being in any wise molested or troubled, and to carry on a commerce not only directly from the ports of an enemy to a neutral port, but even from one port of an enemy to another port of an enemy, whether it be under the jurisdiction of the same or of different Princes. And as it is acknowledged by this treaty, with respect to ships and merchandizes, that free ships shall make the merchandizes free, and that everything which shall be on board of ships belonging to subjects of the one or the other of the contracting parties shall be considered as free, even though the cargo, or a part of it, should belong to the enemies of one or both, it is nevertheless provided that contraband goods shall always be excepted; which being intercepted, shall be proceeded against according to the spirit of the following articles. It is likewise agreed that the same liberty be extended to persons who may be on board a free ship, with this effect, that, although they be enemies to both or either of the parties, they shall not be taken out of the free ship, unless they are soldiers in the actual service of the said enemies.

ARTICLE VIII

This liberty of navigation and commerce shall extend to all kinds of merchandizes, except those only which are expressed in the following article, and are distinguished by the name of contraband goods.

ARTICLE IX

Under the name of contraband or prohibited goods shall be comprehended arms, great guns, cannon-balls, arquebuses, musquets, mortars, bombs, petards, granadoes, saucisses, pitch-balls, carriages for ordnance, musquet-rests, bandoleers, cannon-powder, matches, saltpetre, sulphur, bullets, pikes, sabres, swords, morions, helmets, cuirasses, halbards, javelins, pistols, and their holsters, belts, bayonets, horses with their harness, and all other kinds of arms and instruments of war for the use of troops.

ARTICLE X

These which follow shall not be reckoned in the number of prohibited goods, that is to say: All sorts of cloths, and all other manufactures of wool, flax, silk, cotton, or any other materials; all kinds of wearing apparel, together with the things of which they are commonly made; gold silver coined or uncoined, brass, flesh, salted fish, cheese, butter, beer, oil, wines, sugar; all sorts of corn or pulse, tobacco; all kinds of spices, salted and smoked flesh, salted fish, cheese, butter, beer, oyl, wines, sugar; all sorts of salt and provisions which serve for the nourishment and sustenance of man; all kinds of cotton, hemp, flax, tar, pitch, ropes, cables, sails, sail-cloth, anchors, and any parts of anchors, ship-masts, planks, boards, beams, and all sorts of trees and other things proper for building or repairing ships. Nor shall any goods be considered as contraband which have not been worked into the form of any instrument or thing for the purpose of war by land or by sea, much less such as have been prepared or wrought up for any other use: all which shall be reckoned free goods, as likewise all others which are not comprehended and particularly mentioned in the foregoing article, so that they shall not by any pretended interpretation be comprehended among prohibited or contraband goods. On the contrary, they may be freely transported by the subjects of the King and of the United States, even to places belonging to an enemy, such places only excepted as are besieged, blocked, or invested; and those places only shall be considered as such which are nearly surrounded by one of the belligerent powers.

ARTICLE XI

In order to avoid and prevent on both sides all disputes and discord, it is agreed that, in case one of the parties shall be engaged in a war, the ships and vessels belonging to the subjects or inhabitants of the other shall be furnished with sea-letters or passports, expressing the name, property, and port of the vessel, and also the name and place of abode of the master or commander of the said vessel, in order that it may thereby appear that the said vessel really and truly belongs to the subjects of the one or the other party. These passports, which shall be drawn up in good and due form, shall be renewed every time the vessel returns home in the course of the year. It is also agreed that the said vessels, when loaded, shall be provided not only with sea-letters, but also with certificate containing a particular account of the cargo, the place from which the vessel sailed, and that of her destination, in order that it may be known whether they carry any of the prohibited or contraband merchandizes mentioned in the 9th article of the present treaty; which certificates shall be made out by the officers of the place from which the vessel shall depart.

ARTICLE XII

Although the vessels of the one and of the other party may navigate freely, and with all safety, as is explained in the 7th article, they shall, nevertheless, be bound, at all times when required, to exhibit, as well on the high seas as in port, their passports and certificates above mentioned; and, not having contraband merchandize on board for an enemy's port, they may freely and without hindrance pursue their voyage to the place of their destination. Nevertheless, the exhibition of papers shall not be demanded of merchant-ships under the convoy of vessels of war, but credit shall be given to the word of the officer commanding the convoy.

ARTICLE XIII

If on producing the said certificates it be discovered that the vessel carries some of the goods which are declared to be prohibited or contraband, and which are consigned to an enemy's port, it shall not however be lawful to break up the hatches of such ships, nor to open any chests, coffers, packs, casks, or vessels, nor to remove or displace the smallest part of the merchandizes, until the cargo has been landed in the presence of officers appointed for the purpose, and until an inventory thereof has been taken; nor shall it be lawful to sell, exchange or alienate the cargo or any part thereof, until legal process shall have been had against the prohibited merchandizes, and sentence shall have passed declaring them liable to confiscation, saying nevertheless as well the ships themselves, as the other merchandizes which shall have been found therein, which by virtue of this present treaty are to be esteemed free, and which are not to be detained on pretence of their having been loaded with prohibited merchandize, and much less confiscated as lawful prize. And in case the contraband merchandize be only a part of the cargo, and the master of the vessel agrees, consents, and offers to deliver them to the vessel that has discovered them, in that case the latter, after receiving the merchandizes which are good prize, shall immediately let the vessel go, and shall not by any means hinder her from pursuing her voyage to the place of her destination. When a vessel is taken and brought into any of the ports of the contracting parties, if upon examination she be found to be loaded only with merchandize declared to be free, the owner, or he who has made the prize, shall be bound to pay all costs and damages to the master of the vessel unjustly detained.

ARTICLE XIV

It is likewise agreed that whatever shall be found to be laden by the subjects of either of the two contracting parties, on a ship belonging to the enemies of the other party, the whole effects, although not of the number of those declared contraband, shall be confiscated as if they belonged to the enemy, excepting nevertheless such goods and merchandizes as were put on board before the declaration of war, and even six months after the declaration, after which term none shall be presumed to be ignorant of it, which merchandizes shall not in any manner be subject to confiscation, but shall be faithfully and specifically delivered to the owners, who shall claim or cause them to be claimed before confiscation and sale, as also their proceeds, if the claim be made within eight months, and could not be made sooner after the sale, which is to be public: provided, nevertheless, that if the said merchandizes be contraband, it shall not be in any wise lawful to carry them afterwards to a port belonging to the enemy.

ARTICLE XV

And that more effectual care may be taken for the security of the two contracting parties, that they suffer no prejudice by the men-of-war of the other party or by privateers, all captains and

commanders of ships of His Swedish Majesty and of the United
States, and all their subjects, shall be forbidden to do injury or
damage to those of the other party, and if they act to the contrary, having been found guilty on examination by their proper
judges, they shall be bound to make satisfaction for all damages
and the interest thereof, and to make them good under pain and
obligation of their persons and goods.

ARTICLE XVI

For this cause, every individual who is desirous of fitting out
a privateer, shall, before he receives letters-patent, or special
commission, be obliged to give bond with sufficient sureties, before
a competent judge, for a sufficient sum, to answer all damages
and wrongs which the owner of the privateer, his officers, or
others in his employ may commit during the cruise, contrary to
the tenor of this treaty, and contrary to the edicts published by
either party, whether by the King of Sweden or by the United
States, in virtue of this same treaty, and also under the penalty
of having the said letters-patent and special commission revoked
and made void.

ARTICLE XVII

One of the contracting parties being at war and the other
remaining neuter, if it should happen that a merchant-ship of the
neutral Power be taken by the enemy of the other party, and be
afterwards retaken by a ship of war of privateer of the Power at
war, also ships and merchandizes of what nature soever they may
be, when recovered from a pirate or sea rover, shall be brought
into a port of one of the two Powers, and shall be committed to
the custody of the officers of the said port, that they may be
restored entire to the true proprietor as soon as he shall have
produced full proof of the property. Merchants, masters, and
owners of ships, seamen, people of all sorts, ships and vessels,
and in general all merchandizes and effects of one of the allies or
their subjects, shall not be subject to any embargo, nor detained
in any of the countries, territories, islands, cities, towns, ports,
rivers, or domains whatever, of the other ally, on account of any
military expedition, or any public or private purpose whatever,
by seizure, by force, or by any such manner; much less shall it
be lawful for the subjects of one of the parties to seize or take

anything by force from the subjects of the other party, without the consent of the owner. This, however, is not to be understood to comprehend seizures, detentions, and arrests, made by order and by the authority of justice, and according to the ordinary course for debts or faults of the subject, for which process shall be had in the way of right according to the forms of justice.

Article XVIII

If it should happen that the two contracting parties should be engaged in a war at the same time with a common enemy, the following points shall be observed on both sides:

1. If the ships of one of the two nations, retaken by the privateers of the other, have not been in the power of the enemy more than 24 hours, they shall be restored to the original owner, on payment of one-third of the value of the ship and cargo. If, on the contrary, the vessel retaken has been more than 24 hours in the power of the enemy, it shall belong wholly to him who has retaken it.

2. In case, during the interval of 24 hours, a vessel be retaken by a man-of-war of either of the two parties, it shall be restored to the original owner, on payment of a thirtieth part of the value of the vessel and cargo, and a tenth part of it if it has been retaken after 24 hours, which sums shall be distributed as a gratification among the crew of the men-of-war that shall have made the recapture.

3. The prizes made in manner above mentioned shall be restored to the owners, after proof made of the property, upon giving security for the part coming to him who has recovered the vessel from the hands of the enemy.

4. The men-of-war and privateers of the two nations shall reciprocally be admitted with their prizes into each other's ports; but the prizes shall not be unloaded or sold until the legality of a prize made by Swedish ships shall have been determined according to the laws and regulations established in Sweden, as also that of the prizes made by American vessels shall have been determined according to the laws and regulations established by the United States of America.

5. Moreover, the King of Sweden and the United States of America shall be at liberty to make such regulations as they shall judge necessary respecting the conduct which men-of-war and privateers respectively shall be bound to observe, with regard to vessels which they shall take and carry into the ports of the two Powers.

Article XIX

The ships of war of His Swedish Majesty and those of the United States, and also those which their subjects shall have armed for war, may with all freedom conduct the prizes which they shall have made from their enemies into the ports which are open in time of war to other friendly nations; and the said prizes upon entering the said ports shall not be subject to arrest or seizure, nor shall the officers of the places take cognizance of the validity of the said prizes, which may depart and be conducted freely and with all liberty to the places pointed out in their commissions, which the captains of the said vessels shall be obliged to shew.

ARTICLE XX

In case any vessel belonging to either of the two States, or to their subjects, shall be stranded, shipwrecked, or suffer any other damage on the coasts or under the dominion of either of the parties, all aid and assistance shall be given to the persons shipwrecked, or who may be in danger thereof, and passports shall be granted to them to secure their return to their own country. The ships and merchandizes wrecked, or their proceeds, if the effects have been sold, being claimed in a year and a day, by the owners or their attorney, shall be restored, on their paying the costs of salvage, conformable to the laws and customs of the two nations.

ARTICLE XXI

When the subjects and inhabitants of the two parties, with their vessels, whether they be public and equipped for war, or private or employed in commerce, shall be forced by tempest, by pursuit of privateers and of enemies, or by any other urgent necessity, to retire and enter any of the rivers, bays, roads, or ports of either of the two parties, they shall be received and treated with all humanity and politeness, and they shall enjoy all friendship, protection, and assistance, and they shall be at liberty to supply themselves with refreshments, provisions, and everything necessary for their sustenance, for the repair of their vessels, and for continuing their voyage; provided always that they pay a reasonable price; and they shall not in any manner be detained or hindered from sailing out of the said ports or roads, but they may retire and depart when and as they please, without any obstacle or hindrance.

Article XXII

In order to favour commerce on both sides as much as possible, it is agreed that, in case a war should break out between the said two nations, which God forbid, the term of nine months after the declaration of war shall be allowed to the merchants and subjects respectively on one side and the other, in order that they may withdraw with their effects and movables, which they shall be at liberty to carry off or to sell where they please, without the least obstacle; nor shall any seize their effects, and much less their person, during the said nine months; but on the contrary, passports which shall be valid for a time for their return, shall be given them for their vessels, and the effects which they shall be willing to carry with them. And if anything is taken from them, or if any injury is done to them by one of the parties, their people and subjects, during the term above prescribed, full and entire satisfaction shall be made to them on that account. The above-mentioned pass-ports shall also serve as a safe conduct against all insults or prizes which privateers may attempt against their persons and effects.

Article XXIII

No subject of the King of Sweden shall take a commission or letters of marque for arming any vessel to act as a privateer against the United States of America, or any of them, or against the subjects, people, or inhabitants of the said United States, or any of them, or against the property of the inhabitants of the said United States, from any Prince or State whatever, with whom the said United States shall be at war. Nor shall any citizen, subject, or inhabitant of the said United States, or any of them, apply for or take any commission of letters of marque for arming any vessel to cruize against the subjects of his Swedish Majesty, or any of them, of their property, from any Prince or State whatever, with whom his said Majesty shall be at war. And if any person of either nation shall take such commissions or letters of marque, he shall be punished as a pirate.

Article XXIV

The vessels of the subject of either of the parties coming upon any coast belonging to the other, but not willing to enter into port, or being entered into port, and not willing to unload their cargoes or to break bulk, shall not be obliged to do it, but on the contrary, shall enjoy all the franchises and exemptions which are granted by the rules subsisting with respect to that object.

ARTICLE XXV

When a vessel belonging to the subjects and inhabitants of either of the parties, sailing on the high seas, shall be met by a ship of war or privateer of the other, the said ship of war or privateer, to avoid all disorder, shall remain out of cannon shot, but may always send their boat to the merchant ship, and cause two or three men to go on board of her, to whom the master or commander of the said vessel shall exhibit his passport, stating the property of the vessel; and when the said vessel shall have exhibited her passport, she shall be at liberty to continue her voyage, and it shall not be lawful to molest or search her in any manner, or to give her chase or force her to quit her intended course.

ARTICLE XXVI

The two contracting parties grant mutually the liberty of having each in the ports of the other, Consuls, Vice-Consuls, Agents, and Commissaries, whose functions shall be regulated by a particular agreement.

ARTICLE XXVII

The present treaty shall be ratified on both sides, and the ratifications shall be exchanged in the space of eight months, or sooner if possible, counting from the day of the signature.

In faith whereof the respective Plenipotentiaries have signed the above articles, and have thereto affixed their seals.

Done at Paris the third of April in the year of our Lord one thousand seven hundred and eighty-three.

(SEAL)   B. FRANKLIN.

(SEAL)   GUSTAV PHILIP COMTE DE CREUTZ.

SEPARATE ARTICLE (a)

The King of Sweden and the United States of North America agree that the present treaty shall have its full effect for the space of fifteen years, counting from the day of the ratification, and the two contracting parties reserve to themselves the liberty of renewing it at the end of that term.

Done at Paris the third day of April, in the year of our Lord one thousand seven hundred and eighty-three.

(SEAL)   B. FRANKLIN.

(SEAL)   GUSTAV PHILIP COMTE DE CREUTZ.

SEPARATE ARTICLES

ARTICLE I

His Swedish Majesty shall use all the means in his power to protect and defend the vessels and effects belonging to citizens or inhabitants of the United States of North America, and every of them which shall be in ports, havens, roads, or on the seas near the countries, islands, cities and towns of His said Majesty, and shall use his utmost endeavours to recover and restore to the right owners all such vessels and effects which shall be taken from them within his jurisdiction.

ARTICLE II

In like manner the United States of North America shall protect and defend the vessels and effects belonging to the subjects of His Swedish Majesty, which shall be in the ports havens, or roads, or on the seas near to the countries, islands, cities, and towns of the said States, and shall use their utmost efforts to recover and restore to the right owners all such vessels and effects which shall be taken from them within their jurisdiction.

ARTICLE III

If, in any future war at sea, the contracting Powers resolve to remain neuter, and as such to observe the strictest neutrality, then it is agreed that if the merchants ships of either party should

---

(a)   See footnote on p. 182.

happen to be in a part of the sea where the ships of war of the
same nation are not stationed, or if they are met on the high sea,
without being able to have recourse to their own convoys, in that
case the commander of the ships of war of the other party, if
required, shall, in good faith and sincerity, give them all necessary
assistance; and in such case the ships of war and frigates of
either of the Powers shall protect and support the merchant-
ships of the other: provided, nevertheless, that the ships claiming
the assistance are not engaged in any illicit commerce contrary
to the principle of the neutrality.

ARTICLE IV

It is agreed and concluded that all merchants, captains of merchant-ships or other subjects of His Swedish Majesty, shall have
full liberty in all places under the dominion or jurisdiction of the
United States of America, to manage their own affairs, and to
employ in the management of them, whomsoever they please;
and they shall not be obliged to make use of any interpreter or
broker, nor to pay them any reward unless they make use of them.
Moreover, the masters of ships shall not be obliged, in loading or
unloading their vessels, to employ labourers appointed by public
authority for that purpose; but they shall be at full liberty, themselves, to load or unload their vessels, or to employ in loading
or unloading them whomsoever they think proper, without paying reward under the title of salary to any other person whatever;
and they shall not be obliged to turn over any kind of merchandizes to other vessels, nor to receive them on board their own,
nor to wait for their lading longer than they please; and all and
every of the citizens, people, and inhabitants of the United States
of America shall reciprocally have and enjoy the same privileges
and liberties in all places, under the jurisdiction of the said realm.

ARTICLE V

It is agreed that when merchandizes shall have been put on
board the ships or vessels of either of the contracting parties,
they shall not be subjected to examination; but all examination and
search must be before lading, and the prohibited merchandizes
must be stopped on the spot before they are embarked, unless
there is full evidence or proof of fraudulent practice on the part

of the owner of the ship, or of him who has the command of her; in which case only he shall be responsible and subject to the laws of the country in which he may be. In all other cases, neither the subjects of either of the contracting parties who shall be with their vessels in the ports of the other, nor their merchandizes, shall be seized or molested on account of contraband goods, which they shall have wanted to take on board, nor shall any kind of embargo be laid on their ships, subjects or citizens of the State whose merchandizes are declared contraband, or the exportation of which is forbidden; those only who shall have sold or intended to sell or alienate such merchandize being liable to punishment for such contravention.

Done at Paris, the third day of April, in the year of our Lord one thousand seven hundred and eighty-three.

(SEAL)   B. FRANKLIN.

(SEAL)   GUSTAV PHILIP COMPTE DE CREUTZ.

ADDRESS ON JOHN HANSON BY MR. SCHIRM OF MARYLAND[1]

To John Hanson belongs the distinction of having held the highest Federal office ever conferred upon a Marylander, that of President of the United States in Congress assembled, and of having done more than any other one man in the colony to destroy the supremacy of Great Britain. John Hanson was born at Mulberry Grove, Charles County, Md., on April 3, 1721. The Hanson family was a large one, and many of them found their way into the public service. His grandfather, Colonel Hanson, fell at Lützen for the cause of religious liberty; his oldest brother, Judge Walter Hanson, was commissary for Charles County; his brother Samuel was a patriot, and presented to General Washington £800 sterling to provide shoes for his barefoot soldiers; William, the youngest brother, was examiner-general of Maryland; his son, Alexander Contee, was a patriot and intimate with Washington. He was one of the first judges of the general court and chancellor of the State; he was an elector for Washington, and compiled the laws of Maryland; his son, Samuel, was a surgeon in the Life Guards of Washington, and his son, Peter Contee, of the Maryland Line, was wounded at Fort Washington.

The first mention of John Hanson in public life is as a delegate from Charles County to the lower house of assembly, in which he served nine terms. The disputes which arose between the two houses of assembly upon the burning questions of the day brought to the lower house, composed of the representatives of the people in the province, the ablest men in Maryland. He carried to that body a matured mind, which was there trained for the higher and more important responsibilities that awaited him in a broader field. At the close of the French and Indian war the tide of immigration turned to the fertile regions of Frederick County, and thither, in 1773, John Hanson followed

[1] From *Proceedings in the Senate and House of Representatives upon the Reception and Acceptance from the State of Maryland of the Statues of Charles Carroll of Carrollton and of John Hanson*, pp. 106-111. The statue was erected in Statuary Hall in the Capitol, and was formally accepted on January 31, 1903.

the long train of sturdy home builders. In his new environment his personal magnetism was soon felt; his sound judgment and honesty of character won for him the respect and confidence of the people. His advice was eagerly sought in those times of growing dissatisfaction, and, through his efforts, the citizens of Frederick County became devoted to the principles of the Revolution and firm in their resistance to the oppressions of the mother country.

His influence constantly increased and he was the leading spirit among a band of determined patriots during the transition of Maryland from a dependent, proprietary province into a sovereign State. During this period of transition there gradually grew up side by side with the proprietary government another government—a government of the people. The latter was an outgrowth of the restless desire for freedom, and its formidable character was not suspected until it became too powerful to be checked. This new government consisted of a general convention of the province and its council of safety, while in the counties there were mass metings and committees of observation, with an embryo department of state called a committee of correspondence. Hanson was a member of the convention and served as chairman of both the committee of observation and the committee of correspondence in Frederick County. To these honors was added that of treasurer of the county, and to him were intrusted all the funds to pay the soldiers and the Delegates to Congress.

John Hanson was a silent, but no less effective, power. His activity was of that character as to require secrecy to make his plans effective. When, however, the crisis had been reached, when bold and fearless words were needed to arouse the resolution and strengthen the purpose of his compatriots, he arose in the convention in July, 1775, and with the unflinching determination of Patrick Henry declared that they would "repel force by force," and pledged himself to support the "present opposition." These were timely words. Enthusiasm was rekindled; other colonies heard them and rejoiced. From that day the colonists in Maryland were bound in closer union. Upon John Hanson primarily devolved the task of organizing and equipping the army. Money was scarce, arms and ammunition were scarcer, but his resourceful mind knew no obstacles.

Under his direction two companies of riflemen were sent to join the army at Boston, and these were the first troops that came from the South to Washington's assistance. Forty companies of minutemen were organized, and the whole of Maryland was put upon the defensive. Arms were manufactured, powder mills erected, and money provided through voluntary contributions. So thorough was his work that when 13,800 militia were required to reënforce the army, Maryland furnished much more than her full quota. That he had the confidence of the Government is evidenced from the fact that President Hancock made him one of a committee of two to transmit $300,000 to General Washington for the maintenance of the army in Canada, and by the further fact that he was one of the committee of four deputized to reorganize the Maryland troops, for which purpose Congress furnished the committee with blank commissions to be issued, under the advice of General Washington, to officers who reënlisted after the term of their enlistment had expired.

John Hanson rendered one service to his country that can not be too greatly extolled. Lord Dunmore, the proprietary governor of Virginia, conceived the plan of arming the Indians on the frontier and to make a simultaneous attack upon the colonies from the back country and from the coast. It was planned first to fall upon Fort Pitt, in Pennsylvania, and thence to work their way eastward to Alexandria, Va., in which vicinity there was a fleet of 90 British ships prepared to continue the onslaught along the waterways. The designs of Lord Dunmore were soon detected by Hanson and by his vigilance frustrated. Dr. John Connolly, one of the chief conspirators, who had been carrying dispatches from General Gage to Lord Dunmore, and who had been operating with the Cherokee, Swanee, Mingo, and Delaware tribes, with several of his comrades, fell into the hands of the minutemen of Maryland, near Hagerstown, while they were on their way to Detroit. The arrest of these allies of the King and Parliament, of General Gage and Lord Dunmore, was followed by their imprisonment, and the conspiracy died.

About four years later, in 1779, in another sphere of action, John Hanson again proved himself the man of the hour. Maryland had persistently refused to agree to the Articles of Confederation until some provision had been made for settling the question of the Western domain. That Maryland was right in her contention subsequent events have established; but a crisis had been reached upon which may have devolved the very existence of the Union. John Hanson, believing that the failure to effect a union would probably mean the loss of everything that had been achieved and that through union alone the perplexing questions could be solved, set to work to have the bar to a complete union removed. His attitude at this time was not unlike that of President Lincoln at a later period of our national history. Hanson's efforts were rewarded by the passage of an act to empower the Delegates of this State in Congress to subscribe and ratify the Articles of Confederation, and accordingly, on the 1st day of March, 1781, John Hanson and Daniel Carroll, as Delegates of the State of Maryland, put their signatures to the document which was the beginning of the indissoluble Union of the United States. This having been accomplished, he threw his entire force into the debate on the Western land question. That question was settled according to the judgment of Maryland, and out of that vast territory which became the common property of all the States were carved the newer States of Ohio, Indiana, Illinois, Michigan, and a part of Wisconsin.

John Hanson was three times elected to the Continental Congress, and after his third election was elevated to the position of President of that body. During his first and second terms in Congress he was shown the distinction of being elected also to the lower house of the State. After twenty-five years of public service, rich with the honors that become the man with a clear mind and an incorruptible heart, he retired to private life, and spent his last days at Oxon Hill, Prince George County, Md., where he died November 22, 1783.

John Hanson was one of those modest, unassuming great men who seek no glory for themselves, but find their highest reward in the good that accrues from their efforts to the great body of the people. He was essentially a thinker, a contriver, an unraveler of knotty points, a man to whom the people looked when other leaders said, "What shall we do now?" In those days, when there was great diversity of opinion among men of equal ability and patriotism, John Hanson proved himself a master in bringing to the front the central idea and enlisting the support of all men who in their adherence to the chief thought lost sight of minor differences. He was of a reflective temperament, weighing well each proposition, and standing firm by his decisions. Too little tribute has heretofore been paid to those quiet, thoughtful men who have furnished the basic ideas upon which governments have been founded and for which armies have contended. Behind the man behind the gun is the idea, the principle, the conviction, which justifies his use of arms, and without which an army becomes an irresponsible mob. It has been said that it is sweet and beautiful to die for one's country, but it is no less sublime to give to one's country sound doctrine and imperishable tenets. The statue of John Hanson, representing him in a reflective attitude, I now formally present to our country, whose Government he so grandly helped to establish.

An Outline of the French Participation in the American Revolution

Unbiased students of American history will now admit, I think, that of the many circumstances which combined to aid the colonists during the revolution none was as valuable as the support of the French people and government. The fact that France was anxious to humble proud England—her official motive was selfish of course—made her enter into the conflict with mind and soul, and it is reasonably certain that the thirteen colonies would not have gained their independence in 1783 except for the French assistance. Tomes have been written on the subject, and here it is necessary to recall but a few of the more essential features of the French participation, including in the term "French" all foreign elements that served under the flag of France.

Frenchmen, either officially or non-officially, furnished aid to the American colonies throughout the revolutionary struggle. At first, to be sure, Louis XVI and his ministers were opposed to any militant help. But by the year 1776 French "philosophers" and "encyclopedists," through their abstract discussions of changes in the organization of society and government, had unknowingly molded public opinion and fashion to an extent which they had never dreamed; and when American agents arrived in Paris, French individuals were quite ready to listen to them. The philosophers' ideas of freedom could now attach themselves to something tangible. So the authorities were gradually won over, at first privately, and, in February, 1778, publicly, by the proclamation of the alliance with the United States, followed of course by a formal declaration of war against England. It is said that Marie Antoinette embraced the American cause with special fervor, possibly because she wished to lead the fashion in this sphere as well as in everything else; but in any case, America-enthusiasm seems to have been definitely *established* as one of the fashions of the day by the Queen of France, and the colonists could be glad that she had assumed a favorable attitude.

During the years 1776 and 1777 French aid consisted of the voluntary enlistments in our army, by private individuals, such as Lafayette, without official sanction, and of the furnishing of money and supplies. Everything except food—clothing for the troops, arms and military equipment, and financial credit, had to be procured from Europe. The importance of obtaining adequate supplies need not be emphasized here. The author Beaumarchais established a private "commercial house," and the French government sold to this House at low prices and a long credit its own arms, ammunition, and other goods. This House then shipped the supplies to America, bringing back cargoes of indigo, rice, fish, and tobacco. In 1777 clothing, powder, cannon, and muskets were sent, and most of this material arrived in America. Besides, millions of francs in cash were either given outright or loaned to the colonists. American privateers, too, found refuge in the French harbors.

But the British navy did much damage. French ships were captured, and it was realized in America that the control of the sea was an enormous advantage to the English. For this and other reasons an alliance was requested by America to wage the war more effectively. American vessels in French ports were unable to put to sea because of the vigilance of the British cruisers. The coöperation of the French navy became imperative. So the independence of the Colonies was recognized by France; and on February 13, 1778, Paul Jones entered the harbor of Brest on the American man-of-war *Ranger,* carrying for the first time into a foreign port the flag of the new republic. Americans could now in French ports plan operations in Europe and send out cruisers to harry the British coasts and capture British merchantmen. From a French port sailed, in August, 1779, the *Bonhomme Richard* upon the "immortal cruise" which ended in the great night battle with the *Serapis,* and which became the talk of Europe. A part of the war, then, was already being fought in European waters.

Belligerent coöperation with the United States was inaugurated immediately after the treaty of alliance was signed, and this meant, first of all, the participation of all the French naval forces. In July, 1778, a large fleet under Count d'Estaing, bringing the first French minister to this country and a contingent of naval troops, arrived in American waters, after a few minor engagements on the way, and began operations along the New England coast. The combined attack of the Americans and French against

Newport, then held by the British, failed, however, and little was accomplished during the year 1778 "except perhaps to divert the attention of the English and keep them from new undertakings." In November the French fleet sailed for the West Indies, in which France was particularly interested.

In the summer of 1779 the naval campaign was more fortunate. The French—as we have described—captured Grenada and St. Vincent, and d'Estaign defeated the English under Lord Byron, an uncle of the poet. This was a welcome victory; and the French assistance being "earnestly demanded" in the southern states, d'Estaign returned from the West Indies in September, 1779, with his fleet and four thousand troops, and united with the American forces under General Lincoln in the siege of Savannah. The attack was characterized by extraordinary bravery, but ended in defeat, leaving several hundred killed and wounded before the fortifications. As we have seen, it was at Savannah and Grenada that several Swedish officers were present.

In 1779-1780 the scene of the conflict in America had shifted, then, to the South, to Georgia and the Carolinas, the British desiring to cut off the southern states entirely. In the meantime, Spain desired to enter the struggle, being anxious to recover Gibraltar, Minorca, Jamaica, and Florida from the English, and in July, 1779, formed an alliance with the United States. The French and Spanish navies joined, would, it was believed, constitute a force far stronger than that of Great Britain and give control of the seas to the Allies. As a result the sphere of activity was, ultimately, immeasurably increased, geographically, and many naval engagements and military sieges henceforth took place—as we can learn from references to them by Swedish officers, for instance—on remote territories or in remote waters little known by average students of the Revolution. We can not enumerate them all here. There were several lesser conflicts during the year 1780, especially in southern and West Indian waters; but, as a whole, this was a "year of disasters," and in August the situation for a time seemed hopeless. Washington's correspondence revealed the desperate need for money and naval superiority. The latter was obtained through the final union of the French and Spanish fleets, and other needs were satisfied by Lafayette, who had gone back to France in 1779 to plead the American cause, and had returned to the United States in April, 1780, with the promise of an auxiliary army and more substantial aid in other respects.

On July 10, 1780, a French fleet under Admiral de Ternay arrived at Newport, which had previously been evacuated by the British, bringing fifty-five hundred men under the command of Count de Rochambeau. The moral effect alone of this timely assistance had a salutary influence on the spirits of the colonists. The Frenchmen paid for their purchases in real money, instead of in depreciated American paper, and although the French forces were doomed to a life of military inactivity for eleven months, in Rhode Island, the mere presence of the foreigners revived the hopes of some conclusive action in the near future. The opportunity for this action came in 1781.

Early in that year two expeditions were undertaken by the French fleet against the English in Virginia, and though no determining results were achieved, they at least prevented the enemy from undertaking a disastrous offensive. The fleet returned to Newport. Admiral Ternay had died in the interim and been succeeded by Admiral de Barras, and in West Indian waters Count de Grasse with a powerful fleet had replaced Count d'Estaign. An offensive of six weeks duration by the combined French and Spanish forces against the British stronghold at Pensacola, Florida, in the spring of 1781, was successful, and on May 8 the English garrison capitulated. With the French at Pensacola served, as we have noted, some gallant Swedish officers. The time of definitive coöperation of French and American arms was approaching. It was decided to concentrate all efforts against the English at Yorktown, Virginia. The plan was to unite the two French fleets, those of de Barras at Newport and of de Grasse in the West Indies, in or near the Chesapeake Bay, and to unite the armies of Rochambeau and Washington for the attack on land. The French army broke camp at Newport on June 10, marched overland via Hartford, Connecticut, and in the beginning of July the two armies were finally united, on the Hudson. From there the combined forces proceeded cross-country south to Philadelphia and Baltimore.

The Spanish did not coöperate directly with the Americans, but were willing to guard French interests in the West Indies while de Grasse operated in American waters. Thus released from duty in or near his own territory, de Grasse sailed in

August, 1781, for the Chesapeake, defeated the English under Admiral Graves on September 5, and about the same time landed on Jamestown Island thirty-four hundred troops spared from the French possession of San Domingo. Five days later he was joined by the fleet of de Barras, from Rhode Island. Through the enforced withdrawal of Admiral Graves from the Chesapeake region, the allied land troops could be transported unmolested down the Bay by water to Yorktown, where, in October, as we know, a complete victory was won by the Allies. The perfect coöperation of the French and American forces on both land and sea had asserted itself, and had brought the desired result.

The surrender of Cornwallis was the beginning of the end, so far as military operations on the American continent were concerned. The French expeditionary army went into winter-quarters near Williamsburg, Virginia, and in June, 1782, started its journey northward toward the port of embarkation for home. The troops reached Rhode Island in November; were fittingly received and fêted in Newport and Providence; reached Boston, after a disagreeable march, on December 7, some soldiers deserting on the way to make their future home in America; and on Christmas Eve, 1782, the fleet under Vaudreuil sailed for France, carrying with it the French auxiliary army. Duc de Lauzun's legion, however, remained south and did not leave until the following May, "when it embarked at the Capes of Delaware." Rochambeau, who had turned over his command to Baron de Vioménil, sailed on January 11, 1783, for France.

Yet, after the battle of Yorktown the war had been continued by the French,—subsequent home operations by Americans do not concern us here,—especially on water, and was continued for almost two years. Captures of English vessels were made and battles fought everywhere between the American coast and the "mouths of the Ganges." "Exultant over the great success of the Virginia campaign, de Grasse set sail for the West Indies . . . in November, 1781. After a stormy passage of three weeks, the fleet reached Martinique and during the winter months it achieved some small successes." But on April 12, 1782, de Grasse's fleet was completely routed by the English under Rodney, the French losing three thousand men and five ships. De Grasse himself was made a prisoner. What was left of the French fleet found refuge at Cap François, where ten Spanish ships came out and protected

its entrance into the harbor.   The defeat was the most disastrous
that had ever happened to the French navy.   In the Far East,
however, the French carried off the chief honors during the years
1782 and 1783, the significance of which has often been over-
looked.   At all events, Rodney's victory over de Grasse had no
effect on the final peace negotiations, so far as American interests
were concerned, and on September 3, 1783, the formal treaty of
peace was signed by all belligerents.   The United States had won
their independence.

INDEX OF NAMES

(Names of naval vessels are printed in italics.
Names of Swedish officers are designated by an asterisk (*).)

A

Adams, John, 24, 31, 33, 34, 35, 36, 38, 51.
Achif, L', 102.
Actionnaire, L', 106, 128.
Aiguillon, Mme. d', 59.
Alembert, Jean Le Rond d', 59, 65.
Alexander I, Emperor of Russia, 161.
Alexandre, L', 97, 102.
Allen, Andrew, 84.
Alliance, 41.
Amazone, L', 116.
*Aminoff, Feodor Mauritz, 87.
Amitié, L', 124.
Amphion, L', 105, 118.
Amphitrite, L', 118.
Amsterdam, 42.
Amsterdam, brig, 46.
*Anckarloo, David, Capt., 35, 122.
*Anckarloo, Fredrik Magnus, 92, 122.
Andromaque, L', 106, 113, 114.
Annapolis, Md., 133.
Annibal, L', 88, 108.
Anrep, G., 5, 99, 108, 122.
Antilles, The, 17, 112, 154.
Ardent, 21, 88, 110.
Argo, 118.
Ariel, 17, 116.
*Armfelt, E. L., Capt., 90, 122-123.
*Armfelt, Gustaf Mauritz, 123.
Artois, Count of, 123.
Astrée, L', 116.
Auguste, L', 96, 100, 106, 112.
Austria, 41.
Aymar, Chevalier d', 100.

B

Balch, Thomas, 101, 108.
Baltic, The, 11, 13, 45.
Baltimore, Md., 133, 134.

Bancroft, George, 14, 18, 23, 25, 68, 69, 148.
Barras, Count de, 132, 133.
Beaumarchais, Caron de, 59.
Benzelius, Adolph (Benzilstjerna), 70.
Bernadotte, Carl Johan, Prince, 161.
Bernstorff, A. P. Count, Danish minister of foreign affairs, 26, 27, 30, 38, 42.
Betisi, Viscount de, 166.
Biddle, Edward, 84.
*Bildt, Carl Daniel, 123.
Bille, Danish naval officer, 9.
Biscay, Bay of, 97.
*Bjelke, Nils, 94.
Björnstjerna, M. F., Count, 162.
Blanche, La, 100.
*Blessing, David Gustaf, 89, 92, 94, 95.
Boston, Mass., 107, 116, 145.
Bougainville, French naval commander, 100, 116.
Bourgoyne, La, 145.
Brest, France, 107, 116, 124, 126, 132, 152.
Bretagne, La, 110.
Broglie, Victor François, Duc de, 13, 101, 151, 153.
Brown, John, British historian, 25, 38-39.
Brown, Nicholas, 132.
*Brummer, A. F., 90, 92, 95-96.
Bryan, George, 83.
Byron, John, Admiral, 105, 151, 154, 155.

C

Cadiz, Spain, 42, 97.
Carl August, Duke of Augustenburg, 139.

Carlos III, King of Spain, 59.
Caton, Le, 108.
Carlson, Knute Emil, 25.
Carlyle, Thomas, 135.
Carmichael, William, 14, 15, 16, 37, 41.
Carné, de, foreign naval officer in French service, 88.
Castrén, Gunnar, 56, 59, 61.
Castries, Charles Eugène, Marquis de, 18, 94, 95, 103, 104, 115.
Catherine II, Empress of Russia, 25, 37, 63, 161.
Cattegat, 105.
*Cederström, Olof, 96.
Ceylon, island of, 122, 126.
Chabert, Marquis de, 112.
Champagny, de, foreign naval officer, 88.
Charles XIII, King of Sweden, 139.
Charles, Prince of Lorraine, 59.
Charmante, La, 107.
Chastellux, Chevalier de, 4, 134.
Chesapeake Bay, 8, 108, 109, 133, 134.
Chester County, Pa., 81.
Choiseul, E. F., duc de, 59.
Cincinnati, Order of, 129, 136, 138, 139, 159, 160, 161, 167.
Claghan, Capt., 45.
Clozen, French officer in America, 133, 134.
Concorde, La, 118.
Coninck, de, Dutch agent, 38.
Conquérant, Le, 94, 97, 103, 104.
Cooke, Joseph, Capt., 46.
Cooper, Samuel, 41.
Copenhagen, Denmark, 24, 30, 34, 38.
Cordova, Don Louis, Spanish commander, 125.
Cornwallis, Lord, 16, 98, 106, 112, 136, 138.
Coromandel, Asia, 127.
Couronne, La, 107.
Crawford, Gideon, Capt., 44, 45.
Creutz, Carl Johan, 59.
Creutz, Gustav Filip, Count de, 5, 6, 7, 9-13, 16, 20, 30, 49, 56-65, 89,

90-93, 99, 101, 106, 107, 109, 110, 111, 112, 115, 116, 118, 120, 121, 122, 124, 126, 127, 131, 137, 150, 151, 152, 162.
Cronholm, Neander N., 53.
Cuddalore, India, 124.
Custine, de, French officer, 133.

D

Damas, Count de, 132, 133.
Dana, Francis, 38.
Danish officers, 9.
Davis, Charles Lukens, General, 86.
Deane, Silas, 40.
*De Frese, of de la Marck's regiment, 123.
*De Frese, George K., 89, 92, 96, 97, 99.
*De Frese, Hans, 123.
Denmark, 14, 16, 24, 25, 26-27, 31, 34, 54, 55.
Destin, Le, 119.
Deux-Ponts, Counts de, 134.
Diadème, Le, 154.
Diane, La, 109.
Dickenson, John, 83, 84.
Diderot, Denis, 50, 65.
*Diedrichs, 128.
Digges, Thomas, 34.
Dillon, Count Arthur, 149, 152, 156, 162, 166.
*Döbeln, K. von, 122, 123-124.
Dominica, West Indies, 94, 102, 110, 112, 119.
*Du Bordieu, 95.
Dubourg, Cromot-, 133.
Duc-de-Bourgoyne, Le, 101.
Dumas, C. W. F., American minister to The Hague, 37.
Dumas, G. M., Count, French general, 132.

E

East Indies, 9, 44, 90, 94, 97, 123, 124.
*Egerström, A. J., 128.
Egmont, Mme. d', 65.
Ellery, William, 38.

*Engageante, L', 97.
English Channel, 8, 97.
*Enigheten, 97.
Estaing, Charles Hector, Count d', 21, 88, 90, 91, 102, 104, 105, 106, 110, 117, 118, 148, 149, 151, 152, 154, 155, 156, 162-166.
*Eveillé, L', 128.

F

Faust, Albert Bernhard, 69.
*Feif, Carl Donat (the Younger), 92, 97.
*Feif, Gustaf Casten (Kasten), 89, 92, 97.
*Fendant, Le, 105, 106.
*Fersen, Hans Axel, Count von, 1, 2, 4, 23, 65, 90, 98, 129-146, 147, 150, 157, 160, 167.
*Fier, Le, 97.
Finland, 125, 159, 161.
Fisher, Danish naval officer, 9.
Fitz-Herbert, English envoyé, 159.
*Fleming, Herman af Liebnitz, 87.
Florida, 8, 17.
*Fock, Berndt Wilhelm, Baron, 125.
*Fock (Robeck), Johan Henric, Baron von, 90, 98.
*Fondelin, de, 128.
Fort Royal, 111.
Fox, Joseph, 83.
Franklin, Benjamin, 13, 15, 19, 20, 22, 41, 42, 47, 49, 50, 51, 53, 54, 62, 63, 66, 82, 83, 85, 124, 157, 159.
Franzén, Carl Michael, Swedish Bishop, 63, 66.
Frederick the Great, King of Prussia, 40.

G

*Gahn af Colquhoun, Carl Pontus, 125.
Gálvez, Don Bernardino, de, General, 114, 115.
Gardiner, Asa Bird, 129.
Gardiner's Bay, 143.

*Gedda, Georg, 125.
Geer, Baron de, Swedish envoyé, 15.
Geijer, Erik Gustaf, historian, 32, 56.
Genoa, 55.
*Gentile, La, 107.
Geoffrin, Mme. de, 56, 59.
George III, 19.
Germany, 13, 16, 43, 45.
Gibraltar, 17, 90, 96, 111, 112, 125, 126, 127.
*Gloire, La, 101.
Gloria Dei Church, Philadelphia, 70.
*Glorieux, Le, 110.
Good Hope, Cape of, 123.
Gothenburg, Sweden, 30, 44, 45, 46, 48, 49.
Gottland, island of, Sweden, 110.
Gouvion, French officer of engineers, 141.
Grasse, F. J. P., Count de, Admiral, 96, 100, 102, 103, 106, 108, 109, 110, 116, 118, 119, 133.
Graves, Admiral, 103, 112.
Grenada, West Indies, 21, 23, 88, 90, 96, 104, 105, 110, 116, 117, 118, 149, 151, 154, 162-164.
Grétry, A. E. M., 65.
Grimm, F. M., 65.
*Grubbe, Kristoffer, 90, 92, 98-99.
Guadeloupe, West Indies, 17, 90, 102, 112, 116.
Guichen, Luc Urbain, Count de, 17, 88, 96, 97, 100, 101, 102, 105, 112, 113, 120, 124, 157.
Gustavus III, King of Sweden, 9, 14, 19, 23, 29, 42, 46, 48, 49, 50, 60, 61, 88, 90, 92, 93, 96, 105, 115, 118, 121, 126, 127, 129, 130, 138, 139, 148, 150, 153, 160, 164.
Gustavus IV, King of Sweden, 118.
Gustavus Adolphus, King of Sweden, 2, 13.
Gyllenborg, Georg Fredrik, 58.
Gyldenkrone, Baron, Danish minister to Sweden, 29.
*Gyllenskepp, David C., 128.
*Gyllenskepp, S., 90, 92, 99.

H

Hague, The, 37, 41.
Haj, 68.
Halifax, 17.
Hamburg, 43, 46, 55.
*Hamilton, J. H., 90, 125.
*Hammarberg, Adolph, 87.
Hanson, Alexander Contee, 80.
Hanson, John, 78-80, 198-202.
Hardy, Admiral, 112.
Harris, Sir James, 27.
Hartford, Conn., 135, 137, 141, 142.
Hauch, Danish naval officer, 9.
Havrincourt d', French envoyé, 57, 59.
Hector, 101.
Helvetius, C. A., 55.
Hercule, L', 97, 121.
Hermelin, S. G., Baron, 47, 48, 70.
Hesselius, Gustaf, Swedish artist, 18, 70.
*Hohenhausen, Carl Johan von, 2, 90, 99-100, 109.
Holcker, American banker, 141.
Holland, 14, 20, 21, 25, 27, 43, 48, 53, 54.
Howe, Lord, 84.
Hudson Bay, 95.
Hughes, Admiral, 94.
Humphreys, Charles, 83.
Hunter, Miss, of Newport, 4.

I

Illerim, The, 35, 36, 122.
India, 8, 17, 92.
Intrépide, L', 99, 112.
Invincible, L', 96.

J

*Jägerskjöld, Carl Ludvig, 100.
*Jägerskjöld, Christer, 128.
Jason, Le, 132.
Jay, John, American envoyé to Madrid, 16, 41.
Jefferson, Thomas, 136.
Johnson, Amandus, 68, 77, 91.

Jones, John Paul, 17.
*Jönsson, Onnert, 100-101, 117.
Junon, La, French frigate, 21, 88, 110.

K

Kalm, Per, Swedish botanist, 18, 19, 69, 71.
Karlskrona, Sweden, 107, 108, 113, 120, 126.
Keen, Gregory B., 71.
Keen, Måns, 71.
Keppel, Admiral, 121.
Kerguelen-Trémaric,   Yves-Joseph, 100, 101, 102.
*Klick, 128.
Knox, Henry, General, 129, 141.
Koefoed, Danish naval officer, 9, 88.
Krieger, Danish naval officer, 9, 88.
Kyn, Göran, 71.

L

Lafayette, Marquis de, 4, 7, 21, 22, 23, 49, 129, 131, 141, 142, 158.
Lameth, Chevalier de, 153.
Landais, Capt., 41.
Languedoc, Le, 120.
*Lannerstjerna, Adolph Christian, 92, 94, 126.
Laubardiere, French officer, 133.
Lauzun, Duc de (Biron), 1, 4, 88, 98, 133, 134, 135.
Leach, M. Atherton, 81.
Lidner, Bengt, 64, 66.
*Liewen, 101.
*Lilljehorn, Pehr Ulric, 90, 101-102, 139.
Lincoln, American major-general, 133.
Linné, Karl von, 57.
Livingston, Robert R., 16, 47, 50, 51, 54.
Louis XVI, 19, 139.
Lovet, Capt., 46.
Lovisa Ulrika, Queen of Sweden, 58.
Luckassen, Peter, Skipper, 68.
Luzerne, Chevalier de la, 23.
Lynd, Jonas, 70.

M

Macartney, George, Governor of Lesser Antilles, 162.
Macnamara, naval commander in French service, 102.
Madrid, 32, 58, 59.
Magee, Capt., 46.
Magnifique, Le, 102, 106.
Malaga, Spain, 35.
Malling, Mathilda, Swedish writer, 67.
Marck, A. M. R., Count de la, 123, 124, 126, 127.
Marie Antoinette, Queen of France, 1, 65, 132, 134, 135, 139.
Marigny, Chevalier Bernard de, 110.
Marmontel, Jean François, 13, 56, 57, 59.
Marshall, Christopher, 84.
Marstrand, Sweden, 20, 44, 45.
Martinique, West Indies, 17, 103, 109, 112, 116, 120, 154.
Maurepas, Jean Fréderic, Count de, 6, 153.
Medée, La, 120.
Mediterranean, 98.
Merlant, Joachim, Capt., 134.
Mexico, Gulf of, 106.
Minorca, Spanish island in Mediterranean, 35, 127.
Montbarey, Prince de, 153.
Monteille, Admiral, 113.
*Monthell, Peter, 102.
Montesquieu, 12.
Moré, Count de, 4.
Morris, Robert, 83.
Morton, Ann Justis, 86.
Morton, John, 77, 80-86.
Motte-Piquet, de la, French naval commander, 96, 111, 120.
Muhlenberg, Dr. Henry Melchoir, 86.
Murphy, D. I., 49.
*Myrin, 90, 126.

N

Nancy, sloop, 44.
Naples, Italy, 21, 55, 136.

Napoleon, 10, 111, 148.
*Nauckhoff, Henric Johan, 2, 89, 90, 92, 94, 95, 102-104, 116.
Nauman, Dr. Erik, 5.
Necker, Jacques, 153.
Necker, Mlle., 147.
New Amsterdam, 67, 69.
New England, 67.
Newport, Rhode Island, 108; 132; 132; 135; letters from, 140; 142; 143.
Newport *Mercury,* 46, 47.
New York, 17.
Nixon, John, 84.
Noailles, Viscount de, 88, 91, 94, 95, 99, 101, 102, 113, 149, 153, 156, 166.
Nolcken, J. F., Baron de, Swedish envoyé to England, 33.
Nordenflycht, Hedvig Charlotta, 58.
*Nordenskjöld, Otto, Henric, Baron, 89, 92, 96, 104-106, 128.
North, Lord, 31.
North Sea, 105.
Northumberland, Le, 103, 104, 119.
Norway, 43.

O

Odhner, C. T., 23, 28, 30, 31, 44, 49, 89, 90, 91.
Örn, Swedish vessel, 81.
Orth, Samuel P., 71.
Orvillier, Count d', 102, 104, 105, 111, 121.
Ottoman Ports, 55.
Ouezzan, Morocco, 121, 155.

P

Palmier, Le, 96.
*Palmquist, Magnus Daniel, 90, 92, 106-107.
Panin, Count, Russian ambassador to France, 25, 32.
Parker, Sir Peter, 112.
Passy, France, 15, 36, 41, 51.
Pearce, Benjamin, Capt., 46.
Pégase, Le, 98.
*Peijron, Carl, 126.

Penn, William, 81.
Pensacola, Florida, 90, 94, 106, 112, 113-116.
Perouse, de la, French commander, 95, 116.
*Peterson-Rosensvärd, Adolph Fredrik, 89, 90, 113-116.
*Piper, Carl Ulric, 87.
Port Louis, Mauritius, 123, 124.
Porto Cabello, S. A., 145-146.
Porto Rico, 23, 145.
Portugal, 54, 55.
Prevost, English major-general, 164, 165.
Providence, R. I., 45, 133.
Providence *Gazette,* 21, 31, 44-45, 48.
Prussia, 25, 26, 37, 40, 55.
*Puke, Johan, Baron and Count af, 89, 92, 107-108.

Q

*Quanten, Carl Jacob von, 87.

R

*Raab, Carl, 2, 92, 108-109, 128.
*Rajalin (Rayalin), Carl Frederic von, 92, 109.
*Rajalin, Samuel Mauritz, 90, 92, 109, 116.
Rambler, The, 46.
Rapaapo, N. J., 71.
*Rappe, A. A. A., 126-127.
*Rappe, Claës Eric, 127.
Ravennel (Ravenal?), Capt., 107, 114.
*Rehbinder, Carl Gustaf, 89, 90, 92, 99, 110-111.
Reventlou, Ditlev, 29, 30, 42.
Rhode Island, 9; family names of, 72; 116; 130; 140; 148.
*Ribbing, Carl Adolph, 121.
Rising, John Classon, 81.
Robertnier, L. F. B., 4.
Robin, Abbé, 4, 6.
Robuste, Le, 118, 151.
Rochambeau, Count de, 4, 17, 98, 101, 129, 130-134, 136-138, 141, 158.

Rochambeau, Viscount de, 141.
Rodney, Admiral, 17, 97, 100, 102, 105, 110, 142, 143, 145.
Rome, Italy, 55.
*Rosen, Robert Magnus, von, 111.
Rosenstein, Swedish embassy Secretary, 52.
*Rosén von Rosenstein, Magnus A., 92, 111-112, 116.
Roslin, Swedish painter in Paris, 65.
Royal Suédois, French regiment, 13, 87, 127, 131, 148, 157.
Runeberg, Johan Ludvig, 124.
Russell, C. H., 8, 19, 20.
Russia, 10, 13, 16, 24, 25, 27, 46, 55, 110, 161.

S

Sagittaire, Le, 97.
Sandwich, 100.
St. Barthélemy, West Indies, 14, 62, 108, 110.
St. Christopher, West Indies, 108, 109, 112.
Saint-Esprit, Le, 109, 112, 117, 118.
St. Eustache, West Indies, 103.
St. Ildefonso, Spain, 37.
St. Lucia, West Indies, 96, 120.
St. Michel, Le, 100.
St. Petersburg, 32, 34, 38, 161.
St. Vincent, West Indies, 23.
Santo Domingo, West Indies, 95, 103, 106, 108, 112, 120.
Sandels, Swedish general, 89.
Sardinia, 21, 55.
Savannah, Ga., 105, 108, 148, 149, 150, 152, 163, 164-166.
Sayre, Stephen, 15, 42.
Saxony, 55.
Sceptre, Le, 95, 96.
Scheffer, Ulrik, Swedish minister of foreign affairs, 29, 63, 151.
*Schultén, Z., 90, 92, 116.
*Schützercrantz, Johan Herman, 2, 101, 117.
Segur, Count de, 101.
Senegal, 90, 105.
*Sjöstjerna, Aron, 117, 128.

Solitaire, Le, 100, 111, 117.
Solano, Spanish commander, 113.
Soules, François, 4.
South River, 68.
Souverain, Le, 110.
Spa, Belgium, 7, 32.
Spain, 8, 14, 17, 40, 41, 43, 46, 56, 57, 116.
Spanish allies, 8.
Sparre, Carl, 152-154, 158, 160.
Sprengtporten, von, Swedish minister to Denmark, 29.
*Sprengtporten, Göran Magnus, von, 88.
*Staël von Holstein, Gustaf Johan, 87.
*Staël von Holstein, Joachim, 87.
Staël von Holstein, Baron de, Swedish ambassador to Paris, 7, 50, 63, 89, 124, 147, 156, 160.
*Staré, 92, 127.
Staten Island, 84.
*Stedingk, Curt von, Baron, 1, 65, 90, 91, 92, 99, 139, 147-166, 167.
*Stedingk, Victor, von, 89, 117-118, 151.
Steuben, Baron von, 12.
Stjernstolpe, Bothvid Elof, 70.
Stockholm, Sweden, 24, 34.
Suffolk, Lord, 28.
Suffren, Bailli de, 8, 9, 94, 100, 122, 123, 126.
Surtine, A. R. de, 7, 110.
Swedish officers, 1-5, 7, 9, 87-168.

T

Talleyrand, Prince de, 13.
Taraval, painter, 65.
Termées, Admiral, 116.
Ternay, Count de, 17, 103, 107.
Tiger, 116.
*Tilas, Baron, 118.
Tobago, West Indies, 23, 103.
*Toll, C. F. (?), 119.
*Törnquist, 119.
*Tott, 119.
Trincomalee, Ceylon, 124.

Trinité, La, West Indies, 120.
*Tromelin, de, 128.
Tuscany, 55.

U

*Ulfsparre af Broxvik, Johan Carl, 127.
*Ulfvenklou, H. G.(?), 120.
Unicorn, 106, 115.
Union, 17.
"Uppsala Academy," 63.

V

Vaillant, Le, 119.
Vauban, French officer, 133.
Vaudreuil, Marquis de, 94-96, 101, 102, 104, 105, 119, 120, 121.
Vengeur, Le, 110, 111.
Venice, Italy, 55.
Vergennes, Charles Gravier, Count de, 14, 16, 21, 28, 30, 49, 61, 64, 103, 104, 136, 152.
Versailles, 32.
Ville-Vieille, de, foreign officer in French service, 88.
Ville de Paris, La, 112.
Vioménil, General, 145.
*Virgin, Arvid, 120.
Virginia, 67, 133, 144.
Voltaire, 56, 59.

W

Wachtmeister, Hans F., 121.
*Wachtmeister, Klas, Count, 89, 91, 120-121.
Wallin, Johan Olof, Swedish archbishop, 66.
Washington, George, 4, 17, 66, 76, 130, 132, 133, 136, 137, 138, 139, 141, 142, 143, 160.
Wayne, Anthony, General, 84.
Wertmüller, Adolph, Swedish painter, 3, 65.
West Indies, 8, 19, 23, 62, 89, 90, 100, 106, 109, 111.
West Point, Va., 133, 134.
Wharton, Francis, 135-136.
Williamsburg, Va., 133, 144.

Willing, Thomas, 83.
Wilson, James, 83.
Wrangel, Dr. Charles von, 86.
*Wrede, Fabian, Count, 127.
*Wrede, Jöran Casimir, 127.
*Wrede, Henrik, 127.

Y

Yorktown, Va., 90, 98, 103, 106, 112, 134, 136, 138.

Z

*Zachaud, Daniel, 121.